We dedicate this book to the tireless efforts of administrators, faculty, and staff in our school system throughout the nation who have worked hard to eliminate bullying among our young people.

Contents

Tables

Foreword

Bullying has reached a critical mass in our schools, communities, homes, work-places, governmental institutions, airways, and the World Wide Web. Our children are suffering at the hands of social and cultural norms that have rejected the importance of instituting appropriate acceptable social behaviors. Today, we live in a society where "everything goes." Relatively speaking, children cannot clearly decipher between what is right or wrong, unless they are gifted with support systems (parents, effective schools, teachers, mentors) that make concerted efforts to build and shape their moral compasses. Social and emotional development start at home and are further shaped by societal expectations. According Bodrova and Leong (2007), states that children's social and emotional stages of development rely on the expectancy of the adults in the lives and society. However, when there is a breach in the social-emotional constructs of how adults respond to children inappropriately, they begin to create their own social norms and principles to live by. Social accomplishments are almost non-existent. Putting children in the position to build their own mental capacity is irresponsible and detrimental to their personal welfare.

As a result of this paradigm shift, educational lawmakers have conceded to prematurely expose our school-aged children to learning expectations that require the application of higher cognitive functioning before they are mentally ready. The absurdity between metal and cognitive demand can lead to psychological issues, like self-deprecation and victimization of others. During my tenure as an educator, I have seen an array of acts of bullying that range from a group of dysfunctional teachers organizing a cause to resist implementation of best educational practices to a nine-year-old boy influencing two of his classmates to pin down another student, while he took his shoes off and put them in the trash. These types of behaviors are shocking and have caused major damage to all parties involved. To help offset bullying in schools, school officials are heightening the awareness of bullying through programs that require students to adhere to a set of principles, rules, and/or standards to eliminate or minimize bullying. But in some cases, it is not enough. A social issue of this magnitude is not an easy fix; all hands must be on deck to remedy the problem—church leaders, schools, corporations, civic leaders, and parents. The institution of schools has always supported the whole child, until educational lawmakers limited social and emotional curricular and replaced them with more cognitive expectations and processes. This school of thought has caused a significant reduction in the development and use of a child's affective filters, which can lead to pathological behaviors.

School is a microcosm of a community. It reflects the best and worst of what is in our society. School-aged children are among the most at risk groups in our society for many things. They are more likely to victimize and commit crimes. Many children report that they are more frequently victims of crime at school than in any other setting (Dorn, 2003). Now that bullying has reached epic proportions, educators, parents, and community leaders see bullying as a devastating form of abuse that can have long-term effects on youthful victims, robbing them of self-esteem, isolating them from peers, causing them to drop out of school and even prompting health problems and suicide. A recent study conducted by the Family and Work Institute reported that one-third of youth are bullied at least once a month, while six out of ten children witness bullying once a day. Witnessing bullying can also have a lasting effect on children as they often feel helpless or that they maybe the next target (National Crime Prevention Council, n.d.).

Although this information is disconcerting, bullying is a reality that has crippled and produced a generation of children who are desensitized to the need of others. Our children are foregoing their innate ability to show compassion and humility in bullying situations at the expense of others. The lines of moral obligation and responsibility are blurred or almost nonexistent in the mind of bullies. Therefore, as a society, it is critical that we re-establish social norms within every community. Bullying rears its ugly head everyday, and we cannot afford to waste time.

References

Bodrova, E., and Leong, D. J., (2007). *Tools of the mind: The Vygotskian approach to early childhood education*. Upper Saddle River, New Jersey: Columbus Ohio: Pearson Merrill Prentice Hall.

Dorn, M., (2003). *Weakfish: Bullying through the eyes of the child*. Macon Georgia: Safe Havens International.

National Crime Prevention Council., (n.d.) Retrieved from http://www.ncpc.org//topics/bullying

Sonia Martin, Ed.D.
Onslow County Public Schools, NC

Preface

Bullying is a type of violence. In recent years, bullying has come to the forefront and has received national attention. In 2011, President Obama held the first-ever White House Conference on Bullying Prevention to call attention to the school harassment and cyberbullying issues that have ensued. While bullying is not a new phenomenon, new research and resources are increasingly becoming more available to provide guidance and direction to parents, educators, and policymakers to assist in combatting the short and long term negative results of bullying, including cyberbullying.

The phenomenon of bullying deserves special attention by educators, parents, children and communities concerned with violence prevention. As one contributor noted, the nature of bullying does not necessarily lend itself to the same interventions that may effectively reduce other types of conflict among children because it involves harassment by powerful children against children with less power (rather than a conflict between peers of relatively equal status). Therefore, common conflict resolution strategies such as mediation may not be effective.

This book is an extensive work which provides valuable insights for individuals seeking to prevent, intervene, or reduce the effects of bullying not only in the school setting, but also in other environments such as the home (caregiver bullying), in prisons, and on the internet. It not only aids in the understanding of the difference between typical childhood behavior and bullying, but also gives a detailed account on how to recognize the warning signs of bullying, and the role gender equity plays in harassment. The contributors have done an excellent job in raising readers' awareness of the prevalence of bullying and the harm it causes. Not just one, but several areas of bullying are presented and fully discussed, each lending itself to intensive study and commentary. The research demonstrating strategies for effectiveness in both schools and communities is well documented.

The prevalence of bullying and the harm that it causes are seriously underestimated by many children and adults. Any violence prevention strategy must work to raise the awareness of children, school staff, parents, and policy makers regarding the link between bullying and other violent behaviors. The wide-ranging views presented in this book provide a solid base for prevention, intervention and policy efforts.

John Penny, PH.D., TH.D
Chair, Department of Social Sciences
Southern University at New Orleans

Acknowledgments

Our greatest appreciation goes to all of the contributors of the book. A special thanks goes to Dr. Rose Duhon-Sells, who is the founder of the National Association for Peace/Anti-Violence Education. The yearly national conference as well as her vision, wisdom, and love provided the initial spark to proceed with writing this book. A special thanks goes to the reviewers of the texts and editors.

Chapter One

Bullying in the School Environment

Ethel Marie Yeates Fisher
Veronica Lynn Doyle Woodard

Introduction

Students attend schools each day for purposes of learning, responsibility, socialization and to obtain knowledge. These principles are intended to occur in a safe and
comfortable environment. Our schools are intended to be viable places which
provide protection, keeping students out of harm's way. Unfortunately, many students in schools do not feel the security that they should be afforded due to
bullying.

Hazler (1992) states bullying occurs when one or more students, physically or
verbally harass other students without cause (as cited in Holmgren, Lamb, Miller
& Werderitch, 2011). Bullying occurs when students are exposed, constantly and
over time, to negative actions by one or more persons, in which students have
difficulty defending themselves (Olweus, 2001). This definition consists of the
following components:

1. Bullying is aggressive behavior that involves unwanted, negative actions.
2. Bullying involves a pattern of behavior repeated over time.
3. Bullying involves an imbalance of power or strength (pp 3–20).

Bullying is a type of violence. It involves a real or perceived disparity of control, with the more powerful student or group of students attacking those who are
less powerful. This form of harassment may be physical (hitting, kicking, shoving,
spitting), verbal (cruel remarks, name calling, threats), or emotional (spreading
rumors, controlling social relationships, extreme force or intimidation). Bullying

1

can take place in person or electronically (California Department of Education, 2011).

Bullying appears to be a recurrent problem for students in the United States and can be related with a number of short and long term negative results such as depression and poor health (Petrosino, Guckenburg, Devoe & Hanson (2010). According Devoe and Murphy (2011), in the United States, 7,066,000 students, ages 12 through 18, reported that they were harassed at school, in addition to 1,521,000 who stated they were cyber-bullied on or away from school premises (National Center for Education Statistics, 2011).

Although the above statistics of reported bullying have been accounted, studies suggest that numerous occurrences of bullying are not reported to school officials. This makes it difficult for educators to determine the frequency of this negative behavior in schools, which is the initial step in focusing on this problem. Administrators cannot view a complete representation of the conduct of bullying which makes it challenging to help deter the problem (Petrosino, 2010).

Educators and administrators must become aware of the problem of bullying. Some characteristics of bullying and characteristics of victims of bullying are listed below.

Characteristics of Bullies

- Overly aggressive, harmful, enjoys dominating other students (Carney & Merrell, 2001; NSSC, 1995, as cited in Smokowski & Kopasz, (2005).
- Quick-tempered, reckless, low tolerance for frustration (Olweus, 1993, as cited in Smokowski).
- Difficulty processing societal information, many times misinterpreting the behaviors of others as being hostile (Dodge, 1991; McNamara & McNamara, 1997, as cited in Smokowski).
- Popular with other hostile students (Pellegrini, 1998, as cited in Smokowski).
- Positive outlook toward violence, in order to resolve problems or get what they want (Carney, 2001).
- Achieve or retain power and often lacks empathy for their victims (Beale, as cited in Smokowski).
- Often implicated in additional troubled behaviors, such as smoking, drinking, and alcohol and getting into fights (Alude, Adeleke, Omoike & Afen-Akpaida, 2008).
- Poor school achievement and often dislikes school (Nansel, 2001).
- Families of bullies frequently have social problems (Olweus, 1994, as cited in Smokowski).
- Inconsistent discipline in the home (Pellegrini, 1998, as cited in Smokowski).

Characteristics of Victims

- The majority of victims of bullying (about two-thirds) are passive or submissive. The remaining one-third seems to show hostile attitudes (Brokenbrough, 2002, as cited in Smokowski).
- Victims are usually small in physique, weak and frail (McNamara & McNamara, 1997, as cited in Smokowski).
- Victims are often ineffective in sports and other physical activities (Olweus, 1993, as cited in Smokowski).
- They are often insecure, sensitive, have poor communication and problem-solving skills (Schwartz, 1993, as cited in Smokowski).
- Victims often have fewer friends, having minimal relationships with their peers (Nansel, 2001, as cited in Smokowski).
- Relationships are often better with parents and teachers, instead of their peers (Olweus, 1993).
- Victims are inclined to have low self-esteem (O'Moore & Kirkman, 2001, as cited in Smokowski).

Educators must take an active role to help with the incidence of bullying. "To combat bullying, teachers should never ignore a bullying incident but should approach them as teachable moments" (Graham, 2010). Reactions from teachers indicate to those who bully that their behaviors are unacceptable and help victims feel less powerless about their situation (p. 69). One important suggestion to help with the implementation of the prevention of bullying is to create a supportive school environment which encourages students to seek help when they have been harassed or bullied (Eliot, Cornell, Gregory & Fan, 2010).

Interventions, as stated by Penn, (2010), suggest that bullying at schools should be evaluated to find out where and how it takes place. This includes all educators, staff and bus drivers. When the information has been obtained, change the climate of the school so bullies will know that it will not be allowed. Bullying prevention rules should be implemented with the inclusion of the entire student body. In-service training should be provided for teachers and school staff. Increased supervision should be placed where bullying often takes place. Provide bullying activities in the classroom to help eliminate student harassment.

Graham (2010) suggests that many bullying interventions are school-wide methods that encompass all students, parents, educators and staff in the school, with the assumption that bullying is a systematic problem, in which all individuals in the school must have a responsibility to improve or solve this problem. Research has shown that only about one third of such interventions have been successful due to different school settings, demographics and in some cases, the reluctance of some teachers/staff to become involved in bullying interventions. These interventions should not be discarded, however; each teacher should make a serious individual effort to become involved when bullying incidents occur. Teaching tolerance to students should also be emphasized, in order to embrace differences and diversity.

Bullying in the schools is a serious problem in the United States. Our youth deserve safe educational environments that will enable them to become knowledgeable and productive citizens. It is the responsibility of educators, school staff, parents and the community to ensure that our students be provided with surroundings that will allow them to succeed in our nation.

What Happens When the Teacher is the Bully

The teaching profession is perhaps one of the most revered professions in our society. While most educators will not hesitate to tell you the monetary compensation does not come close to being parallel with the amount of responsibility associated with teaching, still teaching is viewed as a trusting, compassionate and caring profession. Each day parents send their children to school entrusting their care and educational preparation to teachers who have been educated and trained to pass on knowledge and information to get students ready to be successful in life. Administrators trust that they have hired competent employees who are committed to making a positive difference in the lives of the students enrolled in the schools. Thus, the idea of the teacher being the bully is practically preposterous.

A survey conducted by Twemlow, Fonagy, Sacco, and Brethour (2006) revealed that 45 percent of 116 elementary school teachers admitted to having bullied as student (p. 194). Hepburn (2000) carried out a qualitative study using discourse and conversational analyses. As part of the study, teachers were asked about teacher bullying of students. Surprisingly, at least one teacher honestly admitted to bullying a student. Results of the study confirmed that teachers who were bullied as students/youth were more likely to bully students and experience bullying by students both inside and outside the classroom, revealing teachers who were both sadistic and a bully-victim type (Twemlow, Fonagy, Sacco, & Brethour, 2006). Adding to the literature regarding teacher bullying of students is a recent study conducted in Ireland by James, Lawlor, Courtney, Flynn, Henry, & Murphy (2008). In this study the researchers investigated bullying at two separate times in a secondary school and concluded that "thirty percent of students said they were bullied by teachers at both times" (p. 160). In 2005 Spitalli suggested ten 'don'ts' of student discipline, specifically cautioning teachers not to bully students stating it is "unconscionable and amounts to professional malpractice" (p. 30). This part of the chapter will reveal information which defines bullying and teacher bullying, common ways that teachers may unintentionally engage in bullying students, and the implications for education.

Bullying and Teacher Bullying Defined

McEvoy (2005) portrays bullying as "repeated physical hurt or psychological distress inflicted by unwanted, offensive, threatening, insulting, or humiliating assaults or any conduct that causes so much stress that it interferes with a victim's educational performance." Additionally, he states, "bullying is usually associated with an imbalance of power in which the bully has perceived, appointed, or self-appointed authority over another due to factors such as the victim's size, age, experience, title, socioeconomic status, or brawn" (McEvoy, 2005). Olweus (1993) defined bullying as "repeated, intentional, and within the context of an unequal power relationship." In 2001, Twemlow, Fonagy, and Sacco conceptualized bullying by offering this compelling viewpoint:

> We can now redefine bullying in schools as the repeated exposure of an individual or group to negative interactions (social aggression) by one or more dominant persons. The person(s) enjoys the discomfort and shame of the victim as if in a sadomasochistic ritual enacted for the perverse public enjoyment of an audience of bystanders who do nothing and may vicariously be aroused as bullies or victims (p. 278).

These general definitions associated with bullying can be carried out by any individual who chooses to engage in this sort of behavior for reasons of trying to gain power or control over another individual.

One definition offered for teacher bullying has been stated as "one who uses his or her power to punish, manipulate, or belittle a student beyond what would be a reasonable disciplinary procedure" (Twemlow & Fonalgy, 2005). Teachers who bully students leave a negative impact that could affect the students for the rest of their lives. Students may think they have no recourse when they feel they have been bullied by a teacher. The common perspective is, administration or other teachers will probably believe the teacher and not defend the student from the abusive teacher. The student may also feel the teacher is seen as an expert and a colleague of other teachers and administration, therefore not believing that the teacher would engage in bullying of a student(s). Because some students may not know how to respond in a situation where the teacher is the bully, it is left up to educators and those who advocate for students, regardless of their age, to be the voice that speaks in behalf of the students. This is especially true even if it means confronting colleagues who openly bully, or are on the border of bullying students.

Some teachers attempt to mask bullying behavior by justifying it as a motivational, mandatory part of providing instruction, suitable as a disciplinary response, or a tool to effectively manage the classroom (Sylvester, 2011). However, these are merely excuses for some educators who choose to engage in bullying students. It may be that these teachers have forgotten the principles and concepts learned during their educational preparation and training prior to having the responsibility of being the person "in charge" in the classroom.

Common Ways Teachers Bully Students

In a recent article, author Ruth Sylvester (2011) offers four common ways that teachers may unintentionally bully students. These are: sarcasm, obscure name calling, refusing to accept late assignments and throwing unidentified assignments in the garbage, and humiliating future students the teacher perceives as a potential behavior problem in the classroom.

Sarcasm is a phrase which usually results in irony when speaking of something or someone as opposite of what is truly meant. It can also be a hurtful remark stated with the purpose of wounding the person for whom the remark is intended. The professional teacher should not use either of these in the classroom. Sarcasm can be interpreted as harmful and hurt to both school-age and adult students. Culturally diverse students who may not be familiar with the intent of sarcasm (even when it is used to suggest humor), can be confused and offended. The teacher should refrain from using sarcastic language in the classroom when responding to a student, reprimanding a student, or evaluating a student's performance. Sarcasm in the classroom is rude and discouraging. A student could be left utterly embarrassed and negatively affected (academically and socially) by the teacher's sarcasm. If sarcastic remarks by the teacher become repetitious, the student can lose respect for the teacher.

Obscure name calling as a form of teacher bullying can occur literally without the teacher meaning for this to happen. An example would be a nursing instructor, agitated that the students in the Fundamentals course are not sure of the names of certain body parts. Frustrated during a demonstration in the lab, he says, "You were supposed to learn this in Biology last semester. Did you already forget what you learned?" This statement could leave the student(s) feeling incompetent or have anger issues with the Biology instructor. As educators, teachers should realize that obscure name calling (even if it is unintentional) is degrading and demeaning to students.

Refusing to accept late assignments or throwing unidentified assignments in the garbage are bullying behaviors (Sylvester, 2011). When a student takes the time and effort to complete an assignment, Sylvester feels the student's work should be accepted and reviewed. Rejecting the assignment or deducting a large number of points from the assignment can be seen as an abuse of power, thus teacher bullying. In Sylvester's opinion, the student should be given the opportunity to explain why the assignment is late. Putting an assignment without a name on the document in the trash can also be interpreted as teacher bullying. An alternative to reinforce to the student the importance of identifying their work would be to place a question mark and the word "name" on the first sheet of the assignment. It may take a few more minutes to identify the student's work that has no name. However, throwing the assignment in the trash can cause feelings of anger and/or hurt on the part of the student. Again, respect for the teacher can be lost.

A statement such as "I know you've heard about me" is an example of teacher bullying that is used to humiliate future students the teacher perceives as a potential behavior problem in the classroom. This practice has been observed directly in some middle and high school teachers. Although there is no research evidence directly associated with this phrase, it could also occur in institutions of higher learning as well. The root cause of such a statement could be the product of gossip or sharing of information in the teacher's lounge, or observing the actions and behaviors of students in the hallways, or in other places on the school campus.

Usually the teacher perceives that the student has the potential for being a problem in his/her classroom in the future. The statement is used as a "power move" to intimidate the student, thereby not becoming a behavioral problem for the teacher in the classroom; "teacher bullying". Sylvester (2011) characterizes this behavior as "deliberate humiliation" which "serves no legitimate academic purpose" (p. 44).

Implications for Education

As a general rule, the majority of professional educators conduct themselves in an ethical manner. These individuals are caring educators, committed to the practice of teaching and educating students, often serving in multiple roles (e.g. counselor, advocate, leader, etc.). However, there are teachers who engage in bullying students. Regardless if these are few in number, the school system/institution must not ignore the problem. Failing to address the problem of teacher bullying can dramatically affect the climate, morale, and productivity of the entire school/ institution, causing monumental harm.

Therefore, it is incumbent on the school/institution to come up with strategies to effectively combat the problem of teacher bullying. One such strategy which can be useful to address this problem is the development of efficient formal policies and procedures which provide a grievance process for students to use to make a complaint against an abusive, bullying teacher. Developing a formal grievance process would allow student(s) to air their grievance regarding a teacher the student feels is engaging in bullying them, and allow a fair investigation of the complaint. This process would not provide "sanction" for the abusive, bullying teacher.

Another strategy for dealing with teacher bullying with implications for education is for educators to introduce opportunities to establish and maintain the students' trust. This encourages the student(s) to report bullying, identify feelings, and address other issues related to being bullied.

Involving faculty and staff in interpersonal strategy has the potential to achieve a positive school culture. Faculty and staff are encouraged to accept diversity and model tolerance themselves. Teachers and para-professionals should participate in ongoing professional development through SafeSchools, an online safety training and tracking system designed specifically for school employees. A course covering bullying is one of the many topics that can be accessed at the website: http:// safeschools.com

The key element for success in any school is the involvement and support of parents, as well as students. Active participation from both students and parents is essential to creating a positive culture in the school which could deter teacher bullying. Using this principle, an urban middle school located in the Los Angeles Unified School District in California encouraged the parents of the students in this school to for an anti-bullying committee. The group held regular meetings collaborating with school administration, and developed an action plan to combat bullying (Murawski, Lockwood, Khalili, & Johnston, 2009).

Perhaps one of the most useful strategies that can be established to combat teacher bullying is to include the community in advocating for a culture of anti-bullying. When administrators, teachers, parents, and students are all actively involved in creating and maintaining an environment that will not tolerate bullying of any kind, especially teacher bullying, then the entire community can feel safe and devote all its effort to the education of the students.

References

Allen, K.P. (2010). Classroom Management, Bullying, and Teacher Practices. *Professional Education, 34(1), 1–15*. Retrieved from EBSCO*host*.

Aluede, O., Adeleke, F., Omoike, D. & Afen-Akpaida J. (2008). A Review of The Extent, Nature, Characteristics and Effects of Bullying Behavior in Schools. *Journal of Instructional Psychology*, 32, 151.

California Department of Education. (2011). Bullying at School. http://www.cde.ca.gov/ls/ss/se/bullyfaq.asp.

Devoe, J., Murphy, C., & National Center for Education Statistics. (2011). Student Reports of Bullying and Cyber-Bullying: Results from the 2009 School Crime Supplement to the National Crime Victimization Survey. Retrieved from EBSCO*host*.

Eliot, M., Cornell, D., Gregory, A. & Fan, X. (2010). Supportive School Climate and Student Willingness to Seek Help for Bullying and Threats of Violence. *Journal of School Psychology*, 48, 533–553.

Graham, S. (2010). What Educators Need to Know About Bullying Behaviors. *Phi Delta Kappan, 92(1)*, 66–69. Retrieved from EBSCO*host*.

Holmgren, J., Lamb, J., Miller, M. & Werderitch, C. (2011). Decreasing Bullying Behaviors Through Discussing Young-Adult Literature, Role-Playing Activities, and Establishing a School-Wide Definition of Bullying in Accordance with a Common Set of Rules in Language Arts and Math. Retrieved from EBSCO*host*.

McEvoy, A. (2005, September). Teachers Who Bully Students: Patterns and Policy Implications. Paper presented at the Hamilton Fish Institute's Persistently Safe Schools Conference, Philadelphia, PA.

Murawski, W. W., Lockwood, J., Khalili, A., Johnston, A. (2009). A Bully-Free School. *Educational Leadership, 67(4)*, 75–78.

Olweus, D. (2001). Peer Harassment: A Critical Analysis and Some Important Issues in Peer Harassment in *Schools*. Ed. J. Juvonen and S. Graham (New York: Guilford Publications), 3–20.

Omizo, M. M., Omizo, S. A., Baxa, G. O., & Miyose, R. J. (2006). Bullies and Victims: A Phemomenological Study. *Journal of School Violence, 5(3)*, 89–105. Doi: 10.1300/J202v05n03_07.

Penn, S. (2010). How to Intervene with Social Bullying in Schools. Retrieved from http://www.eHow.com/how_6246713_intrvene-social-bullying-schools.html.

Petrosino, A., Guckenburg, S., Devoe, J., & Hanson, T. (2010). What Charac-
    teristics of Bullying, Bullying Victims, and Schools Are Associated with
    Increased Reporting of Bullying to School Officials? Issues and Answers.
    Regional Educational Laboratory Northeast & Islands, 092. Retrieved from
    EBSCO*host.*
Smokowski, P., & Kopasz, K. (2005). Bullying in the School: An Overview of
    Types Effects, Family Characteristics, and Intervention Strategies. *Children &
    Schools,* 27(2), 101. Retrieved from Questia.com.
Sylvester, R. (2011). Teacher as Bully: Knowingly or Unintentionally Harming
    Students. *The Delta Kappa Gamma Bulletin, International Journal for
    Professional Educators* 77(2), 42–45. Retrieved from EBSCO*host.*
Twemlow, S. W., Fonagy, P., Sacco, F. C., & Brethour, Jr., J. R. (2006). Teachers
    Who Bully Students: A Hidden Trauma. *International Journal of Social
    Psychiatry,* 52(3), 187–198 Doi: 10.1177/0020764006067234.

Chapter Two
Bullying . . . Even in Retirement

Clifton L. Brown
Ashraf Esmail

Abstract: Bullying to abuse and mistreat the elder adult has not received the scrutiny necessary to determine the depth of the problem. Caregivers are the people who assist the elder adult and may be family members or people of no relation who are contracted to provide expertise in the care of elder adults. Dependence on the caregiver attaches the elder adult through physical, psychological or financial ties that allow the elder adult and/or the bully to fear that a change in behavior will change the elder adult's care. Elder adults with family histories of abuse and violence usually continue to bully, abuse and mistreat family members even after moving out of the abusive situation. Peer on peer bullying is gaining notoriety in elder adult only facilities as more people get older and cognitive impairment becomes more pronounced. Cognitive impairment and/or stroke may affect a part of the brain that is supporting learning and behaving by the elder adult. Given that many of the elderly face the uncertainty of aging, it has forced them to try to influence the treatment of all elders through the media, governmental agencies, and in communities across the country. Because decreasing the opportunity for bullying and over-aggressive behavior by peers, avaricious caregivers, greedy or neglectful relatives will require additional research and codifying of bullying, as well as interested others to recognize, react, and report abuse and/or mistreatment of elder adults.

Introduction

As we get older and our children have children, most of us look forward to retiring from work, but not from life. For many, retirement is viewed as an opportunity to do new and different things. Often things we did not have a chance to do before. Spend more time with the family, take up a hobby, and travel more, are some of the things people have indicated they would do. One of the drawbacks to retiring from work is that we lose a part of our lives. Many of us have established relationships that have existed many years and retirement tends to limit the people, places, and things we participate in. As we now get older, so do most of the people we know. People we know become people we knew as our circle of friends and associates become smaller. Depending on our income, we begin to travel less and our group memberships decrease. If we are fortunate, we remain relatively healthy, suffer only minor pain and discomfort, and take a minimum of prescribed and over the counter medication. We remain active and involved in our families and communities and we understand that getting older does not always mean getting old. Unfortunately, for increasing numbers of us, our getting older is ushering in a new threat . . . one that we thought we outgrew . . . Bullying . . . Even in Retirement.

Bullying is not new. In fact, most of us have heard of instances of bullying since we were children. People taking advantage of others, abusing and harassing others, frightening and even physical violence has been some of the tactics used by bullies. The elder adult population in America is growing continuously and advances in the medical community have pushed the projected life expectancy over 75 years of age (Moody, 2010). Unfortunately, while the improvements have extended the length of life, not all have improved the quality of life. Many of the advances of technology are cost prohibitive and that has limited the number of people who could possibly benefit. Therefore, retirement for increasing numbers of elder adults is creating unanticipated difficulties for them, their families and the community at large. While many elder adults will maintain their independence until very old (Novak, 2006), and continue to perform appropriate behaviors longer than ever before, longevity extends the inappropriate behaviors too. Consequently, increasing numbers of elder adults will have difficulties that will require the assistance of others, and the lack of governmental oversight, and general misinformation about the responsibilities of caregivers, will leave many elder adults unprepared for the challenges of aging (Moody, 2010; Novak, 2006).

Elder adults are the fastest growing segment of the population (Himes, 2001), and will soon rival the number of those younger. The elderly as a group face difficulties different from other segments of the population as every behavior is continually influenced by cognitive and physical changes that hinder their ability to maintain and independently perform appropriate behavior. Simple behaviors become more difficult to repeat as the individual gets older and new behaviors need adoption to become viable, and still provide value to the family and/or the community (Brown, 2011). Physical changes related to age are often subtle. As the individual ages, often becoming more dependent on others, they incur an additional cost for care to maintain current activities. Not being able to drive will require a driver, using a wheel chair often requires an assistant, and limited strength may require a housekeeper. Unfortunately, as the elder adult gets older, the elder adult gets weaker and the more assistance required the more opportunity for abuse. As previously isolated instances of elder adult abuse and mistreatment are becoming more prevalent (Bonnie & Wallace, 2003), it is causing society in general to become more aware of the difficulties faced by the elderly.

Anecdotal stories and reports of bullying are not only increasing in number, but also in degree of mistreatment. For instance, in Ohio, an older couple required additional assistance after being trapped in their home by neighbors bullying, harassing, and mistreating them. From Arizona is the story of Doris Lor who moved into a retirement community and was shunned and ostracized by other elder adults. After complaining and receiving no help from the retirement community administrators, she spends most of her time alone away from the other residents. From Chicago, IL, Margaret Matthews tired of the threats and humiliation from some of her younger neighbors became so afraid that she shot, but did not kill a 12 year old out of fear. In Los Angeles, Maria Lopez's great niece was arrested for inadequate care and later found not guilty of elder abuse, involuntary manslaughter and murder after her aunt died. All of these instances represent a new problem for families, communities and the general society. At what point does the quality of life outweigh the quantity of life. A long life usually means that the individual lived to be as old as possible. However, the number of years that a person could live in an ideal circumstance is probably different from living in continual pain or in fear of being too frail to care for oneself or to receive adequate assistance from others.

Over the past several years, peer-on-peer bullying among elder adults has been gaining national attention (Burgess & Hanrahan, 2006; Moody, 2010) probably because of the increase in elder adult only activities and facilities. While limited research suggests that the majority of older people are not bullied, and that risk factors for bullying do not pose problems for them, the National Center on Elder Abuse believes that the number of elder adults being abused is significantly higher. Combined with the continually deteriorating condition of the elder adult, it becomes increasingly difficult to determine, which type of non-care leads to what level of elder abuse. The National Center on Elder Abuse estimates between one and two million elder adults older than 65 have been mistreated and as the number of elder adults increases, the instances of abuse will increase because of better recordkeeping, increased reporting, and general public awareness. Currently, information about bullying to abuse and/or mistreat the elder adult is extremely limited hindering the ability to effectively forecast accurate behavior or the number of adults being exploited.

It does not appear that any one risk factor can cause or explain bullying. In the majority of instances where bullying is occurring there are a combination of risk factors that may contribute to it (Anetzberger, Lachs, O'Brien, O'Brien, Pillemer & Tomita, 1993). As the elder adult gets older, they face several risk factors that will influence their ability to care for themselves. How ill the elder adult becomes, how active they are, and how much time they spend with others will affect their cognition, physical ability, and physiological condition. For the person responsible for the elder adult's care, stress and lack of support may cause depression (as commonly understood) or offer limited emotional reward to help. Bullying does not appear to occur as isolated instances, but rather in combination with other types of abuse and mistreatment of the elder adult by people responsible for their care and safety. Many of the signs of bullying and mistreatment are wrongly attributed to changes associated with aging (Anetzberger, Lachs, O'Brien, et. al., 1993). Signs and symptoms of bullying may be difficult to detect because cognitive performance influences physical prowess and cognitive impairment often causes one to age faster requiring additional services sooner than might be necessary.

For the elder adult to maintain their independence while aging, it requires they continue to develop cognitively as they age. Bordens and Horowitz (2002) suggest that how people feel about themselves seems to have a direct effect on their cognitive ability, physical health and their emotional well-being. The better we feel, the more satisfied with life we appear the better we are, as Barnes, Wilson, Mendes de Leon & Bennett, (2006) reports that cognitive health and emotional well-being are 'inextricably linked' according to The National Institute on Aging. Cognitive impairment is an interesting phenomenon because it often initially appears as forgetfulness and as memory failures increase, maladaptive and destructive behaviors usually precede dementia. Cognitive decline and dementia appear strongly associated with poorer physical health, mortality, and other debilitating illnesses causing the National Institute of Health to intensify the search for strategies to preserve brain health. If the elder adult is suffering from some form of cognitive impairment, decline or dementia, it will complicate detection of abuse and mistreatment. Dementia is growing in importance primarily because of the resources (public and private) utilized to combat the disease (Farran, 2001; Parker & Philip, 2004). In the case of bullying, the elder adult may not remember they were bullying someone or that they were told not to bully anyone. They also may not remember whether they gave another permission to perform a task or purposely declined to participate in an activity. Consequently, if elder adults diagnosed cognitively impaired are unable to change their behaviors, they become more of a drain on family and institutional resources and more of a burden on the general society.

Dementia is associated with a number of ailments including protein disturbances, vascular difficulties (Schwartz, Glass, Bolla, Stewart, Glass, Rasmussen, et al., 2004), infections, structural brain disorders, neural pathway deterioration (Merzenich, 2000) and depression as understood by general society. Many of these ailments are controlled with medication and too much or too little may aggravate or influence a change in the elder adults' behavior, also creating a greater opportunity for bullying situations. Medication and substance abuse by the elder adult will make it difficult to make decisions or to recognize abuse and mistreatment. However, as societal requirements for individual behavior often call for decisions to be made quickly, for the elderly, hurried decisions lead to mistakes and faulty behaviors. Because the elder adult's condition will worsen with age, many of the signs and symptoms of elder abuse overlap with symptoms of cognitive impairment, and increase the difficulty of identifying elder abuse and mistreatment. Caregivers responsible for elder adults who move to elder adult care facilities should determine if there were any previous problems with the facility to limit the opportunity for elder adult abuse and mistreatment. Because poorly trained, poorly paid, or insufficient staff usually encourages overcrowding and increases the opportunity for bullying, abuse, and mistreatment.

Technology, information and the ability to communicate faster has allowed more people an opportunity for greater participation within the social environment.

Maintaining individual independence in the social environment requires the elder adult to cognitively perform and physically behave to the expectations of others (Novak, 2006). Podewils, Guallar, Kuller, Fried, Lopez, Carlson, et al. (2005) found within a large cohort study of community dwelling elder adults that physical activity may help preserve cognitive function and decrease cognitive decline while protecting against subsequent risk of dementia. Those elder adults bullied by peers are forced to restrict their activities increasing the chances of cognitive impairment and the opportunity for mistreatment and abuse. On the other hand, while those elder adults who bully others may also suffer cognitive impairment, the bully will continue uninhibited and unrestricted to harass and physically abuse other elder adult's by pushing, hitting, punching, or kicking them. Additional bullying behaviors can range from blocking off seats in a general area to stealing and destroying the property of others or any other method that limits the new person's opportunities to participate within the group. These behaviors allow the bully to increase their influence with the others in the group and maintain the abusive behavior.

Most of us do not recognize or take very seriously signs of elder abuse and mistreatment because we think it happens only in rare instances. We give little thought to the elder adult being bullied into behaviors they are not accustomed to or them performing behaviors that may appear to be symptoms of dementia, such as rocking, sucking, or mumbling to oneself (Moody, 2010; Patrick, 2007). We often see only the elder adult aging poorly and becoming frailer. For the family or non-professional caregiver assisting the elder adult, understanding their inability to decide quickly, their feelings of inadequacy, their perception of how it was before, and their physical condition is important to maintaining their self-esteem and sense of accomplishment. Consequently, the elder adult's level of self-esteem is rather important to their ability to comply with changes in caregiver behaviors, possible cognitive impairment, and medical interventions.

Definition of Terms

Bullying is any peer-on-peer aggression by other elder adults, harassment, ridicule, exclusion, ostracism and/or violence by caregivers that include family, friends, institutional employees and others charged with the care of elder adults.

Cognition is the ability to learn and think and is what allows humans to plan, organize, and understand what is appropriate behavior and what is not. Cognitive decline and cognitive impairment can lead to functional difficulties reducing the quality of life among elder adults. The elder adult includes those individuals age 70 and above.

Community dwelling elderly are those elders not confined within a hospice institutional setting. They usually live in their own homes, with an adult child or family member, or in an independent living facility, and for the most part are able to care for themselves with a minimum of outside assistance.

Elder abuse and mistreatment of the elderly is any behavior that harms or injures the elder adult. Elder adult abuse and mistreatment includes bullying, intimidation, threats, physical pain and injury. Elder adult abuse usually falls into five major categories financial abuse, neglect and abandonment, physical abuse, psychological abuse, and sexual abuse.

Resources: *Family and/or private resources* include education, information, and opportunities to amass computable wealth such as money, property, and other sources of revenue to which one has recourse for recovery to offset difficult life situations. It includes the capability or skill needed to diagnose a situation and have the means or ability to plan for a solution to a particular immediate problem. Community and/or public resources include the social service agencies, towns, states, and governments, incorporating various programs that provide relief to those individuals who are unable to provide for themselves the minimum requirements for sustenance.

Senescence is the process of aging through the life course and requires continuous individual cognitive, physical, and physiological changes to match the dynamic of social behavior. Growing older requires the individual to change various behaviors as life situations evolve from child to adult. As most learning is similar and most people find comfort in consistency, cognitive impairment will become increasingly problematic as the population continues to age.

Statement of the Problem

This is the century of old age or, as it has been called, the "Age of Aging" by gerontologist Robert Butler (1927-2010). As more people age alone, maintaining a healthy cognitive existence is important to continually learning new information and understanding changes that occur during senescence (Myers, 2005; Thio, 2005). The aging adult population will invariably require more resources, assistance, and support than other groups as age makes many of their needs greater (Novak, 2006). As a result, healthcare is becoming increasingly important as the elder adult population in America continues to grow. Any person who is 18 years of age or older and may be in need of community care services by reason of mental or other disability, age or illness or unable to protect himself or herself against significant harm or exploitation is considered vulnerable. Therefore, the elder adult is a vulnerable adult. As their positions in society are changing (from producer to consumer), the growing number of elderly having fewer social roles is growing evermore profound. One such change has the maintenance of history (normally the job of the elders) being stored, categorized, and made antiseptic through technology removing human interaction, vicariously lessening the value of the elderly individual (Himes, 2001; Myers, 2005; Novak, 2006).

Bullying, harassment, intimidation, and other forms of elder adult abuse and mistreatment are often subtle and usually classified into five major areas or subsets we associate with elder adult harm, pain, and injury. The abuse can range from physically rough contact and sometimes-physical violence, theft of money and neglect, to psychological and sexual abuse. The emotional and psychological toll involved with any abuse significantly influences the behavior of the elder adult often causing additional pain and discomfort. Research into bullying to abuse and mistreat elder adults has not kept pace with the suspected behavior. School boards around the country have mandated regulations regarding group behavior of adolescents and those younger because bullying does occur in groups. While many of us do not like to think, that any form of bullying happens in our society, much less to older people, it is becoming apparent that group behavior when older mirrors group behavior when younger. The growth in the number of elder adults is given rise to older adult environments where peer on peer bullying is occurring. Bullying can occur with the elder adult bullying other older adults (as in a nursing home), or the elder adult being bullied by other elder adults (senior day care) or being bullied by family/friends/younger adults usually in the home by those caring for the elder adult.

The elderly as a segment of the population will have more difficulty changing any behavior including trying to stop the bullying or to forgive the actor. Unfortunately, elder adults are more likely to suffer a greater number of illnesses including possible cognitive impairment and various other physiological problems such as renal failure diminishing their ability to live independently (Brown, 2011). A faulty short-term memory would disadvantage the elder adult when trying to recall instances of bullying and abuse, as the bully may not remember behaving badly, and the victim may be afraid of repercussions or in the worse case, failing to remember and report the abuse accurately. It is apparent that senescence gets more difficult the longer one lives, but the difficulty can be reduced with the proper assistance to keep the elder adult participating in activities that are both doable and helpful to their continued cognitive development. Learning requires more time as one ages and with limited time to practice the appropriate response, it may contribute to misinformation about the elder adult. Therefore, victims of bullying could exacerbate their situation through failure to report the incident, misrepresent the incident, innocently accuse another or aggravate the bully.

Bullying to abuse and mistreat the elder adult seems to have escaped the widespread inquiry that has followed many of our pressing social issues. In nursing homes, assisted living facilities, and senior centers, elders have to face groups whose association may only be time and familiarity and the unfamiliar is always unsettling. For instance, peer-on peer bullying may occur for non-acceptance, as the elder adult may be the object of bullying for no reason other than they are new to the facility. Elder adult bullies try to enforce behavior by using any means of separation including race, ethnicity, sexual orientation, religion, economic background, and etcetera, to keep the new person from joining the group. This combined with people whose social inputs from the surrounding environment support the elder adult's inability to change situational behavior thus creating an opportunity for mistreatment. The behavior of the bully and the victim in the situation where the abuse is occurring, shape the growth and maintenance of their view of being a victim or a bully (Henslin, 2006; Thio, 2005). Consequently, elder adult cognitive functioning for the bully and the victim appears to be dependent upon previous life course cognitive development (Stevens-Long & Michaud, 2003). People, who were aggressive in their youth and started bullying others, and maintained it through their adulthood, are likely candidates for continuing bullying behaviors as an elder adult.

Types of Abuse and Mistreatment

Financial abuse is primarily the unauthorized use of the elder adult's finances, money, property, and etcetera accumulated by the elder adult for the elder adult. Caregivers, family members and other interested parties should be wary of outside sales people who badger the elder adult to participate in transactions that overwhelm the elder adult. Typical financial abuse may include significant withdrawals from the elder adult's bank or security accounts while there are unpaid bills or lack of medical care, although the elder adult has enough money to pay for them. If there are sudden negative changes in the elder adult's financial condition and increases in spending by the caregiver at the same time, it is possible that items or cash is missing from the elder adult's household. Suspicious changes in wills, power of attorney, titles, and policies as well as adding names to the elder adult's credit or signature cards could be instances of elder adult financial abuse.

Neglect seems the most insidious abuse because it implies that the caregiver or other person charged with the care of the elder adult is aware of the elder adult's needs and are purposely withholding assistance to the elder adult. Neglect also includes abandonment, as the individual responsible for the elder adult's care does not provide any. Neglect seems rather all encompassing and similarly benign because the rules of elder adult abuse and mistreatment are not as clear. The National Center on Elder Abuse suggests that elder neglect, which is usually a failure to fulfill a caretaking responsibility, constitutes more than half of all reported cases of elder abuse. Neglect can occur financially by not providing necessary additional care such as physicians or medical tests, physically by not noticing changes such as bruises, swelling and discolorations. It can be intentional or unintentional, based on factors such as ignorance or denial that an elder adult needs as much care as he or she apparently might. Consequently, while previous investigations of changes in well-being have concentrated on positive and negative effects of life situations (Moody, 2010; Mroczek & Spiro, 2005), little is known about age related change in well-being through bullying to abuse and mistreat the elder adult.

Physical abuse appears to be the easiest form of elder adult abuse and mistreatment to recognize as bruises, discolorations, and other injuries are usually visible. Senescence, the process of aging through the life course requires continuous individual cognitive, physical, and more importantly physiological changes to match the dynamic of social behavior (Brown, 2011). As people get older, their skin loses resiliency, they suffer bone loss, and many begin to lose the physical color we associate with good health. Cuts and scratches take longer to heal; elder adults take longer to move and their decisioning often takes longer to effect. Instances of aging can often look like abuse, determining between actual and apparent elder adult abuse is a problem professional, and lay people alike will sometimes confuse. Additional signs of physical abuse may include broken bones, sprains, joint dislocations, and burn marks. There may be broken personal effects (i.e. dentures or glasses) and probably worst of all there may be restraint marks from belts, ropes, tape, and etcetera, used to secure the elder adult

Physical abuse seems to have a greater effect on the elder adult as the elder adult becomes less physical, frailer and more worrisome. Physical abuse may encompass many forms of non-accidental or purposeful force used upon the elder adult. Physical abuse is accompanied by bullying and intimidation, the elder adult becomes easier to control and the abuse more difficult to detect. Bullying and physical abuse, usually make it more difficult for interested persons to separate elder adult mishaps from caregiver behavior. Bullying is easier with the threat of physical abuse as the elder adult sees their position through one of need. As physical abuse is more visible, frustration is probably greater and the difficulty associated with the elder adults condition, probably increases the likelihood of abuse. Physiological pain, physical injury, and cognitive impairment can occur from hitting, pushing, and shoving. Inappropriate dispensing of drugs also impair the elder adult's condition making abuse and mistreatment easier. Consequently, bullying through physical abuse and mistreatment allows the elder adult little opportunity to fight back or stop the bullying and abuse.

Psychological abuse while not as visible as physical abuse, probably contributes as well to the level of elder abuse and mistreatment that occurs through bullying and intimidation. Cognitive and physical decline naturally affect the aging individual and limits the ability of the elder adult to live independently. Cognitive functioning allows the elder adult to make changes in their behavior to continue to take care of themselves. Memory recall of what we think we know and how we perceive the world around us is a function of the information one has collected over the life course. Myers (2005) suggests it seems more likely that the influence of social contact and behavior would have some bearing on an individual's recollection of an event(s). Psychological and emotional abuse induce changes in the elder adult's behavior as insults; threats and harassment allow bullies to shape, control, and decide, which behaviors the elder adult can perform. As people grow older, aspects of their life become more or less important depending on the relative importance of that behavior within their environment (Novak, 2006; Zerubavel, 2005). Ignoring the elder adult or isolating them from family and friends causes an increase in their dependence on the caregiver and an increased opportunity for abuse and mistreatment.

Sexual abuse occurs as the elder adult is subject to sexual contact that is non-consensual. This may include any contact where the elder adult will not give consent and includes if the elder adult cannot give consent. Sexual abuse is physical and supports bullying behavior by causing pain and discomfort to the elder adult. Showing pornographic material, forced undressing, and unwanted touching are also considered sexual abuse of the elder adult. Bruises around breasts or genitals and/or an unexplained venereal disease or genital infections are usually clues that the elder adult has been abused and can be diagnosed by medical personnel (Rollins, 2006). Unexplained vaginal or anal bleeding and/or torn, stained, or bloody underclothing can be observed by the caregiver or other interested person. Similarly, to physical abuse, sexual abuse can also lead to assault and/or battery on the individual (Burgess & Hanrahan, 2006). Because it can be labeled a criminal offense, rape and sodomy can lead to charges and trials quicker than other forms of elder adult abuse and mistreatment.

Elder adult abuse and mistreatment, which includes bullying and intimidation, are difficult to discern and often when we are very sure, it is too late. However, some of the clues to the elder adult being treated poorly might include unusual weight loss, malnutrition, and dehydration or being left dirty and unbathed. Unsanitary living conditions where dirt, bugs, soiled bedding and clothes are present, usually indicates unsafe living conditions (i.e. no heat, water, electric, and etcetera) and additional physical problems that further incapacitate the elder adult. Observing the caregiver threatening, belittling, or controlling the elder adult may also be a sign of elder adult being bullied and mistreated, however, for many interfering in family concerns of others is often taboo. The reasons chosen not to investigate suspected elder adult abuse range from limited knowledge of the behavior, to they are unaware of what actions to take (Adams, McIlvain, Lacy, Magsi, Crabtree, Yenny & Sitorious, 2002). People are unaware of where to report it, or they feel that the elder adult may lose confidence in them, or unfortunately, they fear making the situation worse. The elder adult may not want to stop the bullying through any action that they consider may harm the alleged bully (if the bully has a mental or physical illness). Moreover, the elder adult may have an illness and not be capable of taking steps to protect themselves or may be reluctant to discuss the abuse. Consequently, bullying to abuse and mistreat the elder adult may include any number of things that may influence the elder adult to overlook the abuse if they believe their care is dependent on the bully.

Caregivers

Caregivers can be divided into two basic types. Non-professional, this usually includes the family and others who provide care to the elder adult and are not being paid as such, and professional, which are primarily, contracted non-family caregivers. It is possible for family members to be a contracted caregiver, but that is usually not the case. Contracted non-family caregivers include those individuals paid to assist the elder adult at home or at a facility such as a driver, nurse or therapist. They are not related, and while not complete strangers, their purpose is to provide care to the elder adult. Almost 2 million elder adults are the victims of abuse each year (Anetzberger, Lachs, O'Brien, et. al., 1993; Patrick, 2007) whether at the hands of a caregiver outside the home, in the home or by a peer at a senior living facility. As elder adults begin to require more assistance, the problem of elder abuse and mistreatment becomes one of identification. Age and cognitive impairment will affect he elder adults' perception and ability to think coherently about the

performance of a behavior (i.e. bullying) and often leads to the elder adult continuing the inappropriate behavior. As continually inappropriate behavior increases,
or the elder adult has difficulty deciding which behavior to perform, the risk of
cognitive decline increases as well as the chance for abuse and mistreatment.

Family caregivers are usually adult children or grandchildren, spouses, nieces,
and nephews of extended family members (which may not be related) usually
located in close proximity to the elder adult. Family caregivers often live with the
elder adult and are often the primary caregiver responsible for assisting the elder
adult. Caregivers are also charged with the safety and security of the elder adult as
well as all decisions affecting the elder adult's wider existence in many instances.
Bullying to abuse and mistreat the elder adult creates a climate of fear. For every
known or reported case, the National Center on Elder Abuse says there could be ten
or more that go unreported. The reliability of victims to recall instances of bullying
and intimidation, or abuse and mistreatment are all factors that affect reporting.
Caregivers' lack of awareness of the signs of abuse and lack of governmental
resources for investigations of bullying are also factors that affect reporting.
Consequently, it appears that either the elder adult's condition rapidly deteriorates
causing abuse like symptoms or caregiver frustration makes it difficult to keep the
elder adult safe and secure.

Familial Non-Professional

Taking care of an elder adult may prove rewarding as the elder adult maintains their
current lifestyle, however, increasing age also means increased scrutiny of the elder
adult's behavior and probably an increase in care. Family and non-professional
caregivers often suffer depression (as commonly understood), which is common
among caregivers as the lack of support from other potential caregivers and the
elder adult's condition worsens. It is also possible that the caregiver's perception
that taking care of the elder adult is burdensome and without a financial or psychological reward may seem so overwhelming that the caregiver seeks any relief
including substance abuse. Unfortunately, in family situations it is also possible that
the elder adult's condition will influence how the caregiver responds to the
demands of caring for the elder adult (Farran, 2001). Serious illnesses or dementia
will make care difficult for the caregiver. If the elder adult and caregiver are alone
together almost all the time or if the previous relationship was hurtful or abusive
and/or there is a history of violence in the home, the relationship between the
caregiver and the elder adult is going to be stressful. It appears that for many, elder
abuse, though real, is unintentional. Caregivers may not mean to hit or yell or
ignore the needs of the elder adult, but caregiver inability to relieve the stress of
taking care of the elder adult may push them beyond their financial resources,
and/or their physical and psychological capabilities.

Family caregivers are less forgiving probably because of the pre existing
relationships. Adult children (sons and then daughters) are most abusive because
of the control exerted throughout the care-giving situation. Elder adults being
excluded from family events, ostracism, and violence may be clues to a hidden

problem becoming more visible. Frequent arguments or tension between the caregiver and the elder adult as well as changes in personality or behavior of the elder adult may also signal bullying and/or a problem of abuse. When the elder adult becomes less responsive, requires more assistance, and as their dependence becomes greater, the stress felt by the caregiver increases as does caregiver responsibility. Sometimes the inability of the caregiver to provide more assistance creates stress that can lead to impatience, caregiver mental and physical health problems, and possible burnout trying to satisfy all of the elder adults needs. Consequently, instances of bullying (physical, psychological, social), to mistreat the elder adult through financial mismanagement, denial of healthcare, and neglect are more likely to occur and often are not reported because of fear of being wrong or wanting to protect the abuser.

Professional Non-Familial

Non-family or professional caregivers are trained and compensated for their services. It is possible that they will also be family members, but not usually. The expertise that professional caregivers share with the family is supposed to help maintain the care of the elder adult. In home professional caregivers such as occupational therapists, home care nurses, and transportation drivers come into the home to deliver services and respond to caregiver and patient concerns about the care of the elder adult. Even caregivers in institutional settings can experience stress at levels that lead to bullying, elder abuse, and mistreatment. Nursing home staff may be prone to elder abuse if they lack training, have too many responsibilities, are unsuited to care giving, or work under poor conditions. Consequently, an unscrupulous caregiver might misuse an elder's personal checks, credit cards, and other accounts. They may steal cash, income checks, or household goods, forge the elder adult's signature or engage in identity theft.

Professional caregivers outside the home include doctors, nurses, therapists and other medical personnel who work at hospitals, clinics, community centers and elder adult living facilities assisting the elder adult. The myriad of government agencies, medical supply firms, and products offered to elder adult's increases information and the opportunity for abuse and mistreatment by unethical doctors, nurses, hospital personnel, and other professional care providers. Often the elder adult is solicited for unnecessary services, goods, prescriptions, and/or subscriptions. Moreover, they may incur the cost of doctors and other medical staff, which may include duplicate billings for the same medical service or device. Often the price of the service is exorbitant and the care inadequate even when the bills are paid in full. Other instances of health care fraud include kickbacks for 'referrals to other providers, over medication or under medication, or recommending fraudulent remedies for illnesses and other non-existent medical conditions are instances of elder abuse and mistreatment.

Bullying

Bullying to abuse and mistreat the elder adult seems to be committed primarily by two groups; caregivers, (which is anyone charged with the welfare of the elder) and peers (other elders of approximate age) at varying facilities designed for elder adult care. Caregivers often include family and professional staff from local social service agencies and if in an elder adult facility, administrators, medical staff and support staff. As behavior it appears, does not radically change over the life course without the introduction of some type of trauma (Shute, 1997), bullying, abuse, and elder mistreatment changes the behavior of the elder adult in several ways. As the elder adult can perform fewer physical activities their security is compromised, psychological abuse affects the cognitive abilities of the elder adult. The elder adult's memory may be affected causing periods of self-neglect or there may be increasing frustrations because of decreasing ability by the elder adult. Additionally, the caregiver's response to the behavior unfortunately, could negatively influence the elder adult's response to continued care. Consequently, elder adults limited in their ability to change their behaviors become more of a drain on family resources, which may exacerbate the level and type of abuse and place more of a burden on the general society through monitoring and reporting abusive behavior.

It's difficult to take care of a senior when he or she has many different needs, and it's difficult to be elderly when age brings with it infirmities and dependence. The elderly often remember their youth and when they were younger much clearer than things occurring presently. Consequently, what experience teaches becomes the lynchpin of everything else known and perhaps, because time strengthens memory, it also gives rise to apparent decreases in short term memory possibly affecting their cognitive development and performance (Goldstein, Ashley, Freedman, et al., 2005). Those individuals who may make material decisions affecting the wider existence of the individual have to be careful of so many possible instances of elder adult mistreatment. Both the demands of care giving and the needs of the elder can create situations in which abuse is more likely to occur. Many non-professional caregivers (spouses, adult children, other relatives and friends) find taking care of an elder to be rewarding. Nevertheless, the responsibilities and demands of elder care giving, which escalate as the elder's condition deteriorates, can also be extremely stressful. The stress of elder care can lead to mental and physical health problems that make caregivers burned out, impatient, and unable to keep from lashing out against elders in their care.

Individual and societal stereotypes about the elderly have a tremendous effect on the perceptions and behaviors of others toward the elderly. How we perceive their capability is quite important to what we believe they can do. Bullying changes the behavior of all in the situation and forces the victim into non-participation. For the caregiver assisting the elderly, understanding their inability to decide quickly, their feelings of inadequacy, their perception of how it was before, their physical condition and their self-esteem is also important to their ability to remember past events and why some behaviors were performed. Their sense of self worth and life satisfaction depends on their ability to continue being productive in some manner (Brown.2011). As the importance of limiting elder adult mistreatment rests on individual independence that allows the individual to continue contributing to the family, community, and the general society bullying, elder abuse and mistreatment limits the ability of the elder adult to function appropriately. Consequently, in an attempt to understand old age, it may be necessary to determine at what level of independence or lack of ability requires society to contribute to the continued functioning of the individual.

Caregiver Bullying

Familial abuse seems the most unforgiving as our society generally values life above all else and because many believe the family is the foundation for everything that matters. In most societies, family is the strongest bond that the individual makes and that allows us to never be alone. While there is a difference between being alone with one's thoughts and suffering periods of loneliness, (where the elder adult feels alone and helpless), it is important that the caregiver, medical personnel or other interested party notice the changes that occur in the elder adult no matter how subtle. The National Center on Elder Abuse in their 2006 report indicates that by far the major perpetrators of elder abuse were adult children. As they would seem to be in contact more often with the elder adult, that is not surprising. Spouses and those more intimate tend to abuse less often than other family members and strangers. However, children, spouses, relatives, and friends are the people we expect the highest degree of care from and are very disappointed when we find that they have behaved inappropriately. Because elder adults have fewer support systems, the impact of abuse and mistreatment and subsequent neglect is magnified and may be responsible for the elder adult's condition deteriorating quicker (Administration on Aging, 2000).

Caregiver bullying to abuse and mistreat the elder adult often includes financial abuse, neglect, physical abuse, psychological abuse, and to a lesser degree sexual abuse of the elderly. Unauthorized use of monies or property taken by force or intimidation or illegally obtained benefits from taking advantage of the elder adult because of perceived inability to make adequate decisions also borders on neglect. Failure to adequately care for the elder adult is mistreatment through neglect, which has psychological implications when considering how the elder adult will then cope with their changing life situation. Declining cognitive function is a detriment to the elderly individual and their families as it decreases the elder adult's ability to perform the activities of daily living (eating, dressing, communicating, sleeping and physical hygiene) and/or to modify behavior as necessary, which often leads to increased oversight, and limits the elder adult's ability to live independently (Peterson, 2006). Physical abuse is easily the most obvious because the elder adult will not heal as when younger and the bruises, discolorations, and other injuries can be observed. Sexual abuse also can be readily observed if the elder adult can report the abuse in a timely manner. Of course, caregivers and medical personnel as well as other service, facilities, organizations and staff will have to determine if the incident is abuse or an instance of elder adult frailty (a senior moment as they say).

Elder adult mistreatment through bullying and abuse lessens elder adult independence. Adapting and changing behavior through continued learning, enhanced by changes in cognition allows the elder adult to recognize adverse situations such as intimidation and other instances of abuse. Unfortunately, elder adult perception of their general well-being is strongly associated with physical decline and subsequent cognitive and/or physical illness will cause an increased dependence on others for assistance. Kinsella & Phillips (2005) suggest that people grow old in a social and economic context that effects their psychosocial development. Greater resources are associated with increased longevity and the older one gets the greater the chance that the elder adult will require the assistance of others. Zastrow & Kirst-Ashman (2004), suggest that economic limitations create more difficulties for the elder adult and in poorer families, the difficulties become immeasurable. Elder adults unable to adapt to changing environmental stimuli increase their emotional and psychological stress and it lessens the ability to learn in any context (Cavanaugh & Blanchard-Fields, 2002). Consequently, bullying and other forms of elder adult mistreatment adversely affect the wider existence of the individual, their familial relationships, and often forces an increased use of community resources and services.

Peer-on-Peer Bullying

Peer-on-peer bullying usually occurs in social settings. The bullies use exclusion and ostracism more often to make the elder adult feel as an outsider and not welcome in the group. The harassment can range from more classic types of bullying behaviors, such as verbal intimidation, to dirty looks, and even physical violence (Payne, 2000). Elder adult males tend to be more direct with their bullying, using verbal harassment, while females tend more towards passive aggressive tactics, such as gossiping and/or spreading lies about others. Mroczek & Spiro, (2005) suggest that the individual's level of extraversion affects their ability to participate fully in family or individual activities. Life activities such as organization memberships, friendships, and employment lessen as one ages. Fewer relationships cause the elder adult to rely even more on the social settings that include other elder adults and when treated as an outsider bullying can be difficult for the individual and detrimental to the entire group. Targets of bullying and abuse tend to be those individuals who have difficulty with specific tasks (eating, reading, personal hygiene, leisure activities, and etcetera.) or who are new to the facility. Unfortunately, when people become frailer, they feel more vulnerable (Payne, 2000). Therefore, some people adjust to getting older, while other people develop difficult and destructive behaviors toward themselves and sometimes bully others.

Unfortunately, people who were bullies when they were younger and other elder adults who have become bullies are now terrorizing residents in long-term care facilities, assisted living facilities, senior centers, and retirement communities around the country. Elder adult bullying in these primarily elder adult only facilities or elder adult communities tend form cliques just as when younger and criticize, ridicule, and lie about those who do not meet their standards of acceptance. The belief that the elderly have fewer assets (financial, mental or physical) may influence the perceptions of those responsible for determining the types of responses and services the elder adult receives to peer on peer bullying (Kinsella & Phillips, 2005; Newman, 2002). Changing facility (administrative) perceptions of aging and understanding of bullying behavior and mistreatment will allow development of procedures to reduce aggressive behavior, bullying and intimidation. Often situations occur and the elder adult's perception of behavior is overlooked as incorrect perceptions of the elder adult's cognitive ability negatively affect the wider social existence of the individual. To others, the bully's action seems harmless enough, but the victim is sure there is intent and if the situation is summarily dismissed the elder adult becomes more fretful about their safety. Consequently, elder adults being bullied by caregivers or others may equate their response to behavior to the services they may receive. Therefore, those who have relatives in elder adult only facilities should be vigilant in checking that they are being properly cared for.

Conclusions

As the number of elderly people continues to rise, government assistance will decrease and as fewer children are born, more people will age alone making it more important than ever that one continues to develop cognitively as they age. As the average age of American adults continues to rise, it will be increasingly important for individuals to maintain their independence well into old age (Novak, 2006; Sloan & Wang, 2005). People experience abundant subjective well-being when they feel many pleasant and few unpleasant emotions or when they experience many pleasures and few pains (Pavot & Diener, 1993), when they are engaged in interesting activities (Diener, 2000), and when they are satisfied with their lives (Mroczek & Spiro, 2005). Improving the performance of expected behaviors while reducing the need for external assistance, invariably allows the elder adult more opportunity for independent living. Consequently, when one is successful adapting their behaviors to maintain much of their previous level of independence, the more the individual, family, and community will benefit. For people who are bullied and do not understand why the mistreatment, it is quite possible that their overall health is also being affected and that invariably will have a direct effect on their cognitive ability, physical health and their emotional well-being.

The continued growth in the number of elderly has led to greater study of dementia, a condition characterized by global decline in cognitive functioning (Podewils, Guallar, Kuller, et al., 2005). Dementia is growing in importance as more people get older and more suffer some degree of cognitive decline and impairment causing increased use of health services. Measuring cognitive decline and impairment is imprecise (Sloan & Wang, 2005), and it affects the elder adult's performance of subsequent behavior. Unfortunately, an inaccurate measure of cognitive functioning will expose the elder adult to increased screening and a greater chance of a mistaken diagnosis of dementia (Parker & Philip, 2004). An incorrect diagnosis of dementia added to facing the frailties of age, and confronted with bullying or over-aggressive behavior, probably weakens the overall condition of the elder adult allowing them to deteriorate quicker.

As the number of elder adults increase, the number of those diagnosed with some type of cognitive impairment increases. Cognitive impairment will increase the opportunity for bullying behavior as the bully and the victim may behave inappropriately. Social learning theory (Bandura, 1977) and behaviorism (Mead, 1934) suggest that much of our learning is through repetition, and bullying over a lifetime allows many opportunities for aggressive behavior. The expectations of others may require unfamiliar responses from the elder adult bully as repeated bullying adds to the emotional suffering experienced by the victim. Therefore, maintaining and improving elder adult independence and to limit bullying within families and at elder care facilities, the elder adult must adapt and change their behavior through continued learning, enhanced by changes in cognition.

Limited performance and fewer repetitions make additional learning difficult and the decrease in self-esteem and limited opportunity to contribute to the maintenance of family and community will further diminish the activities the elderly might perform (Oysterman, Kemmelmeier, Fryberg, Brosh, & Hart-Johnson, 2003). Post Positivism suggests that those experiencing reality view the world differently, therefore society and the individual jointly create reality and failure to accurately identify cognitive deficits of elder adults increases the instances of cognitive misdiagnosis, poses a threat to their physical well-being, and increases the cost of care (Parker & Philp, 2004; Zerubavel, 2003). Consequently, that failure has prompted The National Institute on Aging to suggest a new paradigm that focuses on what maintains brain health rather than dysfunction. The premise is that cognitive health and emotional well-being are 'inextricably linked' to limiting cognitive decline (Barnes et al., 2006), which will invariably allow the elder adult more independence and a better opportunity to recognize bullying and/or over-aggressive behavior, abuse, harassment, intimidation and mistreatment.

Each of the 50 states, District of Columbia, Guam and Puerto Rico has laws that are designed to protect elderly citizens from abuse and mistreatment under the federal older Americans Act (42 U.S.C.). In general, federal statutes require that elder adults not be subjected to discrimination, intimidation or coercion. Most states provide grievance procedures and a Long Term Care Ombudsmen Program, which assists seniors with complaints against those suspected of abusing elder adults. They monitor nursing homes, assisted living facilities and other types of residential in-home care facilities. Interestingly enough as the number of elder adults increase, more states are enacting criminal penalties against people found to have abused or mistreated elder adults. Moreover, basic criminal laws such as assault, battery, rape, and murder are being used more often to prosecute people committing harm, injury or pain against the elder adult. For anyone who suspects elder adult abuse and mistreatment the "eldercare locator" is a national network of local agencies that provide assistance and help for the abused and mistreated elder adult.

The ultimate goal for the human services professional, is to prevent people in need from being mistreated and overlooked and to provide those resources that will allow for continued independence. Bullying by the caregiver or by a peer will affect how the elder adult subsequently behaves. Counselor/health professional/caregiver effectiveness unfortunately, is judged by the outcome of the elder adult's behavior, which is a function of how productive, satisfying, and self-sufficient the elder adult may become. Consequently, the most important aspects in developing a relationship with the elder adult and possible subsequent intervention are honesty and confidentiality. Patience and vigilance are necessary not to intimidate, but to maintain respect and not bully or abuse the elder adult (Peterson, 2006). Therefore, it appears that without a most encompassing ethical approach by the professional and/or non-professional caregiver to the elder adult, the decrease in bullying, abuse and mistreatment will be minimal and possible gains could be short lived. Continual cognitive development throughout senescence allows the elder adult to contribute to the family and the community and enhances their level of self-respect and self-efficacy. Continued cognitive performance will allow the individual to be independent longer and that will lessen the chance of caregiver and peer bullying.

Two things seem abundantly clear. Medicine and technology are going to assist people to live longer and therefore, there will be more elder people living longer with a greater chance of developing an ailment that will require the assistance of another. While that will create employment opportunities, it will also create many more opportunities for abuse and mistreatment. Secondly, as more people get older it will spur greater public awareness of bullying to abuse and mistreat the elder adult and that will encourage increased reporting of abusive instances, better record keeping and methods to measure behavior. Increasing the recognition of elder adult abuse and mistreatment may spur innovations to improve elder adult health and limit the opportunity for caregiver's and peers to bully, abuse and mistreat the elder adult, and as the elderly does better, it will allow all of us to feel better about getting older.

References

Adams, W.L., McIlvain, H.E., Lacy, N.L., Magsi, H., Crabtree, B.F., Yenny, S.K., & Sitorious, M.A. (2002). Primary care for elderly people: Why do doctors find it so hard? *The Gerontologist, 42,* (6) 835–842.

Administration on Aging. (2000). *Profile of older Americans.* Washington, DC U.S. Department of Health and Human Services.

Anetzberger, G.J., Lachs, M.S., O'Brien, J.G., O'Brien, S., Pillemer, K.A., & Tomita, S.K. (1993, June) Elder mistreatment: A call for help. *Patient Care. 27,* 11 93–94.

Ayres, R. (2004). September/October). The economic conundrum of an aging population. *World Watch Magazine, 45–49.*

Bandura, A.J. (1977). *Social learning theory.* Englewood Cliffs, NJ: Prentice-Hall.

Barnes, L.L., Wilson, R.S., Mendes de Leon, C.F., and Bennett, D.A. (2006). The relation of lifetime cognitive activity and lifetime access to resources to late-life cognitive function in older African Americans. *Aging, Neuropsychology, and Cognition, 13* 516–528.

Bonnie, R., and Wallace, R. (2003) *Elder mistreatment: abuse, neglect, and exploitation in an aging America.* National Research Council.

Bordens, K.S., and Horowitz, I.A. (2002). *Social psychology* (2nd ed.) Mahwah NJ: Erlbaum.

Brown, C. L. (2011). The impact of satisfaction of life on cognitive functioning in Black elder adults: A correlational study (Doctoral dissertation). Retrieved from ProQuest. (34436230).

Burgess, A., and Hanrahan, N. (2006). *Identifying forensic markers in elderly sexual abuse.* Washington, DC. National Institute of Justice.

Cavanaugh, J.C., and Blanchard-Fields, F. (2001). *Adult development and aging* (4th ed.) Belmont, CA: Wadsworth/Thomson Learning.

Diener, E. (2000). Subjective well-being. *American Psychologist, 55* (1) 34–44.

Farran, C.J. (2001) Family caregiver intervention research; Where have we been? Where are we going? *Journal of Gerontological Nursing. 27* (7) 38–45.

Goldstein, F.C., Ashley, A.V., Gearing, M., Hanfelt, J. Penix, L., Freedman, L.J., and Levy A.I. (2001). Apo lipoprotein E and age at onset of Alzheimer's' disease in African-American patients. *Neurology 57* 1923–1925.

Henslin, J.M. (2006). *Social problems* (7th ed.) Upper Saddle River, N.J: Pearson.

Himes, C.L. (2001, December). Elderly Americans. *Population Bulletin.* 3–8.

Kinsella, K., and Phillips, D.R. (2005, March). Successful aging. *Population Bulletin.* 32–34.

Mead, G.H. (1934). *Mind, self and society.* Chicago, ILL: Univ. of Chicago Press.

Merzenich, M. (2000). *A learning revolution: Dr. Michael Merzenich and brain plasticity.* Impact, The UCSF Foundation On-Line magazine. Retrieved June 30, 2003.

Moody, H.R. (2010). *Aging concepts and controversies* (6h ed.) Thousand Oaks, CA: Sage.

Mroczek, D.K., & Spiro, A. (2005). Change in life satisfaction during adulthood: Findings from the Veterans Affairs normative study. *Journal of Personality and Social Psychology, 88* (1) 189–202.

Myers, D.C. (2005). *Social psychology* (8th ed.) Boston, MA: McGraw-Hill.

National Center on Elder Abuse (2004). *Survey of state adult protective services: Abuse of adult 60 years of age or older.* Washington, DC. National Center on Elder abuse.

Newman, D.M. (2002). *Sociology: Exploring the architecture of everyday life* (4th ed.) Thousand Oaks CA: Pine Forge

Novak, M. (2006). *Issues in aging.* Boston, MA: Pearson.

Oysterman, D., Kemmelmeier, M., Fryberg, S., Brosh, H., & Hart-Johnson, T., (2003) Racial-ethnic self-schemas. *Social Psychology Quarterly, 66* (4) 333–347.

Parker, C., & Philp, I. (2004). Screening for cognitive impairment among older people in Black and minority ethnic groups. *Age and Aging, 33* (5).

Patrick, P.K.S. (2007). *Contemporary issues in counseling.* Boston MA: Pearson

Pavot, W., & Diener, E. (1993). Review of the satisfaction with life scale. *Psychological Assessment 5* (2), 164–172.

Payne, B.K. (2000). *Crime and elder abuse: An integrated perspective.* Springfield, IL: Charles C. Thomas

Peterson, C. (2006). *A primer in positive psychology.* New York: Oxford University Press.

Podewils, L.J., Guallar, E., Kuller, L.H., Fried, L.P., Lopez, O.L., Carlson, M., et al (2005). Physical activity, APOE genotype, and dementia risk: Findings from the cardiovascular health cognition study. *American Journal of Epidemiology, 161* (7) 639–651.

Rollins, J.N. (2006, July). Keep alert for signs of abuse in elderly patients. *Family Practice News, 36* (14) 55

Shute, N. (1997, June). A study for the ages. *U.S. News and World Report,* 67–72.

Stevens-Long, J. & Michaud, G. (2003). *Theory in adult development.* In J. Demick & C. Andreoletti (Eds.) Handbook of Adult Development. 3–22. New York, NY: Kluwer Academic.

Schwartz, B.S., Glass, T.A., Bolla, K.I., Stewart, W.F., Glass, G., Rasmussen, M., et. al., (2004). Disparities in cognitive functioning by race/ethnicity in the Baltimore memory study. *Environmental Health Perspectives, 112* (3) 314–320.

Sloan, F.A., & Wang, J. (2005). Disparities among older adults in measures of cognitive function by race or ethnicity. *Journal of Gerontology; Psychological Sciences, 60B* (5) 242–250.

Thio, A. (2005). *Sociology: A brief introduction* (6th ed.) Boston MA: Pearson.

Zastrow, C. H., & Kirst-Ashman, K. K. (2004). *Understanding human behavior and the social environment.* (6th ed.). Belmont, CA: Thomson, Brooks/Cole.

Zerubavel, E. (2003). *Time maps: the social topography of the past.* Chicago, IL: University of Chicago Press.

Chapter Three

'Bully-Proofing' the Academe:
Dealing with the *Bunch* and *Bullies*
in a Whole School-Approach

Perla Palileo-Brame
Vanessa Caguicla Bivens

Introduction

School bullying is a widespread problem of epidemic proportion that is shared by educational institutions serving students from Kindergarten through High School across all kinds of communities—'bullying' nowadays can just happen anywhere, anytime; and, chances are those who are bullied won't even tell.

There are many reasons why people are bullied. Some people are picked on because of their religion or race, while others are chosen because of their weight, the clothes they wear or because they're clever—things that no-one should be ashamed of fundamentally or basically.

Bullying is an intentional and persistent aggressive behavior that may include physical violence, teasing and name-calling, and intimidation. Bullying can be related to the harassment of racial and ethnic minorities: gay, lesbian, and bisexual youth.

Surveys indicate that 11 percent of American schoolchildren in the sixth through the tenth grades have been bullied, 13 percent have engaged in bullying, and six percent have been both perpetrators and victims of bullying (Nansel, et al. 2001).

According to Parker and Brain, "school bullying is a hot topic among educators" (Parker Peters, and Brain, 2010). Other agree (Brown & Taylor, 2008; Card & Hodges, 2008; Nordahl, Poole, Stanton, Walden, & Beran, 2008).

Educators often seek ways to reduce or eliminate violence in the schools. This sometimes involves examination of bullying behaviors, including who is performing and receiving the bullying. In a recent study, 22.7 percent of high school students reported that they had been victimized in the past month. In the same study, more than 30 percent of students reported that they had bullied another student during the last month (Bradshaw, Sawyer, & O'Brennan, 2007).

Bullying as a Global Issue

Bullying is a global issue. There are many recent reports about bullying around the world. In "Bullying Among Children and Youth," Susan Limber and Maury Nation state:

> bullying is a common and potentially damaging form of violence among children. Not only does bullying harm both its intended victims and the perpetrators, it also may affect the climate of schools and, indirectly, the ability of all students to learn to the best of their abilities (Limber & Nation, 2013).

Moreover, the link between bullying and later delinquent and criminal behavior cannot be ignored. Although studies of comprehensive anti-bullying programs are scarce in the United States, evaluation data from other countries suggest that adopting a comprehensive approach to reduce bullying at school can change students' behaviors and attitudes, reduce other antisocial behaviors, and increase teachers' willingness to intervene.

Stimulated by the pioneering work of Dan Olweus in Norway and Sweden (Limber & Nation, 2013), researchers from several nations—Australia, Canada, England, Ireland, Japan, Norway, and the United States—have begun to explore the nature, prevalence, and effects of bullying among school children. Their findings provide compelling reasons for initiating interventions to prevent bullying. Its high prevalence among children, its harmful and frequently enduring effects on victims; and, its chilling effects on school climate are significant reasons for prevention and early intervention efforts in schools and communities.

The phenomenon of bullying deserves special attention by educators, parents, and children concerned with violence prevention for two significant reasons. First, the prevalence of bullying and the harm that it causes are seriously underestimated by many children and adults. It is critical that any violence prevention strategy work to raise the awareness of children, school staff and parents regarding the link between bullying and other violent behaviors.

The nature of bullying does not necessarily lend itself to the same interventions that may effectively reduce other types of conflict among children. Because it involves harassment by powerful children against children with less power (rather than a conflict between peers of relatively equal status), common conflict resolution strategies such as mediation may not be effective.

The Extent of Bullying in the United States

U.S. Secretary of Education Arne Duncan has challenged the parents, school administrators and students to "break the cycle of bullying in America." On April 13, 2011, Duncan said, "Bullying is a serious problem that can have tragic consequences; and, more needs to be done to recognize and address the issue." (Duncan, 2011) In remarks to the Anti-Defamation League's 2011 Shana Amy Glass National Leadership Conference, held April 3–5 in Washington, D.C., Secretary Duncan discussed the impact of bullying in our nation's schools, and called bullying a "a moral and educational issue." Secretary Duncan told an audience of nearly 500 ADL leaders from across the country:

> Last fall, our nation witnessed the tragic impact that bullying can have on individual lives. Over the course of one month, five young people took their lives after being bullied or harassed. The deaths reminded all of us that we need to stand up and speak out against intolerance in all its forms (Duncan, 2011).

Although there have been few studies of the prevalence of bullying among American schoolchildren, available data suggest that bullying is quite common in U.S. schools. In a study of 207 junior high and high school students from small Midwestern towns, 88 percent reported having observed bullying, and 77 percent indicated that they had been victims of bullying during their school careers. A study of 6,500 students in fourth to sixth grades in the rural South indicated that 1 in 4 students had been bullied with some regularity within the past 3 months and that 1 in 10 had been bullied at least once a week. (Limber & Nation, 2013)

Approximately one in five children admitted that they had bullied another child with some regularity in the previous three months. These figures are consistent with estimates of several other researchers. Furthermore, contrary to popular belief, bullying occurs more frequently on school grounds than on the way to and from school. (Limber & Nation, 2013)

The prevalence of bullying among US youth is substantial (Nansel, 2001). Given the concurrent behavioral and emotional difficulties associated with bullying, as well as the potential long-term negative outcomes for these youth, the issue of bullying merits serious attention, both for future research and preventive intervention (Hoover, Oliver & Hazler).

More than 3.2 million (nearly one in six) are victims of bullying each year, while 3.7 million bully other children in sixth through tenth grade. Preventing kids from becoming bullies and intervening to stop bullying, however, cannot only protect children from the pain that bullying inflicts immediately, but can protect all of us from crime later on. Whereas programs have been developed that can cut bullying and future arrests by as much as fifty percent, these programs need to be implemented in America's schools. These were the recent findings by Fox and Elliott in their support for Washington, D.C.'s campaign FIGHT CRIME: INVEST IN KIDS as supported by Center for Problem-Oriented Policing.

The questions should be: *Why do kids bully? What causes these bullying and where does it come from?* Bullying in the classroom is not new. Bullies have been around for ages and if the teacher cannot understand why the child is bullying, she may never really be able to help the child. *So where do bullies come from?*

Jacqueline Chinappi writes that:

> When people think of a bully they may imagine a larger than life kid who goes around picking on kids half his or her size. Many times though this is simply not true. Bullies can come in many sizes and forms. They can be short or tall, a boy or a girl, have glasses or no glasses, etc. Some popular television and movie bullies are actually girls! One of the most popular "girl bullies" was Nellie Olsen from *Little House on the Prairie* who was always tormenting Laura Wilder and was constantly cheating, stealing, and most of all lying (Chinappi, 2009).

Different types of bullying that can be manifested through:

- Verbal abuse: name-calling, putting someone down, teasing, insulting others, and threatening others.
- Physical abuse: punching, kicking, biting, shoving, making others do things they do not want to.
- Covert abuse: telling others you will spread rumors about them if they do not do something, rejecting people and not talking to them, talking badly about people behind their backs.
- Cyber abuse: overt or covert bullying behaviors using digital technologies. Examples include harassment via a mobile phone, setting up a defamatory personal website or deliberately excluding someone from social networking spaces (The Department of Education and Early Childhood Development's Building Respectful and Safe Schools, 2010).

It seems that bullies thrive on attention and unfortunately it is a negative attention. This negative attention puts a damper on the children's class time and education time. Kids and even adults who are bullies try to push others down to feel a sense of power. For one reason or another, the constant demeaning of other people makes the bully feel good about him or herself. When the bully feels good then they feel as if they are "better than other." This bullying not only brings attention to them but also brings a personal gain.

It is clear that one doesn't have to be physically beaten up or hurt to be a victim of bullying. Teasing, being threatened and name calling can all be classed as forms of bullying. With the rise of technology, bullying can happen by mobile phone nowadays. Mobile phone is now a venue for bullying. One who receives a rude or scary text message directly to his phone, or a voicemail message sent through that might be threatening or a photo message which may make one feel uncomfortable, is also considered, bullying. It means that bullying cannot just happen face to face with someone, but also over the phone or even on the Internet—in that case, it is called cyber—"bullying."

Anyone can be the target of bullying. However, numerous research studies report that certain groups are more likely to experience bullying and are more vulnerable to its harmful impact. This was what Janssen and his co-authors found out in their research in 2004 regarding the "School's Role to Help Prevent Bullying" and added that " children and adolescents who have certain physical or emotional traits or sexual orientation are at greater risk for physical, verbal and relational bullying. For example, multiple studies find that overweight and obese children are more likely to be bullied than their normal-weight peers" (Janssen, Craig, Boyce & Pickett, 2004).

Causes of Bullying

What really causes bullying? Perhaps a good one-shot question would be: *Why are there bullies and why are people "bullied?"*

Kids and even adults who are bullies try to push others down to feel a sense of power. For one reason or another, the constant demeaning of other people makes the bully feel good about him or herself. When the bully feels good then they feel as if they are "better than other." This bullying not only brings attention to them but also brings a personal gain. It seems bullies thrive on attention, unfortunately it is negative attention. This negative attention puts a damper on the children's class time and education time.

There are numerous reasons why people are bullied. Some people are picked on because of their religion or race, while others are chosen because of their weight, the clothes they wear or because they're clever—things that no-one should be ashamed of.

Bullies can be acting this way for several reasons. This is the only way they know how to act: perhaps they have been pushed around, beaten down or abused at home. These types of bullies do not know anything else, they have not been taught any other way. They do not get attention at home. These types of bullies are seeking attention and love but they do not know how to go about it. So they turn into bullies and receive negative attention. The first time they do something wrong and get attention, they feel good about themselves. So instead of trying to do something for positive attention, they continue down the road for negative attention. This is the only way they know how to act. Perhaps they have been pushed around, beaten down, and abused at home. These types of bullies do not know anything else, they have not been taught any other way. They do not get attention at home. These types of bullies are seeking attention and love but they do not know how to go about it. So they turn into bullies and receive negative attention. The first time they do something wrong and get attention, they feel good about themselves. So instead of trying to do something for positive attention, they continue down the road for negative attention.

Children who are bullied are often singled out because of a perceived difference between them and others, whether because of appearance (size, weight, or clothes), intellect, or, increasingly, ethnic or religious affiliation and sexual orientation.

Leslie Pappas of the *Philadelphia Inquirer* wrote:

Only after Ryan Halligan hanged himself did his father realize what the 13-year-old had been doing online. Through three months' worth of links and instant messages saved on his home computer, Ryan's growing pain —and the callousness of his online tormentors—became clear. "You're a loser," one message jabbed. There were other taunts, Web searches on suicide, and, ultimately, threats to kill himself to get back at school bullies. "Tonight's the night," Ryan finally typed. "It's about time," the screen replied. This nightmare situation continued after Ryan's death on October 7, 2003, when his father, after clicking on his son's saved links, found months of horrible messages directed to Ryan (Pappas, 2005).

It can be further explained that Ryan's situation was extreme but sadly, not an isolated case. Cyberbullying is a huge deal to the youth experiencing it. They can often feel even more alone than if the bullying was occurring in person. At least with non-cyberbullying, someone may hear something or see something and possibly help. Cyberbullying can be terrifying because it is such an isolated experience for the victim.

Who Bullies and Why?

Bullying is usually defined as a subset of aggressive behavior characterized by repetition and an imbalance of power (Olweus, 2004). The definition "a systematic abuse of power" also captures these two features (Smith & Sharp, 1994, p. 2. The behavior involved is generally thought of as being repetitive, i.e., a victim is targeted a number of times. Also, the victim cannot defend himself or herself easily, for one or more reasons: He or she may be outnumbered, smaller or less physically strong, or less psychologically resilient than the person(s) doing the bullying.

People sometimes assume that only boys bully, but that is not true. Girls also bully others. Boys tend to use methods such as hitting, fighting, and threatening. These face-to-face behaviors are easy to observe. Girls do bully using physical and verbal attacks, but they often use behind-the-back methods that are harder to see. These more subtle behaviors include getting peers to exclude others and spreading rumors and gossip. It's important to remember, though, that girls and boys use both face-to-face and behind-the-back methods.

Why Do Children Bully?

There is no universal reply to the question why do children bully. Usually a child bullies when he is insensitive to others' needs and desires and oversensitive about his own needs and desires. However, each child has to be analyzed as individual case.

Bullying is a behavior. Every behavior is either inherent or learned. Inherent behavior is what a child is born with. Learned behavior is something that the child has learned from surrounding people and environment. From an online newsletter that read: "The root causes for habitual or hardcore bullies are different from temporary bullies. Every such child might be having a different reason for bullying" (http://www.child-discipline-with-love.com/why-do-children-bully.html) Some of the common reasons why kids bully are:

Born Bully

A born bully starts bully behavior even when he is a toddler, though the symptoms are milder. If we are sure that the child is behaving that way ever since toddler stage and there has been no source to teach aggressive or bullying things to him, we can conclude that the child is inherently like that.

Some children may have some different type of neurological constitution. An example is Attention Deficit Hyperactivity Disorder (ADHD). These children are very impatient, impulsive, energetic and extremely active. These traits make them bully when they don't get what they want.

Trained Bully

A child who is otherwise peace loving and normal by birth may also turn into a bully if he finds an aggressive or bullying atmosphere in the family, where he finds everybody being insensitive to others. The family members have problem in sharing feelings and belongings. Nobody in the family is affectionate. There is a culture of violence in the family.

Parents of bullies are inconsistent on the issues of discipline and consequences. They are not bothered about the behavior of their children. They do not even think it necessary to monitor the activities of their children. Physical punishment is very common in such families. The bonds between parents, children, and siblings are not very strong. Being angry about petty things, pushing, pulling, slapping is a common behavior. Violent movies, TV shows and video games add fuel to the fire. The child learns this behavior and with the passage of time he becomes a fully trained bully. The child does not even realize that something is wrong with this kind of behavior, because he does not come across any sensitive behavior with which to compare.

Temporary Bully

Some children bully all the time in all places. These are habitual bullies. On the other hand, there may be children who are not bullies otherwise but they may bully sometimes. These are temporary bullies. The reason for temporary bullying may be: suffering from some trauma like death of a parent, relative, close friend or pet, parents' divorce, birth of a new baby, boredom or frustration, being under pressure to succeed at all costs etc.

Hardcore Bullies

The root causes for habitual or hardcore bullies are different from temporary bullies. Every such child might have a different reason for bullying. Some of the common reasons are: (a) Desire of being powerful and popular, (b) Pampered and spoiled, (c) Reaction to bad experiences, (d) Unaware of being a bully, (e) Having fun. Let us examine each of these categories bearing the reasons why children tend to bully others:

(a) Desire of being powerful and popular—Bullies are generally bigger and stronger than their victims; and, they use intimidation to get what they want. They like the feeling of being powerful and in charge of the scene. They believe that aggression and violence is the only way to get things done their way. Power makes them feel good about themselves. They feel like tough super heroes that they see in comics and movies.

(b) Pampered and spoiled Bullies—Some parents pamper their children to the extent of spoiling them. They fulfill all of their kids' desires. They don't teach their kids to differentiate between acceptable and unacceptable behavior. This makes the kids realize that it is acceptable to demand any thing at anytime. It also teaches them to misbehave if their desires aren't fulfilled. They try to impose this behavior on everybody expecting everyone to do what they say.

(c) Reaction to bad experiences—Some children are themselves victim of abuse or bullying at home, school or playground; and, take out their anger and humiliation on others. They may be bullied by their siblings or even their own parents. Some children are bullied when they are younger, and they turn into a bully themselves when they are a few years older.

Some children might have problems in more than one areas of their life like studies, communication, playing, etc. Something or someone is making them feel insecure, inadequate, humiliated or having no sense of accomplishment. Bullying makes them feel better.

Their parents, siblings, teachers or peers might have been neglecting them. With the passage of time the feeling of being 'neglected' grows into the feeling of being 'rejected'. They look for opportunities to grab attention of their peers, teachers and parents. Acting bully makes them feel that other are paying attention to him.

Some children might be jealous of the victim because people like the victim for some of his qualities. A bully has a strong desire to dominate and overpower this victim.

(d) Unaware Bully–Some bullies don't even know that their behavior is hurting others so much and how it makes the victim feel. In fact, you may be a bully yourself and not know it, and wonder why children bully.

(e) Having Fun—Some bullies enjoy troubling others for fun only. They know that they are hurting others. But they do it because they enjoy seeing others crying, being hurt, in pain.

Basically, children bully for a variety of reasons. Sometimes they pick on other children because they need a victim—someone who seems emotionally or physically weaker, or just acts or appears different in some way—to feel more important, popular, or in control. Although some bullies are bigger or stronger than their victims, that's not always the case.

Sometimes children torment others because that's the way they've been treated. They may think their behavior is normal because they come from families or other settings where everyone regularly gets angry, shouts, or calls names. Some popular TV shows even seem to promote meanness—people are "voted off," shunned, or ridiculed for their appearance or lack of talent.

School children beware: "Kick me" can get you kicked out. A Manhattan fourth-grader was suspended from school for two days for sticking a Post-it note reading "kick me, please" to a classmate's back, the *New York Post* reported. The tough punishment was the result of New York City public schools' zero-tolerance anti-bullying policy, implemented in 2008. The principal was just following the rules, says an education department representative. The students, for their part, do not seem to be too scared of the "bully." The suspended boy "either teases you or he tells you he's going to start hitting you, but never does," said one (*New York Post*, 2008).

The following is an eye-opener to everyone. We can never know that there are valid reasons why children or even teens perform this unbecoming behavior. However, this will be our responsibility from beginning to end. Being adults, we have the responsibility to get this full orientation about bullying of all sorts and make a move to help prevent it. We should remember that bullies also tend to continue their behavior throughout their lives. Their bullying actions become a cycle, in that bullies have children that they bully, and then their children become aggressive, and then they bully others too.

According to Frank Peretti, there are two basic reasons why kids bully. One reason a child bullies is because he (or she) *has a deep troubling need of his own* and is picked on or feels that he does not have a very successful life. Bullies may be experiencing trouble at home, be underachievers in school, and for whatever reason they feel they have to make themselves better by picking on someone else. On the outside bullies may look fine, but they may be very lonely or may deliberately try to hurt themselves or have trouble eating or sleeping (Peretti, 2001).

Another reason kids bully is that they may fall into a trap by thinking that bullying is just *the cool thing to do*, especially in front of their friends. Sometimes bullies are those kids who are good students, athletes, or the kids who seem to have everything going for them. In *Time Magazine*, it was reported that even though bullies often will have high self-esteem, they "tend to be victims of physical damage as well." Most bullies live in families in which parents discipline them "inconsistently or through physical means" (Winters, 2000).

Unfortunately, there are people who reward others who bully. The bullies are made to feel that they are "fitting in" with the others, or are "being cool" when they are acting like a bully. Mostly these kids do not feel very good about themselves, and bullying takes away that feeling. "Too often a bully's behavior is encouraged and not stopped. Some bullies become popular ringleaders with other kids, but not all bullies are the cool kids. Some are troubled students who may have been bullied themselves" (Time for Kids - see citation below)

Another reason why kids bully others is that adults do not give kids the skills they need to be able to tolerate and appreciate the differences of others. When the bully sees other people who are different, they lash out and make fun of them. Many feel that bullies engage in this behavior because it makes them feel important.

They learn that being physically aggressive is a way to get what they want and a way to control people.

Signs of Bullying

Often, children are taught that it is a sign of weakness to ask for help, and they hold back from telling anyone when they are being bullied for fear of appearing weak. Many children feel shame and assume, "Something must be wrong with me! Why else would they target ME?" Unless your child tells you about bullying—or has visible bruises or injuries—it can be difficult to figure out if it's happening. But there are some warning signs. Parents might notice their children acting differently or seeming anxious, or not eating, sleeping well, or doing the things they usually enjoy. When children seem moodier or more easily upset than usual, or when they start avoiding certain situations, like taking the bus to school, it might be because of a bully.

Many children, particularly boys and older children do not tell their parents or adults at school about being bullied, so it's important that adults are vigilant to possible signs of bullying. Here's a guide to recognizing the signs of bullying, and getting it to stop. The following are the warning signs for both parents and teachers to be aware of:

- Possible warning signs that a child is being bullied include:
- Comes home with torn, damaged, or missing pieces of clothing, books, or other belongings
- Has unexplained cuts, bruises, and scratches
- Has few, if any friends, with whom he or she spends time
- Seems afraid of going to school, walking to and from school, riding the school bus, or taking part in organized activities with peers (such as clubs)
- Takes a long, "illogical" route when walking to or from school
- Has lost interest in school work or suddenly begins to do poorly in school
- Appears sad, moody, teary, or depressed when he or she comes home
- Complains frequently of headaches, stomachaches, or other physical ailments
- Has trouble sleeping or has frequent bad dreams
- Experiences a loss of appetite
- Appears anxious and suffers from low self-esteem (Stop Bullying, 2010).

More likely, the following questions are important for the parents and the teachers. These are guidelines that will make us understand and really accept that bullying is an issue that should be addressed. Parents need to be aware of the warning signs when their children may be experiencing depression, severe anxiety, or PTSD due to bullying. The following is a list of red flags to look for:

(1) Is your child disconnecting from people and isolating him/herself in their room? Although teens usually separate from the family, they normally connect more often with their friends.

(2) Has your child developed physical problems such as stomachaches and headaches that interfere with their life?

(3) Has your child's schoolwork recently suffered, and is it difficult for your child to concentrate?
(4) Does your child have trouble falling, or staying asleep or experience frequent nightmares?
(5) Does your child seem listless, unenthusiastic, and disinterested in life?
(6) Have you noticed that your child seems hyper-vigilant, extremely nervous, depressed, or emotionally explosive (beyond the normal teenage angst and moodiness)?

As Ted Zeff, states on his website:

> Approximately 160,000 children miss school every day in the United States for fear of being bullied; more than 50 suicides have been linked to prolonged bullying; and approximately 85 percent of school shootings have revenge against bullies as a major motive. The costs of bullying are high, but, unfortunately, many children suffer alone, keeping their bullying experiences to themselves (Zeff, 2013).

If you suspect bullying but your child is reluctant to open up, find opportunities to bring up the issue in a more roundabout way. For instance, you might see a situation on a TV show and use it as a conversation starter, asking "What do you think of this?" or "What do you think that person should have done?" This might lead to questions like: "Have you ever seen this happen?" or "Have you ever experienced this?" You might want to talk about any experiences you or another family member had at that age. Let your children know that if they are being bullied —or see it happening to someone else—it is important to talk to someone about it, whether it is you, another adult (a teacher, school counselor, or family friend), or a sibling.

Bullying: Does it Matter?

The 1993 National Household Education Survey, based on the responses of 6,504 students in grades 6-12, reported that unsafe conditions at school are a reality for most students. The report found that 56 percent of the respondents had personally witnessed some type of crime or victimization at school, including bullying, physical attack, or robbery, and that 71 percent reported that such incidents happened at their schools. Another study shows that out of 15,000 6th-10th graders at public and private schools, 30 percent of these students reported being either bullies, victims or both (Lusden, 2002). Recent statistics show that the percentage of students who reported being bullied increased between 1999 and 2001 (Bureau of Justice Statistics, 2003).

Bullying really matters, because: Children who are bullied are at risk for developing a number of emotional difficulties, including depression and anxiety symptoms. Children who are particularly traumatized may go on to develop a specific type of anxiety disorder called, post-traumatic stress disorder (PTSD). PTSD is usually brought on by a terrifying physical or emotional event or series of events. Some of the symptoms of PTSD include trouble sleeping, withdrawal from normal activities, a lack of concentration, and emotional numbness. When children are suffering from PTSD, they are prone to develop strong physical symptoms in situations where they feel unsafe and in danger. They appear disconnected from others, and they experience an intense physical response from their nervous system that involves angry outbursts, jumpiness, and hyper alertness. This reaction is the nervous system's response to potential danger, whether real or imagined, creating constriction, disassociation, and helplessness in order to protect the body.

Dr. Zeff further relates that when children experience trauma, they often become frozen and exhibit feelings of helplessness and shame, rendering them nearly unable to defend themselves when attacked or put under pressure. These traumatized children then bring this frozen state of helplessness to many other situations that they perceive as threatening throughout their lives. And, the more withdrawn these children become, the more fearful and helpless they feel, the stronger the likelihood that they will slip into serious emotional trouble. With all of these, we don't want to have our students or our children act like zombies and all through the time, traumatized (Zeff, 2009).

If you suspect that your child is suffering from any of the above symptoms and you have not been able to help alleviate their suffering, you should consider having your child evaluated by a licensed psychologist, licensed marriage and family counselor, or licensed social worker. If you can't afford to pay for private therapy sessions, virtually all cities have low-cost therapy clinics (check with your city or county department of mental health).

What Parents Should Know about Bullying?

The many myths about bullying include the notion that bullying is a harmless childhood activity and a normal part of growing up. Confusion about the difference between conflict and bullying can fuel this myth. Although occasional peer conflict is inevitable, bullying is not inevitable. In a conflict, both sides have equal power to resolve the problem. But bullying involves the intentional, one-sided use of power to control another. Its harmful consequences can affect people seriously for the rest of their lives . . . this means that bullying is NEVER a normal part of growing up.

Bullying jeopardizes children's safety and potentially creates both short-term and long-term problems for all children involved. Children who are bullied are more likely to develop future academic problems and psychological difficulties. Serious problems such as depression and low self-esteem can result, and they can continue into adulthood.

Children who bully and continue this behavior as adults have greater difficulty developing and maintaining positive relationships. Research shows that without effective intervention, children who regularly bully others may grow up to become perpetrators of domestic violence, child abuse, hate crimes, sexual abuse, and other illegal behavior. In fact, children with bullying problems at age 8 are six times more likely to be convicted of a crime by age 24 than children who do not bully. This is the only way they know how to act: perhaps they have been pushed around, beaten down, and abused at home. These types of bullies do not know anything else, they have not been taught any other way. They do not get attention at home. These types of bullies are seeking attention and love but they do not know how to go about it. So they turn into bullies and receive negative attention. The first time they do something wrong and get attention, they feel good about themselves. So instead of trying to do something for positive attention, they continue down the road for negative attention.

Bullying among children is aggressive behavior that is intentional and involves an imbalance of power or strength. A child who is being bullied has a hard time defending him or herself. Usually bullying is repeated over time. Bullying can take many forms such as physical, verbal, emotional and cyberbullying. Signs that your child might be bullied: torn clothes, loss of appetite, mood changes, reluctance to go to school, bruises or injuries that can't be explained, Signs that your child might be engaging in bullying behavior: impulsiveness, no empathy for others, a desire to be in control may be an arrogant and boastful winner and poor loser in competitive games

What Parents Should Do If They Suspect Their Child Is Being Bullied?

There is a good chance that some children will not be verbally up to say: I'm getting bullied in school." If the following seem to be happening frequently, parents should likely look for signs that their children are being bullied.

For boys, one classic symptom is that they are teased so much about being gay or being atypical that they're terrified to go to the bathroom. Since there's only one way in and one way out of a bathroom, it's an ideal place to tease other kids. Boys who are bullied often won't go all day, which can lead to lifelong intestinal issues. This could potentially be a sign—if your child races home and goes to the bathroom every day after school. These are all possible signals that your child might be the target of teasing at school.

Bullying expert, Peggy Moss says:

> In this age of MySpace, cell phones, and instant messaging, it has never been more important to ensure that you are a part of your daughter's life: the real and the virtual. It is no surprise that girls are enamored with social communications as a way to make connections and keep in touch. By the time they are ten or eleven, they may be developing their own websites, and creating fun emoticons, avatars, and colorful texts for their emails (Moss, 2013).

In the scope of cyber-bullying, Rachel Simmons, author of *Odd Girl Out*, talks about the dangers of Internet correspondence going something like this: Let's say there are two teen girls named "Julie" and "Anne." One day, Julie gives Anne a funny look in science class. Anne recoils, but does not do anything about it until she gets home and types, "R U mad at me?" Julie responds, "U R 2 sensitive." Rather than picking up the phone and straightening it out, Anne then sends a message about Julie to forty of their closest friends, beginning a progression of misunderstandings and frustrations that eventually leads to someone—Anne, Julie, or maybe someone else—being ostracized, teased, and left out in the cold (Simmons, 2011).

In an interview conducted by Peggy Moss of Lyn Mikel Brown, Brown noted that the above is an unpleasant and likely-sounding scenario, but however unsettling, is not the norm that it is sometimes portrayed to be. Girls have not stopped talking to each other directly and by telephone, as many parents can attest. While it is true that girls who have been raised not to show anger or deal with conflict directly continue to dodge face-to-face confrontations, the behavior itself is not new. The tools of expression have simply changed (Moss, 2013).

These new tools, however, do call for increased education and responsibility. The Internet can be a very private-seeming place when one sits alone in front of a computer screen in a bedroom, but in reality, it can be devastatingly public. Many parents have found that keeping the computer in a public space helps to bring home the message to kids that they are dealing in the public realm when they type messages. As a rule of thumb, remind your child that she should not send any message or photo that she would regret having copied and dispersed widely, and that she should not share her password with anyone. Remind them that if there is a conflict, it is likely to be more easily resolved face-to-face than by email or in a text message.

Bullying can worsen the mental health of teenagers who are already dealing with stress and adolescents who experience teen bullying are more likely to report thoughts of suicide and suicidal behavior. All too often, media reports about bullying-related suicides give a face to this extreme consequence of teen bullying. In addition, targets of cyberbullying are more likely than those who haven't been harassed to use alcohol and other drugs, receive school detention or suspension, skip school, or be bullied in person.

Parents are often reluctant to report bullying to school officials, but bullying may not stop without the school's help. Parents should never be afraid to call the school to report that their child is being bullied and ask for help to stop the bullying. Sometimes children believe it is their own fault, that if they looked or acted differently it wouldn't be happening. Sometimes they are scared that if the bully finds out that they told, it will get worse. Others are worried that their parents will not believe them or do anything about it. Or children worry that their parents will urge them to fight back when they are scared to do so.

D'Arcy Lyness and Michelle New suggest that if your child tells you about a bully, focus on offering comfort and support, no matter how upset you are. Children are often reluctant to tell adults about bullying because they feel embarrassed and ashamed that it is happening, or worry that their parents will be disappointed in them (Dodrill, 2010).

- Praise your child for being brave enough to talk about it. Remind your child that he or she is not alone—a lot of people get bullied at some point. Emphasize that it is the bully who is behaving badly—not your child. Reassure your child that you will figure out what to do about it together.

- Sometimes an older sibling or friend can help deal with the situation. It may help your daughter to hear how the older sister she idolizes was teased about her braces and how she dealt with it. An older sibling or friend also might be able to give you some perspective on what's happening at school, or wherever the bullying is happening, and help you figure out the best solution.
- Take it seriously if you hear that the bullying will get worse if the bully finds out that your child told. Sometimes it's useful to approach the bully's parents. In other cases, teachers or counselors are the best ones to contact first. If you've tried those methods and still want to speak to the bullying child's parents, it's best to do so in a context where a school official, such as a counselor, can mediate.
- Talk with your child. Be supportive and gather information about the bullying. Report suspected bullying to your child's school. In Broward County Florida, you may make an anonymous report by using the anonymous reporting box located inside your school's main entry, area or district site anonymous reporting box or by going to www.browardschools.com. Anonymous reports can also occur by calling the school district's emergency hotline at 754-321-0911.

Bullying is just one of the many challenges children face today. Any number of factors, including bullying, can contribute to a child's change in demeanor or behavior. Let us keep in mind that not every child who is bullied will experience the negative consequences. The key is for us parents and teachers to be observant: Noticing a difference is the first step to finding out what the problem is. Parent, teachers, coaches, and even friends can benefit from learning what signs to look for that may indicate a deeper problem.

The Challenge:
What Can Be Done to Stop Cyber-bullying?

Nine students are being prosecuted for bullying a fellow student, Phoebe Prince, who committed suicide after being taunted and threatened. What, if anything, could and should the school have tried to protect Ms. Prince? What can and should teachers and administrators do at any school where students are bullying other kids? (Eckholm & Zezima, 2010).

In their article "9 Teenagers Are Charged After Classmate's Suicide," Erik Eckholm and Katie Zezima consider what happened at South Hadley High School in Massachusetts, and the legal fallout: "In the uproar around the suicides of Ms. Prince, 15, and an 11-year-old boy subjected to harassment in nearby Springfield last year, the Massachusetts legislature stepped up work on an anti-bullying law that is now near passage" (Eckholm & Zezima, 2010). The law would require school staff members to report suspected incidents and principals to investigate them. It would also demand that schools teach about the dangers of bullying. Forty-one other states have anti-bullying laws of varying strength.

An 11-year-old boy committed suicide and his family says it was because of relentless bullying at a DeKalb Elementary School. Regardless of whether bullying led to Jaheem Herrera's tragic death, his suicide is making a lot of people talk about bullying in schools (Eckholm & Zezima, 2010). In line with this, the next questions follow:

- *Have principals or districts provided any training or guidelines over how to handle bullies?*

We know bullying is commonplace in schools, but it can become excessive.

- *When do you step in and when have you decided not to intervene? How do you make the decision?*

Understanding bullies from their point of view would give us valuable in depth understanding of the problem. We need to have a bond with the child so that the child can talk to us open heartedly. We need to find out what does the child feel like while bullying. If he enjoys it, we need to find out some other acceptable behavior where he can enjoy without hurting anyone, and replace that behavior with bullying.

- *The HB 1366, the School Violence Prevention Act*

Over the past years, both parents and educators have asked supporters to let the legislature know why HB 1366, the School Violence Prevention Act, matters. They've come through with hundreds of emails and so many moving stories and intelligent arguments.

HB 1366—School Violence Prevention Act

Legislation HB 1366 was sponsored by Rep. Rick Glazier (D-Cumberland). The measure would require that public schools in North Carolina adopt policies to address the problems of bullying. Although, this HB 1366 is very controversial, we still believe that in the context of protecting schools from bullying and preventing this to happen, HB 1366 would direct local school boards to adopt policies to prohibit bullying and harassing behavior in the state's public schools. The bill defines bullying or harassing behavior as: "acts reasonably perceived as being motivated by any actual or perceived characteristics, such as race, color, religion, ancestry, national origin, gender, gender identity or expression, physical appearance, sexual orientation, or mental, physical, or sensory disability." (Special Report, May 16, 2007). Here are some more highlights shared from the report:

I was bullied as a school child and survived. I am a retired teacher of emotionally disturbed children and ended my career as a school psychologist and have seen the damage inflicted on children first hand by their caregivers and "teachers."

"You've got to be taught to hate." Please don't aid and abet this crime against children.—Franklin

As a native North Carolinian who chose two years ago to return to this state that I love, I am very concerned about the lack of protection for all children against bullying. I am also a licensed Marriage and Family therapist and have worked with numerous children who have been deeply scarred by verbal and physical assault within their school system. I have witnessed the long-term deleterious emotional effects of such abuse. I am hoping that you share my concerns.—Durham

As a former middle-school teacher, I wish I could look you in the eye and tell you about Javon, a student I taught who was bullied because he was smaller than other kids and was mercilessly teased because other students thought he was homosexual. At that time two years ago, what could I do--what could anyone do? Almost nothing. But this summer, your committee can help change lives like Javon's. Not one more school year should go by with teachers and school staff unable to address and prevent this kind of abusive behavior.—Raleigh

As a 37-year teacher in CMS secondary schools it has been my consistent experience that teachers and principals overlook or even denigrate complaints from students who are harassed because they are perceived to be gay. If they're not listed then they're not going to be helped. Verbal violence and harassment in middle schools and high schools too often lead to real violence.—Davidson (Special Report, May 16, 2007).

Taking out sexual orientation and gender identity/expression protections of House Bill 1366, the School Violence Prevention Act, which is intended to protect all students from bullying and harassment, instills a sense of fear in those students who feel threatened, bullied, or harassed for their sexual orientation and gender identity or expression in North Carolina schools. These students know now that their school will not stand by them when they are bullied, harassed because of who they are.

Four out of five gay, lesbian, bisexual and transgender (GLBT) students report that they have faced verbal, physical, or sexual harassment at school (Gay Lesbian Straight Education Network). These kinds of harassments have resulted in higher suicide rates; drop out rates, lower academic confidence and progress among GLBT students.

We cannot afford to let North Carolina's GLBT students continue to feel the same way because they do not feel safe in our schools. North Carolina's GLBT students deserve better than the second class attention they have received by the revoking of their protection in the revised version of HB 1366.

All children deserve a safe place to learn, grow, and become better individuals, students and citizens of our world. To deny any student these protections and our support diminishes the chances, hopes, and dreams of our students, and we strongly urge the School Prevention Act to be amended to its original standing, which included protections for sexual orientation and gender identity/expression.

Based on the researches and readings presented, there are lots of reason for why do kids bully. Every child has a different reason to bully. Based on the analysis of the information, we can find out what triggers the bully behavior in the child. *Is bullying an inherent behavior or is it learned?* If the root cause is an inherent behavior only, we need to take steps accordingly. Fix appointments with a doctor, developmental therapists, child-psychologists etc. and explore why your child bullies.

If we totally rule out the Inherent behavior, we need to find the sources from where the child could have possibly learned that behavior. Then, we need to look at ourselves first, what kind of source we are to teach behavior to our kids. We parents and teachers are the biggest influence on the child's and students' behavior. To underscore, WE educators and parents cannot stop this if we are not aware of what is really happening. And once we are, we can intervene because we all know that everyone has to right to be able to attend school without being harassed. The school and the home should take this obligation seriously. How can we educators then, cyber-proof our schools?

Interventions to Stop Bullying

Bullying can worsen the mental health of teenagers who are already dealing with stress and adolescents who experience teen bullying are more likely to report thoughts of suicide and suicidal behavior. All too often, media reports about bullying-related suicides give a face to this extreme consequence of teen bullying. In addition, targets of cyberbullying are more likely than those who haven't been harassed to use alcohol and other drugs, receive school detention or suspension, skip school, or be bullied in person.

Teen bullying is also associated with higher rates of weapon carrying and fighting that leads to injury. Investigations of several school-based shootings— including those in Pearl, Mississippi; West Paducah, Kentucky; Jonesboro, Arkansas; Springfield, Oregon; and Littleton, Colorado—pointed to bullying as a factor that contributed to the outbreak of violence.

In an interview with a bullying expert Susan Swearer mentioned the most effective steps to take in order to protect victims of bullying and underscored that: Parents and teachers MUST intervene when they see bullying take place. First, they must tell the student(s) who are doing the bullying to stop. They need to document what they saw and keep records of the bullying behaviors. Victims need to feel that they have a support network of kids and adults. Help the student who is being bullied feel connected to school and home. Students who are also being bullied might benefit from individual or group therapy in order to create a place where they can express their feelings openly (Swearer, 2010).

When she was asked: Who is more at risk for suicide if bullied? In other words, are there personality traits or markers that parents and teachers should look for when they know a child is being bullied? Dr. Swearer answered: "There really is no "profile" of a student who is more at risk for suicide as a result of bullying" She also mentioned book *Bullycide in America*, citing the author, Brenda High's comment, that 'mothers of children who have committed suicide as a result of being bullied share their stories. Their stories are all different, yet the commonality is that the bullying their children endured resulted in suicide (Swearer, 2010). And emphatically states that:

> We do know that there is a connection between being bullied and depression, and we know that depression is a risk factor for attempting suicide. Therefore, parents and educators should look for signs that a child is experiencing symptoms of depression (Swearer, 2010).

The following question was posed to Dr. Swearer about the so relevant and salient point to both parents and educators in the quest to prevent bullying to happen:

> You have been conducting research on a program called "Target Bullying: Ecologically Based Prevention and Intervention for Schools" that looks at bullying and victimization in middle-school-aged youth. Your findings suggest there are certain psychological and social conditions that fuel bullying. What are they and what are the best interventions to stop the cycle? (Swearer, 2010).

This was Dr. Swearer's equally important reply:

> I have been conducting research on bullying since 1998 and during this time, I have become increasingly convinced that bullying is a social-ecological problem that has to be understood from the perspective that individual, family, peer group, school, community, and societal factors all influence whether or not bullying occurs. The question that I ask students, parents and educators is: "What are the conditions in your school (family, community) that allow bullying to occur?" The answers to that question are then the areas to address for intervention. We write about how to do this in our book *Bullying Prevention and Intervention: Realistic Strategies for Schools* [by Susan Swearer, Dorothy Espelage and Scott Napolitano, published in 2009 by Guilford Press]. Interventions should be based on evidence. Since bullying will vary across schools and communities, each school in this country ought to be collecting comprehensive data on bullying experiences. Then, schools can use their own data to design effective interventions in order to change the conditions that are fueling the bullying in their own school and *community* (Swearer, 2010).

Based on Dr. Swearer's comments, it is clear that there are different types of bullies around. In fact, becoming a bully then from an early age, have big chances that he or she will continue to bully into adulthood.

In summary, bullying should be considered as a social-ecological perspective. Dr. Swearer repeats that 'there is no way to profile a bully." She is strong in presenting that conditions in the environment are supportive of bullying . . . and that almost everyone can bully. And as an example, she said: "In fact, the mother of a daughter who committed suicide after being bullied once told me that the girls who bullied her daughter were just 'regular kids'—this means that the conditions in their small town and small school were breeding grounds for bullying" (Swearer, 2010).

In addition, Dr. Swearer elaborated that:

Technology has definitely impacted bullying. What used to be a face-to-face encounter that occurred in specific locations is now able to occur 24 hours a day, seven days a week. Technology—computers, cell phones and social networking sites—are all conditions that allow bullying to occur. One way to protect our children is to limit and/or monitor their use of this technology. I ask parents, "Would you let your 12-year-old daughter walk alone down a dark alley?" Obviously, the answer is "No." The follow-up question is, "Then why would you let your 12-year-old daughter be on the computer or be texting unmonitored?" Parents and kids don't realize the negative side to technology and social networking sites (Swearer, 2010).

She shared more:

My research has also looked at the dynamic between bullying and victimization. In one study, we found that kids who were bullied at home by siblings and/or relatives were more likely to bully at school. So, you can see that the dynamic is complex and crosses all areas in which we all function – in our community, family and schools. We do know that if left untreated, children who learn that bullying is an effective way to get what they want are likely to continue bullying behavior into adulthood. Thus, it is critical to intervene and stop the bullying during the school-age years (Swearer, 2010).

The Role of the School in Preventing Bullying

A positive school climate is one that cultivates several positive characteristics, including a sense of safety for each and every student. Bullying that goes un-checked can shatter a young person's sense of well-being and safety, making it difficult if not impossible to learn.

Upper Merion Area Middle School has come together as a community and a family to create a positive environment of caring and respect. In order to combat bullying it is imperative to develop a comprehensive, multifaceted approach which focuses on the entire school culture. It is a process that takes much planning and collaboration among stakeholders, dedicated leadership and diligence.

Their report about "Creating a Culture of Respect in Order to Maintain a Bully Free Environment" from Upper Merion Area Middle School King of Prussia, Pennsylvania" mentioned that:

Ten years ago, during Strategic Planning, our stakeholders discussed strengths and concerns about our school in order to develop a plan for school improvement. Our goals were to:
• Improve student engagement
• Improve scores
• Improve attendance
• Decrease suspensions
• Decrease bullying

- Improve rapport/relationships between peers,
- Students and teachers
- Increase parent involvement and community partnerships (Upper Merion Area Middle School, 2011).

To underscore, the stakeholders based on this research, learned that the common denominator for student success in all of these goals was to create a positive, caring, respectful and supportive climate. They studied several researches driven K-12 programs and chose Community of Caring to guide the process. According to this report, there are five values needed to stop bullying in school: *Caring, Respect, Responsibility, Trust and Family* which serve as a foundation for positive culture and an umbrella for school initiatives and activities. In short, the goal of this research is to recommend "Values Through the Curriculum." And this was what they had to say:

> It is important that character education is "active education," that it is documented throughout the curriculum, and that all teachers utilize the same vocabulary, teachable moments, and weave the anti-bullying message throughout the curriculum. For example, students in the 5th grade read *The Kid in the Red Jacket*. They learn to make everyone feel respected and cared for. Inclusion is important to them. In 6th grade students read Maniac McGee about a bully and discuss prejudice. They make posters against bullying and develop plans about how to stop bullying if they see it. They learn the importance of not being a negative bystander. In grade 7 students read Crash and write No-Bullying Pledges along with daily Public Address Announcements about Stamping Out Bullying. They also read The Watsons Come to Birmingham and plan how to unite people and celebrate diversity. Grade 8 students read about the Holocaust and discuss tolerance. With each of these Literacy works students take the lead in a movement to promote respect and stop harassment and bullying. Thus the adults are working with the students to actively stop bullying. This is carried through all core subjects and Unified Arts as well and lessons are shared on the web (Upper Merion Area Middle School, 2011).

With all these findings, it was extremely important for the administration to assess their school climate and see if it is 'bully-proof' and seemingly, the outcome was fairly positive to which the following have been recommended:

- The school remains in close contact with parents reporting incidences before they escalate and enlisting parental support in teaching their children to treat all peers respectfully as members of our school family.
- Parent programs include Making Good Choices, Parent Coffees in which parents may ask questions or supply information about bullying, Internet Safety and Cyberbullying Programs, Pro Social Programs, Suicide Prevention, Community of Caring Trainings and Diversity Trainings. Parent involvement in schools is encouraged and stellar communication keeps the parents and community informed about all concerns relating to violence, bullying and cyberbullying.

- The Student Assistance Team and mentors provide support for students at the first sign of bullying.

Based on the above recommendations, we can say that our students feel safe and would want to come to school regularly if they are aware what bullying is and if they are knowledgeable to report the conflict to an adult immediately, should they be victims by the act. Parents should agree that their children should feel safe and enjoy coming to school and that, when they have information about bullying—they should right away call or email their teachers, counselors and/or principals. In this way everyone is coming together to maintain respect for the school family and community. Without the fear of being bullied students are empowered to focus on their academics and on character, leadership, scholarship and service, the mission of our middle school. Lest we forget: *All children, regardless of differences, deserve to be safe, healthy and supported in their classrooms, schools and communities* (Upper Merion Area Middle School, 2011).

A Bully-Proof Educational Environment

We all need some bully-proofing. We aren't likely to get pushed down on the playground at work (as adults) but we might feel like that's what happened. The question is: Have we ever felt like a victim of "drive by bullying behavior"? We often may not have known what happened until it was over and the "the person's tail lights were rounding the hallway corner." And the only evidence of the assault would be something new to our personal "to do list" and the emotional tracks on our faces . . . "I was bullied!"—and each time we find ourselves going along just to "get along" and ask ourselves the question: Have I just been bullied?—is there then a creative way to wear bully-proof suit?

Margaret S. Ross, president of the Kamaron Institute, in her book *Casey and The Amazing Good Finder* which helps adults and children succeed in life, school, work, and relationships asks the following important questions:

- Do you have a zero tolerance bullying policy?
- What program do you have in place to preempt bullying behaviors?
In order to address the questions, which both parents and teachers are so "reliable" for the responsibility in creating a caring environment?

And Ross adds: "The locations may vary, work place, neighborhood, Internet, school or bus, but the bully's weapon of choice remains constant—WORDS" (Ross, 2005).

Bullying School Causalities

Causalities Are Mounting

The National Education Association reports that every day 150-thousand kids miss school due to fear of attack, peer intimidation or bullying. A 2001 study by the

American Association of University Women found that 83 percent of girls and 79 percent of boys report experiencing ridiculing/harassment at school. One in four reported that it happens "frequently." Dreading going to school impairs a child's ability to learn. Dreading going to work impairs an adult's ability to earn.

Since, bullying's most frequent face is verbal—teasing, taunting, threatening, name-calling—or more subtle through malicious gossiping, spreading rumors, and intentional exclusion. Violence can and should be stopped at the name-calling level. The most effective way to do this is to proactively replace it. We need to move beyond bullying prevention to bullying pre-emption.

What Is "Bully-Proofing"?

Numerous studies report that many children across the nation are fearful in their schools and in their neighborhoods. This fear is not only due to the more extreme forms of school violence that have been reported in the media, but to the high incidence of bullying and harassment that takes place daily in U.S. schools, this was a report shared by the National Center for School Engagement (NCSE). The NCSE is one of the organizations we have in the country whose aims has one that is toward the prevention of bullying, in general. This center was established based on over a decade of educational research conducted by Colorado Foundation for Families and Children. NCSE has generated many resources about school attendance, attachment, and achievement. NCSE provides training and technical assistance, research and evaluation to school districts, law enforcement agencies, courts, as well as state and federal agencies—to name a few.

Bully-Proofing Your School (*BPYS*) is a nationally recognized school safety program, implemented in school districts throughout the United States and Canada, with a scientifically proven track record since its inception in 1992. BPYS is a critical element in the creation of safe, civil and caring school culture that, in turn, promotes student attachment to school, attendance at school and achievement in school. BPYS is a comprehensive program for handling bully/victim problems through the creation of a "caring majority" of students who take the lead in establishing and maintaining a safe and caring school community. The program focuses on converting the silent majority of students into a caring majority by teaching strategies that help them to avoid victimization and to take a stand for a bully-free school. In schools which have implemented the program, incidences of bullying behaviors have declined and feelings of safety among the students have increased

Bully-Proofing Our Children

In the article "Can We Bully-Proof Our Kids?," Lisa Jensen, Children's Program Coordinator for the University of Hawai'i Family Education Center, emphasized that:

The key to having bully-proof kids is to give them the opportunity to identify and develop their talents, gain recognition, and build self-confidence, Jensen says. "A confident child draws friends and won't get bullied because they'll get pulled in by the group and be protected. And they won't be as susceptible emotionally. (Woo, 2006).

Since bullying is not a normal rite of passage. It can have serious consequences. We can help our children learn how to prevent bullying. These tips can help:

* Help your child understand bullying. Explain what bullying is. It is more than physical; it can be done in person or over the phone or computer.
* Keep open lines of communication with your child. Check in with your child and listen to any concerns about friends and other students.
* Encourage your child to pursue their interests. Doing what they love may help your child be more confident among their peers and make friends with other kids with similar interests.
* Teach your child to take a stand against bullying. Give guidance about how to stand up to those who bully if it is safe to do so.
* Talk to your child about seeking help from a trusted adult when feeling threatened by a bully. Talk about whom they should go to for help and role-play what they should say. Assure your child that they should not be afraid to tell an adult when someone they know is being bullied.
* Know what is going on in your child's school. Visit the school website, subscribe to the student paper—if there is one—and join the PTA list server mailing list. Get to know other parents, school counselors, and staff. Contact the school by phone or e-mail if you have suggestions to make the school a safer and better learning place.
* All adults in a community have a responsibility to help keep kids safe and stop bullying among children, teens and young adults. How can you get involved?

When parents are involved in their children's education, both children and parents are likely to benefit. Researchers report that parent participation in their children's schooling frequently:

* enhances children's self-esteem
* improves children's academic achievement
* improves parent-child relationships
* helps parents develop positive attitudes towards school and a better under-standing of the schooling process.

Despite these advantages, it is not always easy for parents to find time and energy to become involved or to coordinate with schedules for school events. For some parents, a visit to school is perceived as an uncomfortable experience, perhaps a holdover from their own school days. Others may have their hands full with a job and other children. The availability and cost of babysitters are other factors. Recently, teachers and other school staff have made special efforts to increase communication with parents and encourage involvement in children's learning experiences.

One kind of parental involvement is school-based and includes participating in parent-teacher conferences and functions, and receiving and responding to written communications from the teacher. Parents can also serve as school volunteers for the library or lunchroom, or as classroom aides. In one survey, almost all teachers reported talking with children's parents—either in person, by phone, or on open school nights—and sending notices home (Becker & Epstein, 1982). These methods, along with requests for parents to review and sign homework, were most frequently used to involve parents.

Parents can participate in their children's schools by joining Parent Teacher Associations (PTAs) or Parent Teacher Organizations (PTOs) and getting involved in decision-making about the educational services their children receive. Almost all schools have a PTA or PTO, but often only a small number of parents are active in these groups.

Another kind of involvement is home-based and focuses on activities that parents can do with their children at home or on the teacher's visits to the child's home. However, few teachers involve parents through home-based activities, partly because of the amount of time involved in developing activities or visiting and partly because of the difficulty of coordinating parents' and teachers' schedules.

Bully-Proofing the School

There had been a number of suggestions and recommendations provided for both parents and teachers on how to be involved in making the school an environment of positive development that is in all aspects. For beyond the mental and intellectual needs, the school's responsibility is to raise the students with a strong, peaceful and "perfect" individuals ready for the challenges of their adult lives—and these can only be achieved by providing a "bullying-safe" school environment.

A bully-proof school should have programs that should promote non-violent, confident building, seminars that provide bully education to children and teens. In this way, students will learn to identify the different types of bullying, why bullies pick on other kids, safe people and safe places, who to tell about bullying, and bully prevention.

Preventing and stopping bullying involves a commitment to creating a safe environment where children can thrive, socially and academically, without being afraid. The American Psychology Association (APA) recommends that teachers, parents, and students take the following actions to address bullying.

1. Be knowledgeable and observant. Teachers and administrators need to be aware that although bullying generally happens in areas such as the bathroom, playground, crowded hallways, and school buses as well as via cell phones and computers (where supervision is limited or absent), it must be taken seriously. Teachers and administrators should emphasize that telling is not tattling. If a teacher observes bullying in a classroom, he/she needs to immediately intervene to stop it, record the incident and inform the appropriate school administrators so the incident can be investigated. Having

a joint meeting with the bullied student and the student who is bullying is not recommended—it is embarrassing and very intimidating for the student that is being bullied.

2.   Involve students and parents. Students and parents need to be a part of the solution and involved in safety teams and anti-bullying task forces. Students can inform adults about what is really going on and also teach adults about new technologies that kids are using to bully. Parents, teachers, and school administrators can help students engage in positive behavior and teach them skills so that they know how to intervene when bullying occurs. Older students can serve as mentors and inform younger students about safe practices on the Internet.

3.   Set positive expectations about behavior for students and adults. Schools and classrooms must offer students a safe learning environment. Teachers and coaches need to explicitly remind students that bullying is not accepted in school and such behaviors will have consequences. Creating an anti-bullying document and having both the student and the parents/guardians sign and return it to the school office helps students understand the seriousness of bullying. Also, for students who have a hard time adjusting or finding friends, teachers and administrators can facilitate friendships or provide "jobs" for the student to do during lunch and recess so that children do not feel isolated or in danger of becoming targets for bullying.

4.   Observe your child for signs they might be being bullied. Children may not always be vocal about being bullied. Signs include: ripped clothing, hesitation about going to school, decreased appetite, nightmares, crying, or general depression and anxiety. If you discover your child is being bullied, don't tell them to "let it go" or "suck it up". Instead, have open-ended conversations where you can learn what is really going on at school so that you can take the appropriate steps to rectify the situation. Most importantly, let your child know you will help him/her and that they should try not to fight back.

5.   Teach your child how to handle being bullied. Until something can be done on an administrative level, work with your child to handle bullying without being crushed or defeated. Practice scenarios at home where your child learns how to ignore a bully and/or develop assertive strategies for coping with bullying. Help your child identify teachers and friends that can help them if they're worried about being bullied.

6.   Set boundaries with technology. Educate your children and yourself about cyberbullying and teach your children not to respond or forward threatening emails. "Friend" your child on Facebook or MySpace and set up proper filters on your child's computer. Make the family computer the only computer for children, and have it in a public place in the home where it is visible and can be monitored. If you decide to give your child a cell phone think carefully before allowing them to have a camera option. Let them know you will be monitoring their text messages. As a parent, you can insist that phones are stored in a public area, such as the kitchen, by a certain time at night to eliminate nighttime bullying and inappropriate messaging. Parents should report bullying to the school, and follow up with a letter that is copied to the school superintendent if their initial inquiry receives no response. Parents should report all threatening messages to the police and should document any text messages, emails, or posts on websites.

7. Report bullying and cyber-bullying. It is important for students to report any bullying to a parent or an adult they trust. Often kids don't report cyber-bullying because they fear their parents will take away their phone or computer. Parents will support their child's reports of bullying and not take away their phones as a consequence. It is important for kids to remember that bullying is wrong and should be handled by an adult.

8, Avoid being alone. Whenever possible, avoid situations where there are no other students or teachers. Try to go to the bathroom with a friend or eat lunch in a group. When riding the bus, sit near the front. If you know a student who likes to bully others is in an area where you normally walk to lunch or class, try to use alternative hallway routes (APA, 2013).

The School's Approach to Combat "Bullying"

A child who has to endure bullying usually suffers from low self-esteem and their ability to learn and be successful at school is dramatically lessened. Schools and parents must educate children about bullying behaviors; it will help all children feel safe and secure at school. Children who bully need to be taught empathy for others' feelings in order to change their behaviors and the school must adopt a zero-tolerance policy regarding bullying.

The best and most obvious way to stop bullying in schools is for parents to change the way they parent their children at home. Of course, this is much easier said than done and everyone parents their children differently. Bullies, however, come from homes where physical punishment is used and children have been taught that physical violence is the way to handle problems and "get their way."

Bullies usually also come from homes where the parents fight a lot, so violence has been modeled for them. Parental involvement often is lacking in bullies' lives and there seems to be little warmth.

Early intervention and effective discipline and boundaries truly is the best way to stop bullying, but parents of the victims or therapists cannot change the bully's home environment. Some things can be done at the school level, however.

Most school programs that address bullying use a multi-faceted approach to the problem. This usually involves counseling of some sort, either by peers, a school counselor, teachers, or the principal.

Hand out questionnaires to all students and teachers and discuss if bullying is occurring. Define exactly what constitutes bullying at school. The questionnaire is a wonderful tool that allows the school to see how widespread bullying is and what forms it is taking. It is a good way to start to address the problem.

Get the children's parents involved in a bullying program. If parents of the bullies and the victims are not aware of what is going on at school, then the whole bullying program will not be effective. Stopping bullying in school takes teamwork and concentrated effort on everyone's part. Bullying also should be discussed during parent-teacher conferences and PTA meetings. Parental awareness is the key.

In the classroom setting, all teachers should work with the students on bullying. Oftentimes even the teacher is being bullied in the classroom and a program should be set up that implements teaching about bullying. Children understand modeling behaviors and role-play and acting out bullying situations is a very effective tool. Have students role-play a bullying situation.

Rules that involve bullying behaviors should be clearly posted. Schools also could ask local mental health professionals to speak to students about bullying behaviors and how it directly affects the victims.

Schools need to make sure there is enough adult supervision at school to lessen and prevent bullying.

Conclusion

We are all aware that the best line of defense towards bullying starts at home. Izzy Kahlman author of *Bullies2Buddies* believes that we as a society are doing a lousy job of promoting resilience.

> Rather than helping kids become people who can weather the slings and arrows of life, we are producing a generation of emotional marshmallows—kids who believe they are entitled to a life in which no one upsets them, and can't tolerate any insult to their mind and bodies (Kahlman, 2010).

Raising children to be resilient is crucial in warding off a bully. The child that reacts emotionally distraught to a bully will only encourage the bully.

What can we do as parents to protect our children without turning them into marshmallows a bully will eat for dessert?

So, before the bully gains power while crushing another human being's spirit, our children should be helped in increasing their own self-value and should have all their needs satisfied in order NOT to control others or steal his victim's self-esteem rendering them with feelings of worthlessness . . . .and that is where THE SCHOOL should CONTINUE FROM HOME.

In his article: "Bully-proofing Our Schools," Bob Chase, President, National Education Association agrees to eliminate bullying by not tolerating it. He adds:

> If we adults continue to insist that bullying is a normal part of growing up, even a "character building" experience, then, to be blunt, we have never listened, I mean really listened, to a child who has been victimized by persistent bullying. For children who are constantly picked on, ridiculed, threatened, harassed, or robbed, school becomes torture. As a teenage girl from Naperville, Illinois reported in NEA's recent "Safe Schools Now" television program, the bullying can get so bad that you yearn for death because "then it will stop (Chase, 2013).

A single school assembly will not solve the problem. Every school, elementary or secondary, needs to create a formal code of conduct. And every adult in the school, every student, and every parent should be well briefed in the code as well as the consequences for not living up to it. What's more, students, teachers, and school support staff must be trained in how to intervene effectively. Eliminate the silent bystanders, and we go a long way to eliminating bullying—WE ALL NEED TO

DO MORE! In real life, children don't have such magic at their disposal. Caring adults and concerned communities are all that kids have to protect them.

We can never be sure when this problem will end; as long as there is socialization which is a lifetime process and differences in family upbringing, the issue will continue to emerge in various forms. This is where the schools should approach the bullying. It is the long-term obligation of all school administrators to end bullying by developing the character traits of responsibility, honesty and respect among students. The schools should have a rich curriculum to approach the problem . . . it is not all about competencies and proficiency in reading, math, writing, speaking—it is all an environment rolled into one: A BULLY-FREE ZONE.

The academe can develop a stronger purpose to improve the safety and education of today's children to insure their success. We educators can only aim to give back to our communities, our nation, and our homes—by protecting, educating, supporting and developing our world's future leaders . . . .our children.

Let us all be a PART of this CHALLENGE!!!

References

American Psychological Association. (2013) Bullying: How Parents, Teachers, and Kids Can Take Action to Stop Bullying. http://www.apa.org/helpcenter/bullying.aspx.

Becker, H.J., and J. L. Epstein . (1982). Parent Involvement: A Survey of Teacher Practices. *Elementary School Journal*. 83(2): 85–102.

Bradshaw, C.P., Sawyer, A. L., and O'Brennan, L. M. (2007). The impact of cyber bullying: A new type of relational aggression. http://www.counseling outfitters.com/vistas.

Brown, Patricia Clark. Involving Parents in the Education of Their Children. http://www.kidsource.com/kidsource/content2/Involving_parents.html. Retrieved July 2013.

Brown, S., and Taylor, K. (2007), Bullying, education and earnings: Evidence from the NationalChild Development Study, Economics of Education Review 27, 387-401.

Bully Bill in the House Committee (Special Report May 16, 2007) http://www.ncfamily.org/stories/070516s3.html.

Bureau of Justice Statistics. (2003). School Crime and Safety. Washington, D.C.: Department of Justice.

Card, N. A., and Hodges, E. V. (December 2008). Peer Victimization Among School Children: Correlations, causes, consequences, and consideration in assessment and intervention. *School Psychology Forum* 23(4) 451–461.

Chase, Bob. Bully-proofing Our Schools. http://www.patcom.com/pdf/Bully proofing.pdf. Retrieved July 2013.

Chinappi, Jacqueline. (2009). What Causes Bullying: Where Do They Come From? http://www.brighthub.com/education/k-12/articles/5275.aspx.

College Democrats Statement on HB1366—The School Violence Prevention Act Retrieved from: http://bluenc.com/college-democrats-statement-on-hb1366-the-school-violence-prevention-act#ixzz1d9ZEdyQf.

The Counseling Place, LLC. http://www.thecounselingplace.com.

The Department of Education and Early Childhood Development's Building Respectful and Safe Schools. (2010). Four Kinds of Bullying. http://www. ncab.org.au/fourkindsofbullying/.

Dodrill, Page (2010). Main reasons people are bullyed from *Dealing With Bullying* by D'Arcy Liness and Michelle New. http://paigedodrill.blogspot.com/2010/ 05/dealing-with-bullying-by-darcy-lyness.html.

Downey, Maureen. Should Teachers Stop Bullies? http://blogs.ajc.com/get-schooled-blog/2009/04/21/should-teachers-stop-bullies/

Duncan, Arne. Keynote speech. (2011) Bullying In America, Civil Rights in the 21st Century and the Changing Face of the Mideast Top Agenda at ADL Conference, New York, NY, April 13.

Eckholm, Erik, and Zezima, Katie. (2010). 9 Teenagers Are Charged After Classmate's Suicide. http://www.webofnarcissism.com.

Fox, J.A., Elliott, D.S. Kerlikowske, R.G. Newman, S.A., and Christeson, W. (2003). Bullying Prevention is Crime Prevention. Washington, D.C.: FIGHT CRIME: INVEST IN KIDS.

High, Brenda. (2007). *Bullycide in America*, Los Angeles: JBS Publishing Inc.

Hoover, J., Oliver, R., and Hazler, R. (1992). Bullying: Perceptions of adolescent victims in Midwestern USA. *School Psychology International* 13:5–16.

How to Handle a Bully-Child. http://www.child-discipline-with-love.com/how-to-handle-a-bully..html. Retreived June 2013.

Israel, Sheriff Scott. What Parents Should Know About Bullying. Broward County, Fl: Sheriff's Office. http://sheriff.org/safety/bullying.cfm. Retreived July 2013.

Janssen, Ian, Craig, Wendy, Boyce, William, and Pickett, William. (2004). School's Role to Help Prevent Bullying. http://www.thechallenge.org/16_4_ bullying. html. Retreived July 2013.

Kalman, Izzy. (2010). How We Are Raising a Generation of Emotional Marsh-mallows. http://bullies2buddies.com/how-we-are-raising-a-generation-of-emo tion al- marshmallows/.

Limber, Susan P., and Nation, Maury M. Bullying Among Children and Youth. www.ojjdp.gov/jjbulletin/9804/bullying2.html.

Moss, Peggy. Combat Cyber-Bullying: Be a Part of Your Daughter's Life—the Real and the Virtual. http://www.empoweringparents.com/cyber_bullying. Retreived July 2013.

Moss, Peggy. (2013). Girl Fighting and Your Child. Empowering Parents. http:// www.empoweringparents.com/mean-girls-bullying.php.

Nansel, T., Overpeck, M., Pilla, R., Ruan, W., Simons-Morton, B., and Scheidt, P. (2001). Bullying Behaviors Among U. S. Youth: Prevalence and Association with Psychosocial Adjustment. http://jama.ama-assn.org/content/285/16/2094. full.

Neven, Tom. (2001) The Wounded Spirit: Focus on the Family. http://www. troubledwith.com/ParentingChildren/A000000526.cfm?topic=parenting percent20children percent3A percent20low percent20self-esteem.

New York Post. (2008). 'Kick Me' Can Get you Kicked Out.

Nordahl, J., Poole, A., Stanton, L., Walden, L., and Beran, T. (October 2008). A Review of School-Based Bullying Interventions. *Democracy & Education*.

Olweus, Dan. Olweus Bullying Prevention Programme: design and implementation issues in Norway. (2004). In *Bullying in Schools: How Successful Can Interventions Be?* Edited by Peter Smith, Debra Pepler, and Ken Rigby. Cambridge, UK: Cambridge Univeresity Press, pp. 13–36.

Parker Peters, M., and Brain, S. (2010). Bullying and Victimization Rates among Gifted and High-Achieving Students. http://jeg.sagepub.com/ content/ 34/4/624.short.

Pappas, Leslie. High-tech harassment is hitting teens hard Bullying is nothing new, but it takes on a new and ominous tone in cyberspace. Adults are catching on. *Philadelphia Inquirer*, January 2, 2005. http://www.philly.com/2005- 01-02/ news/25434564_1_online-journals- instant-messages-web-links.

Peretti, Frank E. (2001). *No More Victims*. Nashville, TN: Thomas Nelson Publishing.

Ross, Margaret S. (2005) *Casey and The Amazing Good Finder*. Peachtree, GA: Kamaron Institute Press, Inc.

Simmons, Rachel. (2011). *Odd Girl Out: The Hidden Culture of Aggression in Girls*. New York: Houghton, Miflin, Harcourt.

Skye, Jared. Cyber Bullying Statistics. http://safety.lovetoknow.com/Impact_ of_Cyber_Bullying. Retreived July 2013.

Smith, P. (1999). Who Bullies? http://www.cfchildren.org/programs/hot-topics/ bully/parents1/.

Smith, P., Pepler, D., and Rigby, K. (Eds.) (2004). *Bullying in Schools: How Successful Can Interventions Be?* Cambridge, UK: Cambridge Univeresity Press.

Smith, P., and Sharp, S. (1994). *School Bullying: Insights and Perspectives*. London: Routledge.

Stop Bullying Now. (2010) Signs of Bullying—Warning Signs that Your Child is Being Bullied. education.com. http://www./magazine/article/Warning_Signs_ that_Your_Child/.

Swearer, Susan. (2010). Bullying: What Parents, Teachers Can Do to Stop It. http://www.apa.org/news/press/releases/2010/04/bullying.aspx.

Tamanini, Kara. (2009) How do we Stop Bullying in Schools? http://www. psychcentral. com/lib/2009/how-do-we-stop-bullying-in-schools/.

Upper Merion Area Middle School. (2011). Creating a Culture of Respect in Order to Maintain a Bully Free Environment http://www.character.org/wp-content/ uploads/2011/08/UpperMerionArticleonBullying.pdf.

Winters, Rebecca. (2000) Beware of the In Crowd. *Time Magazine*. August 21, 2000. http://library.thinkquest.org/07aug/00117/whybully.html.

Woo, Georgette. (2006) Can We Bully-proof Our Kids? http://www.island scene.com/ Article.aspx?id=2973.

Zeff, Ted. (2009). Strategies to Prevent your Sensitive Son from Being Bullied. http://drtedzeff.com/news/preventbullying.php.

Chapter Four

Cyberbullying: A By-Product of the Internet

Sherry L. Harrison
Patricia Thurmond

Introduction

The number of Internet users in the United States is multiplying at an exponential rate. The U.S. Department of Commerce: National Telecommunications and Information Research (NTIA) Preview (2011) reported "As of October 2010, the nationwide broadband adoption rate equaled 68.2 percent of households, up from 63.5 percent one year earlier" (p.5).

Part of the Internet's allure can be attributed to the amount of information readily available through search engines. For instance, the Internet provides excellent resources for learning and thus classrooms are being equipped with technology tools such as laptops, iPads, and iTouches to take advantage of these resources. Another allure is social networking sites such as Facebook, MySpace, Google+, and many others. These sites allow users to communicate, document, and share special moments with family and friends a thousand miles away or right next-door. Other sites such as Goggle Docs allow students to work on the same paper simultaneously from different physical locations and apps such as Find My Friends allow students to share their location and movements with friends and family. While these social networking sites and apps allow students to keep in touch with each other, they also provide the perfect environment for cyberbullies to operate.

This chapter explores the double-edged sword of the Internet through the stories of victims of cyberbullying. It brings to light the need to remain vigilant, even in households were Internet usage is heavily guarded or in schools with very strict technology policies. Through these stories, you will understand how and where students are bullied, where victims of bullies turn for help, and the pro-active strategies you as a teacher or parent can implement to try to prevent cyberbullying.

Cyberbullying

When we consider the growth of social networking sites among all age groups, we realize those in authority cannot keep students off these sites forever. In fact, many students who have been told by their parents they may not have a social network account such as Facebook, MySpace, or Twitter find a way to create one away from the watchful eyes of adults. They do so by utilizing a friend's computer or by using other Internet devices such as tablets, smartphones, and game consoles. Therefore, one must assume that at some point the majority of students, even some as early as elementary school or younger, will have some type of social media account now or in the near future.

Once created, students are able to access their accounts away from home at places like fast food restaurants, bookstores, and major shopping malls. Some students even have access to the Internet at school using iBooks and other technology tools designed to enhance the delivery of curriculum, instruction, and assessment. Therefore, it makes sense to teach students how to navigate the Internet as a responsible digital citizen while ensuring they understand the importance of maintaining Internet safety.

One aspect of Internet safety is cyberbullying. Wikipedia (2012), states that "The term 'cyberbullying' was first coined and defined by Canadian educator and anti-bullying activist Bill Belsey, as 'the use of information and communication technologies to support deliberate, repeated, and hostile behavior by an individual or group, that is intended to harm others" (para, 2). Although parents, teachers, and other stakeholders try to prevent students from becoming victims, incidents of cyberbullying remains a growing concern across the nation. The affects of cyberbullying are astounding and touches all age groups from elementary school to high school and beyond. Following are some possible examples of the diverse and creative ways cyberbullies strike. As you read each example, consider the affect on the victim and if the event could have been prevented.

Examples of Possible Cyberbullying

- A victim may be called names on MySpace for others to read
- A victim may receive an email with inappropriate negative comments from a cyberbully who used a free email account with a fake name to bully the victim
- A victim may be terrorized by a bully saying rude and nasty comments within a virtual world such as the virtual worlds many online video games use
- A cyberbully may send texts to the victim's cell phone saying the victim is fat, ugly, and stupid
- A cyberbully may start a false rumor about the victim on Twitter
- A cyberbully may write on the victim's wall on Facebook saying the victim kissed a boy that victim did not kiss

- A cyberbully may create a Tumblr blog making the Tumblr look like it was created by the victim, and then post untruthful information, and images that embarrass the victim
- A victim may place pictures of himself on Facebook, and the cyberbully may click "Do not Like" and then post a negative comment about the pictures, and continually repeat that bullying process every time the victim post pictures
- If the victim is logged into Facebook or has his or her Facebook login information and password saved on the computer, when the victim steps away, the bully may post a sexually inappropriate Facebook status
- Without the victim knowing, a bully could take a female victim's cell phone and text "I like you, and want to go to a movie with you" to a boy, making the text appear as if it was coming from the female victim. Then the bully might spread a rumor on Facebook saying that the victim texted the boy, and asked him to go out.
- When a victim is bullied by one bully, and responds back to the bully trying to get the bully to stop, the bully may get other bullies to post nasty comments on the victim's Facebook
- A bully may use a social question and answer website or respond to a blog with a false statement making the statement look like it was written by the victim
- A bully may take embarrassing video of the victim in the bathroom or locker-room, and place those videos on YouTube for others to see.

These possible cyberbullying examples reveal the hurtful and embarrassing affects of cyberbullying. Victims who are bullied often do not know where to turn for help and may even be too embarrassed to ask for it. This is particularly true when the victim is worried his or her parents might believe the fictitious comments posted by the cyberbully. Even worse, some victims feel being bullied is their own fault. How victims react and the strategies they use vary greatly. Following are reactions victims have to the cyberbullying.

Examples of Possible Victim Responses

- A victim may ask their teacher if they can go talk with their school counselor, and then share with their counselor what is happening
- A victim may ask their teacher if they can share with them what is happening
- A victim may tell their Sunday School teacher what is happening
- A victim may share with their friends what is happening, and one of their friends may tell their own parents, who may tell the parents of the victim, or may tell administrators at the school
- A victim may not have a lot of friends, feel they are all alone, and continue to take the bullying with no response at all
- A victim may tell their parents what is happening, and their parents might print out the hurtful comments their child received on Facebook, and show the school principal, or the police
- A victim may not tell anyone, and just try to handle it without help in hopes that the bully will stop

- A victim may become so depressed the bullying is happening that they commit suicide
- A victim may show their friends the inappropriate comments posted about them on Facebook, and their friends may help them figure out how to contact Facebook to share the bullying that is happening.
- A victim might stand up to the cyberbully, and then due to that, the bully might stop
- A victim might stand up to the bully, and that might make the bullying even worse
- A victim may respond back privately on Facebook to a bully's inappropriate comments, and the bully make take that response from the victim, and post it in a status update for all to see, embarrassing the victim even more

Sometimes cyberbullying may stop after the victim has reported the bullying to a parent, school administrator, police, or the social media company where the cyberbullying occurred. However, often times, cyberbullies do not stop when confronted or will stop for a short time and then later attack the same victim. Unfortunately, in many cases, the bullying was not discovered until after the victim committed suicide.

A Nationwide Movement to Build Awareness

The above examples highlight the seriousness of cyberbullying and the need to build awareness across the nation. Unlike face-to-face bullying, cyberbullies hide behind the anonymity of the Internet, making it harder to find them and stop the harassment. The impact of such attacks does not stop at the victims and their families but also afflict schools, communities, and the nation as a whole. These far-reaching affects were evident in 2010 when the nation saw a rise in suicide among Lesbian, Gay, Bisexual, and Transgender (LGBT) teens and college students. In response, everyday citizens, community organizations, and even government officials banned together to create campaigns of awareness not just for LGBT but for all students who fall victim to bullying, particularly cyberbullying.

One such campaign called the "It Gets Better Project" focused on sending a message directly to LGBT victims using short video clips. Each clip relays a simple message of do not give up; life will get better. Since its September 2010 inception through December 2011, over 30,000 videos were viewed more than 40 million times.

Video submitters to It Gets Better comprise of ordinary citizens, television celebrities, representatives of large corporations, and government officials including President Barrack Obama. In the President's clip, he spoke directly to the victims saying "You are not alone. You didn't do anything wrong. You didn't do anything to deserve being bullied. And there is a whole world waiting for you, filled with possibilities (Obama, 2010, para. 4)." He also spoke to the nation, urging us to stop thinking of bullying as a rite of passage and start ensuring the safety of our nation's children (2010).

The National Crime Prevention Council (NCPC) also has a campaign to spread awareness on their site, http://www.ncpc.org/newsroom/current-campaigns/ cyberbullying. Site visitors can copy banner codes and paste them to their own websites. The site also includes downloadable MP3 public service announcements and other information about bullying.

The NCPC's website is just one of many such sites educating the public on cyberbullying; an Internet search will net dozens of others, including the following:

- www.stopbullyingnow.com (this site provides practical advise and talking points for youths, families, and schools personnel)
- http://www.stopbullying.gov/topics/get_help/index.html (this portion of the site provides suggestions for getting help if bullying continues or gets worse)
- www.thetrevorproject.org/Programs (this site offers crises intervention, including online chats and networking community for LGBT youths)
- www.cyberbullying.us (this site lists cyberbullying laws by state and the latest headlines on cyberbullying)
- http://en.wikipedia.org/wiki/Cyberstalking_legislation (this portion of the site describes cyberstalking/cyberbullying legislation at the state and federal levels)

Each site is different by design but all focus on a common goal, to spread awareness across the nation. Students are going online at younger and younger ages, not just with computers but with video game consoles, cell phones, even Internet enabled wristwatches. Long gone are the days when placing the computer in the family room is enough to protect your student from deviants in cyberspace. Cyberbullies are smart so you must be smarter! Awareness and pro-active strategies are vital to preventing cyberbullying.

The U.S. Department of Education: National Council of Education Statistics reported that "In school year 2006–07, some 8,166,000 U.S. students ages 12 through 18, or about 31.7 percent of all such students, reported they were bullied at school, and about 940,000, or about 3.7 percent, reported they were cyber-bullied (i.e., on or off school property)" (p. 1). Therefore, instead of trying to forbid students from using the Internet or confine them to one room, concentrate on pro-active strategies designed to educate and protect them against cyberbullies.

Pro-Active Strategies to Prevent Cyberbullying

Schools and households across the nation are already incorporating pro-active strategies to help ensure these figures move in a favorable direction. For instance, most schools teach Internet safety and ban social networking sites on school computers. They also discuss with students what to do if they witness bullying of any kind or fall victim to it themselves. Many school districts even provide professional development opportunities for faculty and staff on topics such as bullying and cyberbullying.

In addition to schools, families also incorporate pro-active strategies to prevent cyberbullying. Some place the computer and other Internet capable machines in a common area of the house. Many talk to their students about the dangers and benefits of the Internet and the importance of never giving out personal information. They ask questions about their day and relationships with friends and they listen intently at the answer. These are the basic, more common approaches families and schools take to protect students, others go a step further. Below are a few other strategies for pro-active consideration.

1. Get to know the terms surrounding cyberbullying. A good resource is http://www.cyberbullying.us/cyberbullying_glossary.pdf. If you hear students using such terms, take action.

2. In addition to knowing the terminology, families and schools should know the warning signs of those being bullied and as well as those doing the bullying. Identifying the signs is a proactive step you can use to prevent or at least minimize the attack. Schools could create a simple checklist of warning signs for teacher use. Dr. Meehan (2011) discussed the use of a checklist in his book, *The Right to Be Safe: Putting an End to Bullying Behavior*. He also provided examples as free downloads at http://www.searchinstitutestore.org/The_Right_to_Be_Safe_p/0823-w.htm.

3. Restrict usage on electronic devices. Most devices include built in parental controls to restrict Internet content by rating, restrict purchases for games, movies, and apps, and block sites such as YouTube. On iDevices, you can find parental controls by opening "settings" and clicking on "general" followed by "restrictions." Once you enable restrictions, determine restrictions to impose and then set a password your student cannot guess. Avoid using numbers your student know such as birthdays, alarm codes, pin numbers, or easy combinations such as 1,2,3,4. You can follow a similar process to set restrictions on non-iDevices such as smartphones, electronic pads, and even game consoles. Review the directions that came with the device for steps. Schools can use the same process to restrict access on handheld devices used in the classroom, such as iPads.

4. A smartphone allows students to access the entire Internet while away from the watchful eyes of home and school. Therefore, some families opt to use third-party tools that provide additional protection for smartphones. Some features include the ability to track movement, read text messages, and block phone numbers from calling or sending messages. Most families do not use the tools as a way to spy on their student, on the contrary. They discuss the decision to use them with the student, helping them understand it is about safety, not privacy. Make sure you research your options before purchasing. Some tools are free such as the Apple friendly app Find My Friend and Android friendly app Google Latitude. Other tools charge a one-time fee or a monthly or yearly subscription service and include parental options not available from smartphone manufacturers or apps. Since options, prices, and phone compatibility varies from software to software; you should do your homework. A good place to start is with a comparisons chart like the one found at http:// cell-phone-parental-control-software-review.toptenreviews. com/ or use Google to search for additional charts and information about parental control software.

This type of software is also available for other electronic devices such as computers and tablets.

5. Remember, students can access their Internet accounts from any Internet source; therefore, it is also important to review website restrictions especially on their social networking sites. For a social networking site like Facebook, we recommend a two-step approach for families. First, create your own Facebook account; set your prefaces using the privacy options, and then 'friend' your loved-ones. Becoming a 'friend' allows you to see their postings, pictures, and other entries. Second, as the guardian of the student, log into his or her account and either help to set the privacy controls or set the controls for your student. Set privacy for sharing information with friends and with third-party apps by following steps located in the help center http://www.facebook.com /help/privacy. Also visit Facebook safety page at http://www.facebook. com/help/safety, it offers tools and resources for families, teachers, teens, and law enforcement. In addition, Wired Safety.org (1995–2011) offers additional tips for teens and parents.

6. Not all Internet browsers are created equal. Internet Explorer, Firefox, and Safari privacy settings might be fine for most schools and households but for younger students, consider using a restricted kid friendly browser such as KidZui.com, Zoodles.com, kie-surf.com, Kidoz.net and BuddyBrowser.com. Some kid friendly browsers are free and others charge a fee so be sure to do your research.

Actions to Take if Cyberbullied

Awareness and using pro-active strategies are the best defenses against cyber-bullying. However, sometimes, our best efforts fall short. If this happens, the student should:

1. If asking the cyberbully to stop does not work, do not meet to confront the cyberbully alone or try to handle the situation by yourself. Remember, there are adults around willing to assist.
2. Tell an adult you know and trust such as a parent, family member, school official, etc.
3. Do not retaliate or reply to the message.
4. Avoid reading the messages if possible but do keep them in case you need to contact the authorities.
5. File a complaint with the Internet service provider.
6. If the bullying persists, the guardian should contact an attorney or the police.

Conclusion

The Internet has opened many doors for the use of technology in the classroom as well as life in general. It is unfortunate; however, cyberbullying has become a dangerous by-product of this valuable resource. To protect our children, teens, and young adults against such attacks, households, communities, and political leaders are banning together to promote responsible digital citizenship, Internet safety, and cyberbully awareness across the nation.

References

Meehan, C. (2011). The Right to Be Safe: Putting an End to Bullying Behavior. http://www.searchinstitutestore.org/The_Right_to_Be_Safe_p/0823-w.htm.

Obama, Barack. (2010) President Barack Obama Video Transcript for the It Gets Better Project Washington, D.C. http://www.whitehouse.gov/it-gets-better-transcript.

U.S. Department of Education: National Council of Education Statistics. (2011). Student reports of bullying and cyber-Bullying: Results from the 2007 school crime supplement to the National Crime Victimization Survey. http://nces.ed.gov/pubs2011/2011316.pdf.

U.S. Department of Commerce: National Telecommunications and Information Administration. (2011). Digital nation expanding Internet usage NTIA research preview. http://www.ntia.doc.gov/files/ntia/publications/ntia_internet_use_report_february_2011.pdf.

Wikipedia. (2012). Cyberbullying definition. Retrieved from http://en.wikipedia.org/wiki/Cyber-bullying#Definition.

Chapter Five

First Year Teachers' Perception on Their Self-Efficacy in Bullying Intervention: Teacher Preparation Programs

Sylvia A. Mason
Beverly L. Downing

Introduction

Bullying—The statistics are frightful and the consequences have become tragic. Abraham Lincoln first wrote about bullying to his son's teacher: "He will have to learn, I know that all people are not just, that all men are not true. But teach him also that for every scoundrel there is a hero. Let him learn easily that bullies are the easiest to lick" (as cited in NYC Educator, 2005, p. 1). No longer is simple teasing, whispering in cliques, and writing on bathroom walls of the previous decades the extent of bullying behaviors. These "old school" antics have escalated to new horizons, resulting in serious injury and death.

Bullying is not new. In fact, Battaglio (2006) observed that "school bullying has been a chronic concern for educators since long before Charles Dickens documented its hazards in the schools of his day" (p. ii). Olweus (1973) first discussed early reports of bullying in Scandinavia, in his books *Aggression in the Schools: Bullies and Whipping Boys* and *Bullying at School: What we Know and What We Can Do*. His research has been considered the catalyst for identifying the characteristics, types, and intervention of bullying in the United States. The work of Olweus and other authors (Coloroso, 2003; Cohn & Canter, 2003; Davis & Nixon, 2011; Olweus, 1993; and John, 2011, et al.), brought national attention to this issue, increased data collection, and introduced the characteristics of bullying and victimization.

The incidence of bullying and its effect on children have been staggering. More than 160,000 children fail to report to school each day because they are afraid of being bullied (Info in Preventing Bullying, Harassment, Violence and Online Bullying, 2009). The statistics also reported at least one child out of seven in grades K-12 is either a bully or a victim of bullying. In a time where we are concerned about children not having minimum skills, dropping out, or being globally competitive, one has to wonder if there is a correlation among bullying, school attendance, and academic achievement. In Tatum's (2009) Study, *School Climate, School Safety, Victimization, and Student' Self-reported Grade: a Quantitative Study,* she examines the relation of these variables and their effect on student achievement. In the author's conclusion, she noted that, "Students who are bullied may be at risk of academic failure. Since bullying is a problem at schools, researchers have conducted studies to examine it" (p. 26).

Since the 1990s, the incidence of bullying has increased to critical mass resulting in not only high school absenteeism, but also serious injury, and even death. The National Association of School Psychologists reported, "Between 15 percent and 30 percent of students were bullies or victims. Between 1994 and 1999 there were 253 violent deaths and 52 causalities which were the result of multiple death events; bullying was often the factor in school related deaths" (as cited in Cohn & Canter, 2003, para. 1).

Bullying and the havoc it reeks among school-aged children "is a crime that is not going away anytime soon" (Info in Preventing Bullying, Harassment, Violence and Online Bullying, 2009). Schools, parents, peers, communities, and other stakeholders have begun to understand that "old school" taunts and teasing are not just occurrences that are part of school culture to be endured. The perception was that bullying was a "rite of passage" that every child went through in school. In the last ten years, this idea has not changed, according to a blog by Danielle Mele, Clinical Coordinator for the Assessment Center at the Dominion Education Center, Chesapeake Bay Academy. Mele stated, "A few decades ago many people believed that bullying would help kids toughen up and learn to defend themselves is one that is still prevalent in the United States today" (2011, para. 1). The Center for Disease Control and Prevention warned that, "Bullying, teasing and harassment should not be considered normal rites of passage or 'kids just being kids'" (2011, para. 2).

Behaviors such as talking back, teasing, gossiping, and engaging in cliques, and the occasional schoolyard fight that took place in schools were seen as just a part of going to school and growing up. After all, it happened in "our day" and we survived. Our children will survive, too. This is not true anymore. When children who once thrived and were excited about going to school are suddenly afraid to go to school because they fear being victimized by bullies, then it is time to take action. Since teachers, by public opinion, are the first persons that parents and administrators seek out for answers, they must be prepared to respond and garner the support of all stakeholders to reverse these bullying behaviors.

Definitions

The literature is saturated with definitions and characteristics of bullying (Davis & Nixon, 2011; John, 2011; Swearer, Espelage, & Napolitano, 2009; Hinduja & Patchin, 2008; Olweus, 1999). Nevertheless, all the definitions have held a common theme:

> Bullying is generally defined as an intentional act that causes harm to others, and may involve verbal harassment, verbal or non-verbal threats, physical assault, stalking or other methods of coercion such as manipulation, blackmail, or extortion. Aggressive behavior intends to hurt, threaten, or frighten another person. An imbalance of power of power between the aggressor and the victim is often involved. Bullying occurs in a variety of contexts, such as schools, workplaces, political or military settings and others (U.S. Legal, 2011, para. 1).

Additional researchers have contributed to the literature, sharing similar opinions but also including specific characteristics, types, and duration of bullying to clarify its meaning. Dr. Dan Olweus, founder of the *Olweus Bullying Prevention Program,* provided the most prominent definition:

> A person is bullied when he or she is exposed, repeatedly and over time, to negative actions on the part of one or more other persons, and he or she has difficulty defending him or herself. . . . Bullying can take on many forms: (1) Verbal bullying including derogatory comments and bad names; (2)Bullying through social exclusion or isolation; (3) Physical bullying such as hitting, kicking, shoving, and spitting; (4) Bullying through lies and false rumors; (6) Having money or other things taken or damaged by students who bully; (6) Being threatened or being forced to do things by students who bully; (7) Racial bullying; (8) Sexual bullying; and (9) Cyberbullying [via cell phone or internet] (Hazelton Foundation & Clemson University: Olweus Bullying Prevention Program 2011, paras. 1-4).

Education is not the only profession that has contributed to the definition of bullying. The fields of psychology, nursing, and medicine have also examined bullying behaviors and offered some of the following definitions. The National Association of School Nurses (NASN) defines bullying as "dynamic and repetitive persistent patterns of verbal and/or non-verbal behaviors directed by one or more children on another child that are intended to deliberately inflict physical, verbal, or emotional abuse in the presence of a real or perceived power differential" (as cited by Life and Health Library, CBS Interactive, 2011, para. 3). The American Medical Association's Proceedings (2002) adopted the definition by Olweus (1993a), but added, "Bullying is a pervasive, serious problem with long lasting consequences; it's not just a part of growing up. It happens in schools, which means that parents, teachers, students, and administrators must be aware of the problem and ways to handle it. Bullying can be direct or indirect and is different for boys and girls" (p. 1). Considered a major health issue because of its effects on both bullies and their victims, bullying has been defined by the Center for Disease Control and Prevention "as a form of youth violence that can result in physical injury, social and emotional distress, and even death" (2011, para. 1). The long-term emotional and mental health of bullying victims has earned the concern of the American Psychological Foundation (APA). Dr. Norman Anderson, CEO stated, "Bullying is a form of aggressive behavior in which someone intentionally and repeatedly causes another person injury or discomfort. Bullying can take the form of physical contact, words or more subtle actions, such as cyberbullying—or using the Internet, mobile phones or other digital technologies to harass" (American Psychological Foundation, Anderson, 2011, para. 3).

While the most familiar or widely discussed types of bullying have been physical, racial, sexual, and verbal abuse, the advancement of technology has introduced cyberbullying, a phenomenon that is hard to control and even more serious than one would imagine. Cyberbullying or "cyber stalking" (W.L. Anderson, 2010, p. 18) has global effects since it uses technology as a conduit. Anderson (2010) comments further, cyberbullying involves the use of social media "such as chat rooms, emails, blogs, and is defined as interaction between two minors using the Internet, cell phones, or any type of digital technology" (p. 18). Increased use of classroom technology by teachers for research, instruction, and supplemental learning, has opened the window of opportunity to exacerbate an already difficult global medium to control. Walker (2011) adds, "Traditional bullying and the newer-style cyberbullying is a cause of concern for many children, parents, teachers, school administrators, policy makers, marketplace service pro-viders and other interested stakeholders both in the United States and in other countries most notably, Canada, Australia, and the United Kingdom" (p. 38). Additionally, Feldman (2011) remarked, "Although we may now have a better understanding of these maladaptive behaviors, recent technological advances have created a new forum for bullying" (para. 1). Today's students often come to school more technologically savvy than their teachers do. Though not the intended purpose or use of technology, cell phones, texting, and tweeting have contributed significantly to spreading cyberbullying. These technologies have created a venue where bullies are doing the following:

> Sending huge amounts of buzzers or winks to someone, copying personal conversation and sending them to others, spreading gossip, manipulating pictures of persons and sending them to others, making Websites with humiliating comments about a student, sending threatening emails, misleading someone via e-mail in a open chat room and sending messages with sexual comments (Vanderbosch and Van Cleemput, 2008, p. 501).

During their teacher preparation program, pre-service teachers are evaluated on their through their microcomputer classes, the ability to integrate technology, define fair and appropriate use, and when the use of assistive technology is appropriate. It is reasonable to assume that a conversation about fair and appropriate use occurs in the computer courses but more likely in the context of lesson planning and general legal issues. Additionally, the focus of most microcomputer courses is to meet the technology requirements for integration and portfolio development, not examine how technology has become a vehicle for cyberbullying. In a meeting of the British Education Select Committee, a report entitled *Education's Teachers not trained to handle bullying* (2007) was presented. The report "warned that teachers were not sufficiently trained to tackle the problem" (para. 2). Steve Sinnott (General Secretary, National Union of Teachers) weighed in:

> Cyberbullying brings a profoundly disturbing new aspect to bullying. The Government should convene a high level meeting with internet service providers to explore ways of blocking sites, which allow cyberbullying to happen. While the Government has issued some good advice on targeting prejudice driven bullying, it should be given a much higher profile. The Select Committee's finding on special needs bullying is deeply disturbing. It highlights the need to review inclusive educational practice. The inclusion of children with special educational needs in mainstream schools is being carried out without sufficient preparation and resources (as cited in Education's Teachers, 2007, para.2).

Pre-service teachers should be knowledgeable about traditional and cyber-bullying so they can provide early intervention, especially since their ability to understand appropriate usage and integrate it into their lessons is systemically evaluated.

Defining bullying can be compared to opening the fabled Pandora's Box. The box contained "All the evils of the world. When Pandora opened the jar, all of its contents except for one item were released into the world. The one remaining item was hope" (Wikipedia, 2011, para.1). If this is true, let us try to believe that some hope travels to those who are victimized by bullies, knowing there are people out there who are working to find a way to protect these victims before it is too late.

Theoretical Framework

Children are exposed and raised in broad social systems, which include family, school, and community. Within these systems, or "ecological models" (Brofren-brenner, 1979), children act and react based on what they have learned or observed. The Brofrenbrenner Social-Ecological Model suggests that bullying is a social phenomenon directly related to one's environment. If we consider this model to be part of a child's development, it is reasonable to assume that bullying is a learned and/or reactionary behavior. According to Swearer, Espelage, and Napolitano, 2009):

> Bullying behaviors from this perspective emerges from a complex intersection of children's personality and dispositions, which becomes modified as they enter into various contexts across early childhood and adolescence. . . . We contend that bullying/victimization does not occur in isolation and, in fact, results as a complex interaction between the individual and his or her family, peer group, school community, and social norms (p. 15).

The family is the center of a child's world. There are times, however, that what society perceives as the "traditional" family (house, mother, father, and siblings) is not the environment or system to which children are responding. Family, in the broadest terms, could mean foster care; being raised by older siblings, grandparent, or extended family members; or in the extreme cases, gangs. Regardless of how it is defined, the "family environment can undoubtedly affect a child's behavior and outlook on life" (Powell & Ladd, 2010, p. 196).

If teachers are perceived as the gatekeepers and first defense against bullying, it will be imperative for them to have the knowledge, skills, dispositions, and feelings of empowerment. This feeling of empowerment or "self-efficacy" (Bandura, 1997, p3) originates in knowing that one has been prepared to handle a certain situation. Bandura (1997) described self-efficacy as "one's beliefs in one's capability to organize and execute the courses of action required to produce attainments" (p. 3). When perspective candidates enter teacher preparation programs, they enter with the expectation that, in addition to learning content and pedagogy, they will also gain the knowledge and skills to enable them to create and facilitate environments conducive for learning. Presently, the classroom management course is the only course where teacher education majors receive instruction about classroom management theories, best practices, and effective discipline. The exceptions to this are students who major in Special Education or Psychology, where the focus is etiological and prescriptive.

Bullying and Students with Disabilities

Until recently, data reported for bullying has not filtered incidence, participation, or the victimization of students with special needs (students identified as meeting eligibility requirements by IDEA). Nevertheless, bullying does not discriminate. It has only been within the last decade that increased attention to bullying and victimization has emerged. Rose, Espelage and Monda-Amaya (2009) commented, "At the present time, a majority of the bullying research has been reported in a whole school context, and has neglected to report findings for individual subgroups. This is especially true for the population of students with disabilities" (p. 763). Flynt and Morton's (2010) research in the correlation of bullying and disabilities found that "Although there is a substantial body of literature about bullies and victims, relatively little attention has been focused on how this problem relates specifically to children and youth with disabilities" (p. 331). Children with disabilities have been the target of bullies for decades, because they were "different." Because of their learning, physical, or mental disabilities, the opportunity for harassment was greater for inhumane treatment, insensitive comments and physical and emotional abuse. Schoen and Schoen (2010) noted, "The cruel culture of teasing, bullying, and harassment that exists in the schools is particularly relevant for students with disabilities" (p. 68). The incidence of bullying can actually be more frequent and intense towards students with disabilities than without them. Because the range of disabilities is so vast, the child's ability to tell an adult about the bullying or even defend himself [or herself] against it increases his or her chances of being victimized. Moreover, because laws are in place such as IDEA (Individuals with Disabilities Education Act, and ADA (Americans with Disabilities Act), it was reasonable to surmise that children with disabilities were safe from being victims of bullies. However, the opposite is quite true. Mepham explains, "Bullying and abuse are considered within the context of a broad safeguarding agenda. It is proposed that the increased vulnerability of disabled children is directly related to the marginalization of this group in society and that further action needs to be taken to address these issues" (2010, p. 20). AbiltyPath (One of the many advocacy organizations for persons with disabilities) conducted a study called "Walk a Mile in Their Shoes: Bullying and Children with Special Needs." AbiltyPath reported that, "Since 2005, the issue of bullying has become so important that 45 of the 50 states have passed laws against it. Unfortunately, very few of these laws address the specific issues and needs of children with special needs" (p. 31). Notwithstanding, regardless of ethnicity or disability, bullying has reached critical proportions for school-aged children.

Teachers are perceived as the first line of defense to eradicating this epidemic. The reason is "parents send their children to school with the assumption that they will not only learn, but will be protected" (Beebout-Bladholm, 2011, p. 9). This might have been a reasonable assumption 20 years ago. However, with the onset of bullying, this is more difficult to achieve if pre-service teachers are not prepared to handle bullying behaviors. Teacher education programs must give pre-service teachers the same self-efficacy in bullying and as they do for content and pedagogy.

Bullying—The Media Weighs In

As more attention has been focused on bullying, the public has become both saddened and outraged. The effects of bullying have led to serious injury or death resulting in devastating grief for all parties concerned. The question of "why" sparks anger and disgust at such insensitive acts. In the quest to bring attention and eradication of all types of bullying behaviors, advocates against bullying and victimization have the strongest ally possible: the media. Major television networks and prime time serials have devoted significant airtime to the exposure of bullying behaviors and their consequence.

The ABC News Program *20/20,* commented that they were bringing bullying back to the limelight. It is a story, they said, "that you see in nearly every headline and the passage of time has only made bullying worse" (Duberuil, Jim & Eamon McNiff, 2010). Death by bullying, or Bullycide, is new vernacular meaning, "that a victim of repeated bullying became depressed and then died by suicide" (Poland, 2011, p. 92).

One of CNN News' headlines for March read "Prosecutor: 9 teens charged in bullying that led to girls' suicide. . . . It appears that Phoebe's death on January 14 followed a torturous day for her when she was subjected to verbal harassment and physical abuse" (Cable News Network, 2010, para. 1). The stress of school, getting good grades, passing standardized tests, and having friends is all too powerful for some children. Being skeptical or afraid to tell a trusted friend, sibling, teacher, or parent that they are being bullied exacerbates the matter. Believing there is no solution, many children have resorted to the ultimate escape: suicide. Elvin (2001) shared that bullying is a form of torment leaving some victims to believe that suicide is the only way to escape. He comments "Researchers have found that a significant number of youngsters who are unable to cope with bullying take their own lives. . . . Sad as that may be, it's the one channel kids may take when they cannot handle bullying" (p.48).

CNN's prime time show *Anderson Cooper 360*, which aired October 14, 2011, reviewed the in-depth film of director Lee Hirsch's, *The Bully Project*. Cooper and other guests provided commentary regarding Hirsch's film, research, and stories from bullies and victims. Hirsch states, "For too long, bullying has been shrouded in silence or merely dismissed as kids being kids" (Cooper, para. 2). Hirsch also added comments from the recent jury at Silverdocs Film Festival (n.d.) noting, "The jury at Silverdocs film festival perhaps said it best. The torturous experience of youth is shared by many, but it is bravely revealed in this film through characters who confront their experience and work to reclaim their dignity" (Hirsch, 2011, para. 3).

The rise of bullying has brought celebrities to war against bullying. Powerful representatives such as Ellen DeGeneres, Queen Latifah, Jim Carey, Shaquille O'Neal, Mario Lopez, Daniel Radcliffe, Padma Lakshmi, the Dixie Chicks, and Lady Gaga are just a sample of the celebrities who have given their time and voices to supporting the victims of bullying. In addition, organizations and websites such as Teens Against Bullying, Stop Bullying, and The Trevor Project National Center for Bullying Prevention, ParentFurther.com, and StopBullying.gov are just an example of those whose primary goal is to put an end to bullying. Public and private media have recognized the need to keep this topic in the forefront. Unfortunately, they do this while concurrently reporting the violent, yet sometimes deadly, effect of its victims.

The Classroom Management Course

When pre-service teachers begin their plan of study, a classroom management course is usually required. Strong emphasis is placed on this course. Historically, public opinion was if you have no discipline in your class, then there could be no learning. From the outside, this belief remains popular and is one of the major areas by which pre-service teachers are assessed. A Classroom management course is the core course where pre-service teachers are exposed to best practices for establishing discipline through authors such as Wong and Wong's (2004) work *The First Days of School: How to Be An Effective Teacher,* and Tomlinson and Imbeau (2010) *Leading and Managing a Differentiated Classroom*. RTI (Responsiveness to Intervention) and PBS (Positive Behavioral Support) also have been used in schools to help teachers to create a more effective learning environment and to manage behaviors. Unfortunately, these professional development opportunities are offered within the schools and not available to pre-service teachers during program matriculation.

There are two reasons why classroom management courses are necessary. First, a course in classroom management provides a guide as to how to react to various behavioral issues in the classroom. Historically, the class concentrated on immediate action versus reaction modes that "can provide relief to the teacher, increasing the likelihood of a similar reaction to classroom behavior in the future" (Ducharme & Shecter, 2011, p. 258). Teachers see immediate improvement in the behavior, but long-term changes are rare. Second, classroom management courses provide a foundation for discipline so that maximum opportunities for learning are increased. By tradition, Callahan, Clark, and Kellough, (2002) point out that "classroom management is perhaps the single most important factor influencing student learning" (p. 161). As the gravity of bullying behaviors has had an emotional impact on schools, studying the diversity and culture of bullying behaviors in a classroom management should be addressed. The course should require teachers to examine their own dispositions about bullying, understand how internal and external "ecological models" (Brofrenbrenner, 1979, p. 3) affect bullying, and suggest best practices for culturally responsive strategies for intervention.

Pre-service teacher preparation courses at the bachelors, masters, and altern-ative entry levels require at least one three-hour course in classroom management. This course serves as the foundation for learning theory and effective practices. A series of sequential field experiences culminating in student teaching is the conduit between theory and reality. In Marks's (2010) research into course requirements for classroom management, she commented, "Many universities and colleges require only one management course in their teacher education program. Classroom management courses are often centered on general rules, procedures, and consequences and can be interpreted as a list of 'dos and 'don'ts' (p. 180). Salemah, Al-Omar, and Jumia'an (2011) remarked, "Traditional approaches to classroom management in teacher education programs do not seem to work. [The] Program typically include [s] one specific course in classroom management designed as a survey course where students are introduced to various theories and strategies" (p.13). Pre-service teachers leave these courses, having developed a list of three to five rules they would post on walls and share with students, and parents, in an effort to encourage a positive classroom environment.

The increase of on-line instruction and earning teacher licensure by alternate means has also been questioned during pre-service training. Wide ranging debates question program quality, as well as pre-service candidates' knowledge, skills, and dispositions in classroom management versus traditional students. Hammerness (2011) explained, "In the United States, an increasing number of new teachers are being prepared through alternative or early entry routes into teaching. These new forms of teacher preparation raise important questions about how and in what ways candidates are being prepared, particularly in key areas such as classroom management" (p. 151).

Research indicates that bullying is too frequent an occurrence that is everyone's problem (Davis & Nixon, 2011; John, 2011; Battaglio, 2006; Allen, 2010). As pre-service teachers matriculate through the teacher education program, they are engaged in mock and real- life activities focused on instruction and effective classroom management. Typical bullying behaviors such as shouting out, teasing, and acts of defiance are explored and methods of intervention specific to these behaviors addressed. While these behaviors are indeed present, in reality, they do not come close to preparing pre-service teachers to recognize, understand, and develop strategies for bullying prevention and intervention. For this reason, if pre-service teachers have not been exposed, nor had direct instruction about bullying, they might be reluctant to intervene. After they enter the classroom, pre-service teachers are to be the front line of defense, and they must be trained. Classroom management courses are consistently redesigned to meet contemporary challenges. Teacher preparation programs continually analyze and make data drive decisions about their programs. However, they cannot do it alone. Bullying does not occur in isolation. Teachers must have the support of the family and community. In addition, "If school leaders are going to engage more members of the school community, recent data suggests that much work still needs to be done with classroom teachers" (Levy, 2011, para. 10). We often hear "It takes a village to raise a child," designating teachers as the leaders within the village, believing they have the best chance for success to eliminate bullying.

Self-Efficacy and Pre-Service Teacher Training

While pre-service teachers might be familiar with bullying through previous experiences (possibly being the victim or the bully), their training about their responsibilities for intervention of bullying behaviors should begin in the classroom management course. Since the prevalence and consequences have become more devastating, teacher preparation programs must consider preparing their candidates to address bullying. As previously noted, it appears that no direct or very little attention has been given to understanding bullying behaviors. Howard, Horne, and Joliff (2001) reported, "Teachers will not intervene in bullying behaviors consistently until they feel adequately prepared to act" (p. 184). Teacher education programs ensure that their candidates are prepared in their content areas. Seemingly, then, "Before teachers can prevent or intervene in bullying situations, they have to be able to recognize it; research tell us that many teachers do not possess the knowledge or skills to recognize bullying behaviors among their students" (Allen, 2010, p. 4).

Bandura (1977) suggested that there is a correlation between how well a person believes he or she is prepared for a task and then executing that task (p. 3). This would be especially significant if pre-service teachers are expected by their school administrators and parents to intervene in bullying behaviors. If pre-service teachers do not feel they have the skills to intervene, their lack of confidence may contribute to bullying behaviors. Bauman and Del Rio noted:

Comprehensive training in prevention and intervention of bullying in general, not to mention relational bullying is lacking [*sic*]. The need for pre-service teachers to feel confident or empowered comes from their teacher preparation programs. Their self-efficacy is linked to their motivation in the classroom and the likelihood (even with intervening in bullying behaviors) to remain in the profession (as cited in Holt &Keys, 2004, p. 2).

It is reasonable to assume that pre-service teachers are motivated. His or her motivation to remain successful is contingent on their ability to manage classroom behavior effectively. Pre-service teachers develop the belief that they can be successful in the feedback given to them. The more positive the feedback, the more likely their confidence will increase. By contrast, the opposite is also true. In their research on teacher efficacy, Tschannen-Moran, Hoy, and Hoy (1998) found that "teacher efficacy, as motivational construct, proposed that levels of efficacy affects the amount of teacher effort a teacher will expend in a teaching situation and the persistence a teacher will show in the face of obstacles" (p. 23). If pre-service teachers feel that they are prepared to handle a situation where bullying is taking place, their response time might be quicker, resulting in a decrease or elimination of the behavior. Nicolaides, Toda, and Smith shared personal communications from Mary Baginsky's research on child protection within teacher preparation programs:

> The survey found that bullying was an area in which most students wanted a great deal more input during their initial teacher training courses. They wanted their course tutors to approach the subject in more depth so they felt better prepared to cope with situations they came across in schools (as cited in Nicolaides, Toda, & Smith, 2002, p. 107).

O'Moore (2001) concluded, "It is especially important for teachers that they understand what bullying is and the many forms it can take. [Then] they will then [*sic*] be in a position to identify it and deal with it in an appropriate manner" (p. 101). Content, pedagogy, and effective discipline receive a consistent attention within teacher education programs. Special topic seminars or professional development seminars aid in addressing emerging trends in assessment, discipline, and curriculum. The belief is pre-service teachers will be better prepared to produce an effective learning environment. If this were true, then following would also hold true:

> Teachers who are provided with meaningful training and information on bullying will find their actions are better received and more effective as they have a stronger understanding of bullying and the actions best suited to manage negative behaviors. Lacking sufficient training can be detrimental to a new teacher's ability to recognize and address bullying behavior as well as damaging to the students who may have to endure prolonged bullying to classmates (Lytle, 2010, p. 26).

If we compare bullying to the game of football, teachers would be the linesman to stop any movement of this behavior. It is essential that they identify who has the ball and its movement at all times. If they do not, they cannot be effective. The same is true for bullying. Siaranen and Pfeffer's (2011) research examined whether there was a correlation to trained and untrained teachers in bullying behaviors and their length of service in the profession. The authors found that "Anti-bullying [is] a significant factor in explaining teachers' responses, and all the hypotheses regarding training were supported. Trained teachers reported handling bullying significantly more effectively than [those who were] untrained" (Siaranen & Pfeffer, 2011, p. 338).

According to Kokko and Pörhölä (2009), "Although school personnel have both the legal and an educational obligation to prevent and intervene in school bullying as soon as it occurs, it seems that teachers may not have sufficient knowledge or the requisite skills to deal with this problem (para. 9). *The Times Educational Supplement's* Karen Thompson (2010) reported on research from the British Psychological Society's Association Conference regarding the need for training teacher in bullying. She wrote, "Trainee-teachers need to be tough more about the psychological make-up of child bullies and be given strategies to deal with parents." (p. 10). The research on bullying behavior and victimization has had far-reaching effects. The affects of bullying are felt globally, resulting in new policies and guidelines for pre-service teachers to become prepared to intervene in bullying behaviors. Research by Sewell, Cain, Woodgate-Jones, and Srokosz (2009) report-ed the requirements for trainee teachers in England and Wales. Summarizing the School Standards and Framework of 1998 and subsequent revisions (2001-2007), the authors noted, "The Training Development Agency 2007 requires that trainees must receive some training on the management of bully-victim problems in schools. This raising awareness may have an impact on the extent to which trainee teachers see bullying as an issue not only for their pupils but also for themselves" (Sewell, Cain, Woodgate-Jones, & Srokosz, 2009, pp. 4–5). The prevalence of bullying behaviors in South Korea raised awareness of the Korean Educational Department Institute to examine the need for teaching training. Yoon, Bauman, Choi, and Hutchinson's (2011) comparative on whether training in bullying of South Korean teachers made a difference where anti-bullying programs and policies were in place. The authors found:

> About 37 percent of teachers reported having had anti-bullying training, yet their responses did not differ from those without training. These findings underscore the significant limitations of teacher training programs in terms of effectiveness . . . . Teacher training programs may benefit from a more systematic approach that addresses important know variables while offering ongoing support to teachers as they face the challenges of dealing with bullying and victimization in their schools (Yoon, Bauman, Choi, & Hutchinson, 2011, p. 324).

Lastly, in Turkey, Sahin's (2010) study *Teachers' Perception of Bullying in High Schools: A Turkish Study*, the author concluded, "When bullying in schools is taken into consideration, it is impossible to think of this issue as being independent of teachers. . . . . The teacher education curriculum at education faculties should be updated and redesigned to prove a more realistic and scientific education of preservice teachers" (p. 140).

Bullying's far reaching arm has also infiltrated private and public schools. It is a global matter gaining the attention of many schools outside the United States. Toronto Canada's Catholic school district of Ontario, Chan (2009), shared that teachers must become the "social engineers" (p. 188) to invoke change in bullying and victimization. Chang (2009) further added, "To better prepare teachers for such challenges, it will mean teacher-training courses need to include much more practical and solution-based components in their pedagogy, as well as developmental courses on bullying and victimization" (p. 188).

Implications for the Teacher Education

Research of the literature in the United States and abroad (Salameh, Al-Omari, and Jumia'an 2011; Swearer, Espelage & Napolitano, 2009; Kokko, & Pörhölä 2009; Battaglio, 2006; Tschannen-Moran, and Hoy, & Hoy, 1998) has shown that bullying is not just an American issue. The consensus seems to be that pre-service teachers need specific training in bullying. It seems fair to conclude that bullying and victimization is an international issue. Teachers are seemingly regarded as the front line of defense to provide intervention in bullying. However, it may be difficult for pre-service or practicing teachers to live up to these expectations if they are not prepared to do so.

The goal of teacher preparation programs, traditional or alternative, is to give prospective candidates the skills and tools they need to be successful in the classroom. Teacher education programs are bombarded with frequent criticism about teacher effectiveness, student achievement, raising scores, and responding to initiatives such as NCLB (No Child Left Behind). The Department of Education is calling for teacher education programs to better prepare teachers so they can facilitate learning. Hence, teacher education programs redesign their content curriculum to address these concerns and prepare pre-service teachers to go out and conquer. It seems unfair that they are less prepared to do so about bullying.

As teacher education programs examine the data and effectiveness in preparing teachers as part of continuous improvement, they should also take time to examine the reality of bullying and victimization in schools. Given the magnitude and depth of bullying, it seems unlikely that it will be eradicated anytime soon. Hence, the same momentum given for preparing teachers to meet curricular demands should be equal for preparing them to confront bullying as ironic as it seems, even more so. Maybe we should look at this from a different angle. If children feel their teachers will keep them safe from bullies and being victimized, then maybe they will come to school more often. Serious injuries, emotional and mental harassment, and even death from bullying will begin to decrease. Children will begin to learn, become successful, and globally competitive. Teachers just might be able to teach.

There are professional development programs available such as the Olweus' Bullying Prevention Program (2011) and instructional videos and podcasts to give information and statistics about bullying. Notwithstanding, these opportunities operate outside the teacher training environment unless special arrangements are made for training. Schools and Colleges of should include bullying training within classroom management courses. The teacher preparation program leadership should also ask its P-12 partners offer professional development in bullying and if pre-service teachers may attend. This will help pre-service begin to develop the self-efficacy and skills to intervene in bullying behavior. Given the extent of and devastating consequence of bullying this cannot happen too soon.

References

AbilityPath.org (2011). *Support for parents of children with special needs.* Community Gatepath. Retrieved from http://www.abilitypath.org/areas-of-development/learning--schools/bullying/articles/bullying-special-needs-overview.html.

Allen, K. (2010). Classroom management, bullying, and teacher practices. *Pro fessional Educator, (34), 1,* 1–15. EBSCO*host.*

Anderson, N. (2011, November 14). This is psychology [Video podcast]. Retrieved from http://www.apa.org/news/press/video/this-is-psychology/bullying.aspx

Anderson, W. L. (2010). Cyber Stalking (Cyber Bullying) - proof and punishment. *Insights to a Changing World Journal, 4,* 18–23.

Bandura, A. (1997). *Self-efficacy: The exercise of control.* New York, NY: Freeman.

Battaglio, C. (2006). *School bullying: The inside story.* (Doctoral dissertation). Retrieved from Dissertations & Theses: Full Text. (Publication No. AAT NR19937).

Bauman, S., and Del Rio, A. (2006). Preservice teachers' responses to bullying scenarios: Comparing physical, verbal, and relational bullying. *Journal of Educational Psychology, 98*(1), 219–231. doi:10.1037/0022-0663.98.1.219

Beebout-Bladholm, T. (2010). Teachers' responses to bullying situations. The elements that influence intervention. (Doctoral dissertation). Retrieved from ProQuest Dissertations & Theses: Full Text. (Publication No. AAT NR19937).

British Education Select Committee (2007). Teachers not trained to handle bullying. *Education,* 2007, (30), 263, p. 1. EBSCO*host.* Accession No. 24626820.

Brofrenbrenner, U. (1979). *The ecology of human development Experiments by nature and design.* Cambridge, MA; Harvard University Press.

Bullying. (n.d.). Retrieved October 28, 2011 from Bullying Wiki: http://en.wiki pedia.org/wiki/Bullying.

Cable News Network (2010, March, 30)." Prosecutor: 9 teens charged in bullying that led to girl's suicide." *CNN Wire Staff.* Burbank, CA. Cable News Broadcasting. Turner Broadcasting System, Inc.

Callahan, J. F., Clark, L. H., and Kellough, R. D, (2002). Teaching in the middle and secondary schools (7th ed.). Upper Saddle River, NJ: Merrill Prentice Hall.

CBS Interactive Life and Health Library. (2011). Bullying: It isn't what it used to be. http://findarticles.com/p/articles/mi_m0FSZ/is_3_30/ai_n17207241/.

Center for Disease Control and Prevention (2011). Injury prevention and control: Violence prevention understanding bullying fact sheet. Retrieved from http://www.cdc.gov/violenceprevention/pdf/Bullying_Factsheet-a.pdf.

Chan, J. H. F. (2009). Where is the imbalance? *Journal of School Violence*, *8*(2), 177-190. doi: 10.1080/15388220802074199.

Clement, M. C. (2010). Preparing teacher for classroom management: The teacher educator's role. *Delta Kappa Gamma Bulletin*, *77*(1), 41–44.

Cohn, Andrea and Canter, Andrea Canter (2003). Bullying: Facts schools and parents. *National Association of School Psychologists*. http://www.nasponline.org/resources/factsheets/bullying_fs.aspx.

Coloroso, B. (2003). *The bully, the bullied, and the bystander*. New York, NY: Harper Collins.

Davis, S., and Nixon, C. (2011). What students say about bullying. *Educational Leadership (69)*, *1*, p. 18–23

Elvin, J. (2001). Torment and death from 'bullycide.' *Insight on the news. (17), 21*, p. 48

Farris, R. and Hirsch, L. (2011). Bullying: It stops here. [Television series episodes]. Cooper, A. (Executive Producer), *CNN Anderson Cooper 360*. Burbank, CA. Turner Broadcasting System.

Feldman, B. Feldman, M. (2011) Cyber-Bullying in High School: (Doctoral dissertation). Associated Retrieved November 14, 2011 from Dissertations & Theses: Full Text. (Publication No. AAT 3465630).

Fleming, M., and Towey, K. (Eds.) (2002). "Educational forum on adolescent health: Youth bullying. (May 3, 2003). Chicago, Il. American Medical Association. Print. http://www.ama-assn.org/ama1/pub/upload/mm/39/youthbullying.pdf.

Flynt, S. W., and Morton, R. C. (2004). Bullying and children with disabilities. *Journal of Instructional Psychology*, *31*(4), 330–333.

Garvis, S., Twigg, D., and Pendergast, D. (2011). Breaking the negative cycle: The formation of self-efficacy beliefs in the arts. A focus on professional experience in pre-service teacher education. *Australasian Journal of Early Childhood*, *36*(2), 36-41. EBSCO*host*. Accession number: 15421806.

Hammerness, K. (2011). Classroom management in the United States: A view from New York City. *Teaching Education*, *22*(2), 151-167. doi:10.1080/10476210.2011.567844.

Hazelton Foundation and Clemson University (2011). Olweus bullying prevention program. Retrieved from http://olweus.org/public/bullying.page.

Hinduja, S., and Patchin, J. (2011). Bullying, cyberbullying, and suicide. *Archives of Suicide Research, (14), 3*, p. 206–221.

Howard, N. M., Horne, A. M., and Jolliff, D. (2001). Self-efficacy in a new training model for the prevention of bullying in schools. *Journal of Emotional Abuse*, *2*(2/3), 181–191. EBSCO*host*.

Holt, M.K., and Keyes, M.A. (2004). Teachers' attitudes toward bullying. In D. L. Espealage and S. M. Swearer (Ed.S), Bullying *in American Schools: A social-ecological perspective on prevention and intervention* pp. 121–139). Mahwah, NJ: Lawrence Erlbaum.

John, B. (2011). *Childhood reflections: The effects of bullying experiences on teacher intervention.* (Doctoral dissertation). Retrieved from Dissertations & Theses: Full Text. (Publication No. AAT 3445236).

Kokko, T. H. J., and Pörhölä, M. (2009). Tackling bullying: Victimized by peers as pupil, an effective intervener as teacher. *Teaching & Teacher Education,* *25*(8), 1000–1008. doi: 10.1016/j.tate.2009.04.005.

Levy, P. (2011). Confronting cyberbullying. *T H E Journal, 38*(5), 25–27.

Lytle, M. (2010). *Bullying at school: New teacher perspectives and practices.* (Master's thesis). Retrieved from Dissertations & Theses: Full Text. (Publication No. AAT MR66787).

Marks, D. B. (2010). Preservice teachers' perceptions of classroom management instruction: Theory to practice. *National Teacher Education Journal, 3*(2), 179–201. EBSCO*host.*

Mele, D. (2011, January 13). School Bullying – "Sticks and Stones May Break My Bones But . . ." [Web log message]. Retrieved from http://www.cba-va.org/blog/bid/35819/School-Bullying-Sticks-and-Stones-May-Break-My-Bones-But.

Mepham, S. (2010). Disabled children: The right to feel safe. *Child Care In Practice, 16*(1), 19–34. EBSCO*host.*

McNiff, E., and Ferrari, II R. (2010). Bullied to death in America's schools. [Television series episode]. Dubreuil, J. (Executive producer), *ABC NEWS 20/20.* Burbank, CA. Turner Broadcasting System, Dubreuil.

National Association of School Psychologists (2011). *NASP resources helping children achieve their best. In school. At home. In life.* http://www.nasponline.org/resources/factsheets/bullying_fs.aspx.

Nicolaides, S., Toda, Y., and Smith, P. (2002). Knowledge and attitudes about school bullying in trainee teachers. *British Journal of Educational Psychology, 72*(1), 105. EBSCO*host.*

NYC Educator Blog. (2005, December 31). Abraham Lincoln's letter to his son's teacher. http://www.nyceducator.com/2005/12/abraham-lincolns-letter-to-his-sons.html.

Oliver, R. M., and Reschly, D. J. (2010). Special education teacher preparation in classroom management: Implications for students with emotional and behavioral disorders. *Behavioral Disorders, 35*(3), 188–199. EBSCO*host.*

Olweus, D. (1993). *Bullying at School. What we know and what we can do.* Cambridge, MA: Blackwell.

Olweus, D. (1973). *Aggression in the schools: Bullies and Whipping boys.* Washing, D.C.: Hemisphere Publication Corporation.

O'Moore, M. (2000). Self esteem and its relationship to bullying behavior. *Aggressive Behavior, 26*(1), 99–111.

O'Shaughnessy, J. A. (2001). Is cyber-bullying the next "columbine"? *New Hampshire Bar Journal*, *52*(1), 42–52.

Poland, S. (2011). The phenomenon known as bullicide. *District Administration*, *47*(5), 92.

Powell, M. D., and Ladd, L.D. (2010). Bullying: A review of the literature and implications for family therapists. *American Family Journal*, *(38)*, 3, p. 189–206.

Rose, C. A., Espelage, D. L., and Monda-Amaya, L. E. (2009). Bullying and victimization rates among students in general and special education: A comparative analysis. *Educational Psychology*, *29*(7), 761–776.

Şahin, M. (2010). Teachers' perceptions of bullying in high schools: A Turkish study. *Social Behavior & Personality: An International Journal*, *38*(1), 127–142.

Sairanen, L., and Pfeffer, K. (2011). Self-reported handling of bullying among junior high school in Finland. *School Psychology International*, 32(3), 330–344. doi: 10.1177/0143034311401795.

Salameh, K. M., Al-Omari, A., and Jumia'an, I. F. (2011). Classroom management skills among beginning teachers in Jordan: Preparation and performance. *International Journal of Applied Educational Studies*, *10*(1), 36–48. EBSCO*host*.

Schoen, S. and Schoen A. (2010). Bullying and harassment in the United States. *Clearing House*, *(83)*, 2, p. 68–72.

Selekman, J., and Vessey, J. A. (2004). Bullying: It isn't what it used to be. *Pediatric Nursing*, *30*(3), 246–249.

Sewell, K., Cain, T., Woodgate-Jones, A., and Srokosz, A. (2009). Bullying and the postgraduate. *Journal of Education for Teaching*, *35*(1), 3–18. doi:10.1080/02607470802587087.

Stephens, D. and Vilano, M. (2011). *The Overview: Walk a mile in their shoes.* AbilityPath.org: Support for Parents of Children with Special Needs. Retrieved from http://www.abilitypath.org/areas-of-development/learning-schools/bully ing/articles/walk-a-mile-in-their-shoes.pdf.

Stop Bullying, Harassment, and Violence (2009). *"Bullying Statistics."* Info in Preventing Bullying, Harassment, Violence, and Online Bullying and School Bullying. http://www.umuc.edu/library/libhow/apa_examples.cfm#websites.

Swearer, S. M., Espelage, D. L., and Napolitano, S. A. (2009). Bullying prevention and intervention: Realistic strategies for schools. New Your, NY: Guilford Press.

Tatum, D. (2009). *School climate, school safety, victimization, and students' self-reported grades: A quantitative study.* (Doctoral dissertation). Retrieved from Dissertations & Theses @ Walden University. (Publication No. AAT 3379851).

Tomlinson, C. and Imbeau, M. (2010). *Leading and Managing a Differentiated Classroom.* Alexandria, VA. Association for Supervision and Curriculum Development.

Thompson, K. (2000). Get inside the minds of bullies, staff urged. *Times Educational Supplement*, p. 10.

Tschannen-Moran, M., Hoy, A. W., and Hoy, W. K. (1998). Teacher efficacy: Its meaning and measure. *Review of Educational Research*, *68*(2), 202–248. (Document ID: 33612747).

U.S. Legal (2011). Bullying law and legal definition. Retrieved from http://definitions.uslegal.com/b/bullying.

Vandebosch, H., and Van Cleemput, K. (2008). Defining cyberbullying: A qualitative research into the perceptions of youngsters. *Cyber Psychology & Behavior, 11*(4), 499–503.

Walker, J. (2009). *The contextualized rapid resolution cycle intervention model for cyberbullying.* (Doctoral dissertation). Retrieved from Dissertations & Theses: Full Text. (Publication No. AAT 3392128).

Wong, H., and Wong, R. (2004). *The first days of school: How to be an effective teacher.* Harry Mountain View, CA. Harry K. Wong Publications, Inc.

Yoon, J., Bauman, S., Choi, T., and Hutchinson, A. S. (2011). How South Korean teachers handle an incident of school bullying. *School Psychology International, 32*(3), 312–329.

Chapter Six

Prison Bullying: The Ultimate State for the Battle of Institutional Power and Control

Rose Sabina Griffith Hunte
Ashraf Esmaii

Introduction

Definition

This chapter discusses the issue of bullying in prisons as it relates to the development of power and control in an environment where the inmate has no control. To understand the bullying nature of humans, it is first necessary to define the term, bullying. There has been much debate among researchers to find a common definition for bullying (Monks, Smith, et al, 2009), because it is a behavioral pattern that is found in many different areas of society such as, schools, organizations such as businesses and the work environment, and institutions such as prisons and the military. The debate continues although researchers are beginning to reach common ground. Ireland and Qualter (2008) noted that bullying has proven a difficult concept to define in terms of exact characteristics but that there is a growing consensus that bullying is an all-encompassing term that describes a range of aggressive behaviors. Ireland (2001) noted that present research demonstrated that the personal/descriptive characteristics that adult prisoners brought to the prison environment appeared to be less important in predicting group membership than the behaviors they displayed within the prison. For example, Ireland (2001) noted that drug related and proactive/positive behaviors being more predictive of group membership for male bully-victims while gender differences were demonstrated with negative behavior were more predictive for female bully-victims.

Ireland and Archer (2004) noted bullying as a subcategory of aggressive behavior with its own particular characteristics and that aggression is the term most frequently used to describe bullying. However, they continued by stating that in the case of prisons, the definitions tend to be broader. This may be a reason for the continued debate among researchers in finding a common definition for bullying behavior in prisons. Ireland and Archer (2004) noted interestingly, that in prisons, actions do not and often cannot be repeated to be considered bullying. However, from the recorded prevalence of bullying in prisons, one can infer that bullying can take many covert forms. Ireland, Archer, et al (2007) stated that indirect aggression occurred at the same if not more frequently than direct aggression, which supports the argument for covert aggression among inmates that may not be noticed or is ignored by correctional officers. Monks, Smith, et al (2009) stated that most researchers agree that bullying is an act that is intended to harm and can be defined as physical abuse, verbal abuse, and social isolation or exclusion. Sutton and Smith et al (1999) noted that in contrast to the popular stereotype and research tradition, the oafish bully, lacking in social skills and understanding, is actually a cold, organizing, manipulative expert in the social organizing of gangs, and the use of subtle indirect methods. Hence, they went on to state that bullying can be defined as the systematic abuse of power. Ireland and Qualter (2008) noted that prison based researchers have opted for a broad definition of bullying and stated:

> An individual is being bullied when they are the victim of direct and/or indirect aggression happening on a weekly basis, by the same perpetrator or different perpetrators. Single incidences of aggression can be viewed as bullying particularly where they are severe and when the individual either believes or fears that they are at risk of future victimization by the same perpetrator or others. An incident can be considered bullying if the victim believes that they have been aggressed towards, regardless of the actual intention of the bully. It can also be bullying when an imbalance of power between the bully and his/her victim is implied and not immediately evident.

Ireland and Qualter also noted that it is unlikely that a fixed, measurable, and prescriptive definition will materialize. However, Grennan and Woodhams (2007) argued that since much of the research done on bullying was conducted in schools, it failed to take into account elements of bullying unique to a prison environment. Monks, Smith, Naylor, Barter, Ireland, and Coyne (2009) agreed with Ireland and Qualter on the debate over the definition of the term bullying. They stated that it is agreed that bullying is an act intended to harm, takes place repeatedly, and with an imbalance of power between victim and perpetrator. Monks et al also noted that bullying included physical abuse, verbal abuse, and social isolation in addition that bullying is arguably higher among prisoners than in other settings. Hence, with no consensus on a scientific definition of bullying, in maintaining the title of this chapter, the simplistic definition of Sutton and Smith (1999) that bullying is a systematic abuse of power, will be upheld. Interestingly, this view follows the Biopsychosocial and Ecological Interaction model that will be discussed further in the theories section of this chapter.

Literature

The major issue facing criminal justice research in the United States of America presently is the lack of any current research. Munchkin and Fawcett (1990) described in detail the lack of research in American prisons that dealt with the issue of bullying. First, they noted that the majority of victimization studies conducted in penal institutions were concerned with adults. They cited Farrington and Natter (1980), Fuller and Orsagh (1979), and Bowker (1979), who examined victimization in an adult institution and noted that victimization in a correctional facility is a continuous process, extending through the day and night. Muchnik and Fawcett went on to cite past victimization studies dealing with variables that relate to or have an effect on correctional institutional victimization. These studies can be credited to Nuttal (1980) and Wilson (1977). Recidivism as related to victimization, they credited to Wenk, et al., 1972. The prison environment as related to victimization, they credited to Poole and Regoli (1983), Feld (1981), Nacci (1978), Toch (1978), and Thomas (1975).

Muchnik and Fawcett, (1990) also reviewed the type of offence committed that resulted in confinement and its relationship to victimization. For this work they cited (Bartollas, et al., 1974 & 1976). And last in this category, there is age and race as related to victimization within the correctional setting and was cited from Bartollas and Sierverdes (1981), Toch (1978), Fuller and Orsagh (1977), and Bartollas, et al. (1976). Muchnik and Fawcett additionally cited several studies conducted regarding the role a prison environment has upon victimization, Poole and Regoli (1983), Feld (1981), Nacci (1978), Toch (1978), and Thomas (1975). Many earlier researchers were named by Muchnik and Fawcett, but to continue to cite them would be a repeated citing of studies that reflected and discussed the same issue, bullying.

Patrick (1998) is another American researcher that discussed research on violence between inmates and inmates and inmates and staff in an attempt to understand them from a single perspective. They went on to discuss the environmental problems associated with inmate on inmate violence that creates an unsafe environment. They went on to note that this develops and continues a violent inmate subculture.

More interesting and relevant to this chapter is how current is the research in this area of criminal justice and penology, particularly in the United States of America and can bullying be a behavioral factor of humanity in general.

The studies noted above were all conducted in the 1970s and 1980s. Recent literature on bullying or victimization can be found through European Researchers such as Jane Ireland, Carol Ireland, Rachel Monaghan, Susie Grennan, and Jessica Woodhams. The question of whether or not European research on bullying can be relative to the United States is a very important question that should be answered. The Irelands, who are the most prominent researchers on bullying currently found in the literature, conducted most of their studies in the United Kingdom (England), Ireland, and Australia. As previously stated, this leaves one question: Can research on bullying based on European standards of criminal justice and penology be reliable to a nation such as the United States of America. Commonly known among criminal justice researchers is the fact that the USA has the highest rate of incarceration and the most expansive criminal justice system in the world. This major expenditure of resources to the American penal system and the large housing of inmates in this system can lead to what Tarver 2001 noted as the "graying of the inmate population. Tarver also noted that this aging is expected to increase by 2000 percent and that recent statistics; presumably from the Bureau of Prisons, verify this concern. The opposite standard of this statement is the island nation of Japan. However, since the end of WWII, Japan has gradually Americanized its culture as a nation and is now facing many of the same social problems as America. Issues such as alcoholism among its youth and the rejection of ancient values that maintained a once disciplined and comparatively peaceful Japanese society are no longer in place, thereby, leading to the conclusion of an overall change in their society. However, until recently, the Japanese nation has the lowest incarceration rate in the world, unless current demographics within the nation demonstrate this statement to be invalid. Another problem that can be noted is that much of the research on bullying is based on young children in a school setting. Ireland (2001) discussed the problem noting that it is problematic to apply definitions of bullying derived from school children to a prison environment and that this requires further discussion.

Sociologist textbook writer, Macionis (2011) discusses the sociological terms of reliability and validity. Macionis defines reliability as consistency in measurement, and that to have reliability; the research process must yield the same results when repeated. Macionis, additionally noted that validity is to ensure that in research, the researcher will measure exactly what they intended to measure. This can lead to the argument that American researchers may encounter numerous obstacles, historical and contemporary, in gaining admittance to prisons for updated research on the issue of bullying in prisons. This view is supported by Cicchetti (1998) who noted that editors are knowledgeable in their fields and is possible that they select reviewers who will agree with each other but not have a broad understanding of the content area being evaluated. Hence, the reliance on research completed in what may be termed; culturally-comparative systems, such as the UK (England), Ireland, and Australia may not reflect the circumstances of a nation such as the United States of America. The question, how compatible is the aforementioned nations, their penal institutions, and their prison culture to the United States? This is a matter for future discussion.

Ireland and Qualter (2008) noted that there has not been research within prisons that look at the broader concept of loneliness among prison inmates except for Ireland and Power (2004). The issue of loneliness in regards to bullying will be reviewed further in the theory segment of the chapter.

Ireland (2001) in a study of male and female adult prisoners noted importantly that bullying is repetitive and regular. The results of this study, according to Ireland, suggested that personal descriptive characteristics may not be predictive of group membership and that prison based behaviors may be more important in distinguishing bullying factions.

Ireland and Monaghan (2006) studied perpetrator and victim characteristics noting the perceptions of offenders in defining the term bullying. Their findings illustrated that school-based definitions of bullying are not appropriate and that a broader definition is needed.

Ojala and Nesdale (2004) noticed the influence of group norms in bullying. They stated that this process has not received attention in the children's bullying literature although the power of group norms to elicit antisocial behaviors has been studied in adolescent and adult aggression research.

Hawker and Boulton (2000) discussed the difference between indirect and relational aggression. They importantly noted that European researchers distinguished between physical, verbal, and indirect victimization. Hence, it continues to question the lack of research by American researchers into these new theoretical considerations of bullying.

Lord and Brown (2004) defined the term leadership. They stated that leadership cannot be reduced to a single great mind or individual but that the accomplishments of great people are at best indirect, operating through the accomplishments and actions of others. This definition can be associated with bullying. Obviously, prison bullies are not characterized as great people but they can and do employ indirect tactics through the support of others.

Theories

The literature discussed numerous theories related to bullying in prisons. Additionally, one theory, Leadership Theory, interestingly provided insight into the cognitive skills of bullies. Bullying requires a state of mind. It can be hypothesized that the bully must consider several factors when determining the exercise of their behavior such as victim typology, setting, avoiding capture, acceptance of behavior by peers, and possible reprimand and retribution. The researchers and authors cited in this chapter have provided numerous theories that can be attributed to bullying in all social strata. This section briefly details these theories.

Leadership Theory

This theory posited by Lord and Brown (2004) emphasizes followers as a determinant of leadership because it is through the actions of followers' reactions and behaviors that attempts at leadership can succeed or fail. This emphasis is prophetic in that a bully's success is based on their ability to attract a following. Without the attention of "admirers", a bully's efforts would be in vain. Victimization of another individual through bullying requires the skill to engage the victim successfully through the means of comprehending the individual's weaknesses and avoiding unwanted attention from caretakers. Caretakers can be characterized as correctional officials in a prison, teachers at a school, and coworkers or managerial staff in a work setting.

Farmer et al (2003) noted that the concept of aggressive leaders reflect the ambiguity in research on childhood and adolescent peer relations. They stated that the popular sociometric status, being well-liked by peers, is commonly associated with popularity in the research literature but may not be an adequate measure of an individual's position and influence in the social structure. An example of this can be specific military leaders and politicians whose anti-social behavior is tolerated because of their position and status. Farmer et al explained further by noting that the concept of social aggression may explain why some youth who are perceived as being popular are also not well liked. They defined social aggression as the manipulation of group acceptance through alienation, ostracism, or character defamation. The aforementioned characteristics can be attributed to some individuals that hold powerful roles in a society. This behavioral pattern transcends cultures and is pervasive throughout human civilization and in some non-human species. Although Farmer et al researched school-age children, the conclusions of their research can be attributed to adults. They noted that socially aggressive stratagems were often concealed and had tendency to be used by youth who are central in classrooms or school social networks. Additionally, they noted that youth who are prominent leaders may use both prosocial and socially aggressive strategies to wield influence and thus may not be well like by their peers. This paradigm can be associated with those individuals that hold positions of power in different social strata.

Lord and Brown (2004) cited three examples of powerful leaders and their perceptions of leadership. Walt Disney stated, "You can dream, create, design and build the most wonderful place in the world . . . but it requires people to make the dream a reality." A commonly known fact is that Walt Disney was the founder and leader of Disney studios and several theme parks relating to various productions of his studio. Former United States of America President Ronald Reagan is quoted as stating, "The great leader is not necessarily the one who does the greatest things; he is the one who gets the people to do the greatest things." This can be defined, as a great leader will surround themselves with the people who can make their visions a reality through direct action and involvement. George Stephanopoulos stated that he was " . . . moved by more than what he (Former President Bill Clinton) stood for or how much he knew. It was how I felt around him . . ." A good leader inspires and motivates their subordinates to accomplish great tasks. Lord and Brown went on to note that the first two quotes suggested that the accomplishments of great people are at best indirect and act through the accomplishments and actions of others; while the third is a related idea that was communicated from a subordinate's perspective.

In conclusion, leadership theory serves as a perspective for bullying in all levels of society. Bullies must have the ability to attract a following of approval while maintaining their own immunity to sanctions for their actions. Although the motivation for bullying may vary and differ from the motivations of the above social leaders; the results propel the similarities. This concept of bullying is best noted in the animation children's series Cow and Chicken that is aired on the Cartoon Network and Boomerang channels. In an episode on bullying, Chicken referred to a popular school bully whose power was usurped by a new arrival as ". . . our bully" and proceeded to rally the other students in defending "their" bully. Since this show is targeted to a young audience, continued research on the perceptions of children to bullying prior to and after watching popular media programs may be warranted.

The Need to Belong Theory

Baumeister and Leary (1995) discussed the Need to Belong Theory and proposed that a need to belong, a need to form and maintain at the least a minimum quantity of interpersonal relationships, is innately or nearly universal among humans. They went on to note that this paradigm illustrates human beings as naturally driven toward establishing and sustaining belongingness. This paradigm may also reflect the mob mentality of bullying sessions in which others would cheer the bullying of an individual. It supports an 'us versus them' mentality that can become pervasive during such incidents. It can be argued that this theory might reflect the mentality of close knit organizations such as law enforcement, military companies, and militia groups.

Loneliness

The paradigm of loneliness is discussed in detail because of its discussion on close emotional attachments, which can be perceived as a need of all humans.

In review of the concept of loneliness discussed by Ireland and Qualter (2008), they stated that aloneness means the physical absence of other people and emotional loneliness is a result of absence of close emotional attachments. This is supported by Hawker and Boulton (2000) who defined relational aggression as behavior, which causes or threatens to cause damage to peer relationships and particularly friendship and acceptance. On the other hand, they defined indirect aggression as aggression enacted through a third party or so that the aggressor cannot be identified by the victim. This passive aggressive form of aggression was pointed out by Hawker and Boulton who posited that indirect and relational aggression are conceptually different.

By the very nature of its structure, prison environments cannot be associated with aloneness but can be highly correlated to emotional loneliness. Therefore, inmates that are bullies may be attempting to control their environment and demonstrate power over others leading to acceptance by other inmates who admire their aggression. Some inmates in a prison may see bullying as a way to control their environment and will engage in patterns of bullying. The victims of bullying can be inmates who are smaller physically, those who may have a physical or mental handicap, or those whose crimes place them in a category that causes other inmates to dislike them intensely. The latter can be morally repugnant crimes such as pedophilia, murder of children, and the perpetrators of acts that are seen as the violation of social mores, such as cannibalism or rape. Ireland and Qualter noted that inexperienced victims of prisons would be at an increased risk of social loneliness and those who experience multiple forms of victimization report higher levels of social and emotional loneliness. Since reporting is a qualitative form of measurement, the reports of inmates must be defined to demonstrate how each inmate views their victimization and/or their bullying behavior. To determine the parameters, Ireland and Qualter utilized the DIPC-R, the Direct and Indirect Prisoner Behavior Checklist-Revised, which measured direct and indirect forms of bullying behavior and the SELSA, the Social and Emotional Loneliness scale that provides a measure of three aspects of loneliness. The three aspects of loneliness are as follows, family, romantic, and social. This scale defined family loneliness as a lack of closeness and attachments with family members. This particular measurement supports the finding of Hunte (2010) who noted that the significance of marital status in a study of the effect of life skills education on the generation of misconduct reports might be an indicator in reduced misconducts within an institution. This finding can be verified through further study to determine if marital status is a factor in lower incidents of bullying. It may also indicate that inmates with close family connections may not require a demonstration of power to engage others in a penal environment. In conclusion of the issue of loneliness, Ireland and Qualter noted that the subscale SELSA proved to be reliable by demonstrating $\alpha=.91$ out of the 221 inmates studied. They also found the emotional loneliness scale, which measured family and romantic, also reliable by demonstrating $\alpha=.89$ of the 213 inmates studied. Consequently, this supports Hunte's argument for increased family programs in penal facilities to assist inmates in maintaining their relationships.

Inadequacy vs. Manipulation

Sutton, Smith, and Swettenham (1999) stated that contrary to the popular stereotype of the oafish bully who is lacking in social skills, the bully might actually be a cold manipulative expert in social situations. They went on to note that this perspective entails the organization of gangs and the use of subtle indirect methods. This definition can be representative of pure bullies whose behavior is indicative of just bullying others in contrast to pure victims whose behavior is indicative of being bullied (Ireland and Archer, 2004). However, Monks et al (2009) noted that the above groupings of separating pure bullies, pure victims, bully/victims, and those not involved is a model, which have garnered recent changes. They proposed the development of alternative measures that account for behavioral frequency and that explores bullying/bullied tendency in opposition to categorization. Sutton et al (1999) supported the aforementioned notion that bullying is about power. They stated that bullying is the systematic abuse of power and that the inequality of power implies dominance, which is often associated with social skills and manipulation of belief. Ireland and Monaghan (2006) noted that methods used to measure bullying have evolved and questioned the validity of using these definitions.

In some situations, it can be noted that bullies will provide an impression that the victims deserve their fate. This belief is reinforced by the bully's peer support system. As an example, Sutton and Smith (1999) noted that one fifth of students reported that they might join in the bullying of a victim and that this attitude often translated into actual support for the bully. This same pattern can be viewed in the bullying of adults in all segments of society and its institutions. Bullies are cheered on by others who may just be relieved that they are not the object of the bully's attention and may join in with the bully as a protection from future incidents of victimization upon their person. This is supported by Sutton et al who noted that bullying occurs within social relationships and usually with peers present. Additionally, they noted that these peers might help or reinforce the bully through watching, laughing, and shouting encouragement. The social cognition skills of bullies are demonstrated through indirect or relational forms of bullying that require a manipulation of mental states and beliefs in the form of gossip, rumors, and lies (Sutton et al, 1999). Though Sutton et al conducted their research on young school children, the patterns discussed can also be indicative of bullying among adults in all segments of society. Sutton et al hypothesized that bullies score higher than victims and significantly higher than followers do on scores measuring social cognition. They also hypothesized that teacher-rated indirect bullying correlates with total social cognition scores when physical and verbal bullying are seen as independent variables. In conclusion, Sutton et al noted that it is very possible that the ability to understand the mental states and emotions of others is very adaptive for effective teasing, knowing the most hurtful names, , avoiding detection, choosing the most effective time and method of bullying, and maximizing the victim's vulnerability and minimizing damage to themselves. These scores arguably can be applied to adults. Bullying appears to be an art that requires social-cognitive skills and an understanding of human behavior for maximum effect. Hence, bullies cannot be viewed as inadequate but very adaptive in manipulation and under-standing of social cognitive behavioral processes. However, Ojala and Nesdale (2004) noted that bullying, as a group process, has only recently become the object of empirical research.

Life Events Model and Chronic Stress Models

Ireland and Qualter (2008) discussed both the Life Events Model and the Chronic Stress Models. They posited that the life events model argued that a single life stressor might provoke adjustment difficulties. They noted that both models have been applied to understand the association between victimization, as a source of stress, and social maladjustment, including loneliness.

Ireland and Qualter noted that the life events model argues that a single life stressor might lead to difficulties with adjustment, while the chronic stress model proposes that maladjustment becomes more noticeable as stressful events continue. Addi-tionally, they remarked on the Added Stress Hypothesis, which can be applied to victimization and adjustment difficulties in prisons. The Added Stress Hypothesis might be seen as piggy-backing the Chronic Stress Model because prison existence may be noted as an added life stress that leads to chronic stress for the duration of incarceration.

Four Models of Understanding

Towl (2006) provided four models to assist in understanding the field of prison bullying. He noted that there is a need to develop theoretical models as the next step in the evolution of prison bullying research.

1-Interaction Model

This model reflects on existing aggression literature and includes theories such as material deprivation, indigenous origins, direct importation, social categorization, and evolutionary methodologies (Towl, 2006). Towl continued by noting that the above models are combined with prison literature to form an eclectic model that can explain bullying as an expected behavior in prison. He went on to state that the interaction model is a reflection on how the social and physical aspects of prison environments encourage and maintain bullying.

This model demonstrates the innate nature of criminal behavioral patterns and how these patterns can be continued in a prison setting. Offenders who may have a predisposition towards interpersonal aggression or who deal with situations poorly may continue these predisposed behaviors in a prison setting (Towl, 2006).

2-Applied Social Information Processing Model

Towl (2006) noted that this model emphasizes displays of aggression as an adaptive but not acceptable solution to the threat or actual experience of being bullied and focuses on emotional and normative beliefs. Towl went on to note that this model encompasses the specific role of the prison environment and the emotions of anger and fear. Towl also mentioned that this model focuses on the promotion of internalized guides that determine behavioral responses over non-aggression scripts. There is no shortage of anger in a prison environment and it can be argued that logic dictates that the prevailing anger of offenders will be exhibited through behaviors that demonstrate this anger. Hence, this model can argue that anger and fear is not just the premise of the offender but can also be found among the correctional officers. Correctional officers may demonstrate a heightened awareness of their environment. Inmate bullies tend to bully inmate victims, however, bullies who can intimidate correctional officers in addition to inmate victims, may hold a higher status among their admirers.

3-Applied Fear Response Model

Towl (2006) stated that this model explicitly investigates the responses of victims following their exposure to bullying and the defensive behaviors engaged by offenders to avoid publicity of their behaviors. He went on to note that the model focuses on the motivation factor of fear in explaining the reactions of victims. Towl stated that the perception of the "flight versus fight" response could be referenced to cognitive neoassociation theories of aggression.

The model examines the concepts of the fear response and delayed flight response. Towl defined the "fear response" as outlining how aggressive responses to victimization represents both the fight and flight response while the target of the aggression remains unimportant and can be perpetrators, other prisoners, or correctional staff and can be a motivating factor that serves to protect offenders from bullying in a prison. The "delayed flight" response is defined by Towl as the aggressive response following incidents of bullying that can be manifested through aggression towards others or towards the self and assuming the form of self-injurious behaviors. Interestingly, Towl noted that this delayed-flight response can lead to removal from a prison unit and is considered essential to prisons where an "immediate-flight" response is limited by the restrictions of the physical environment. Towl's discussion is supported by Ireland (2007) who suggested that the use of negative behavior by bully-victims may be a way of attempting to prevent future victimization by conveying to their peers that they are not an easy target and do not deserve to be stigmatized as victims. Offender victims cannot run from offender bullies. Their only recourse may be to demonstrate extreme fear so that they may be placed in a solitary environment where they can avoid offender bullies. However, it can be argued that in a prison setting it may not be possible to escape bullies due to the close and intimate nature of prison units. Hence, it may be preferable to fight back in a vehement fashion, which serves to curtail the stigmatization of victimization.

4-The Biopsychosocial and Ecological Interaction Model

As mentioned earlier in the chapter, Towl (2006) noted that this model focuses on evolutionary functions and cultural regulators and concentrates on the complex interactions between the prison environment and the inmates within. As stated previously, this model according to Towl serves as a strategic solution to the challenges of social competition and accounts for the value of evolutionary theory. Towl described the value of evolutionary theory in illustrating the effect of group living on social interactions and the influence of ecology in the recruitment and success of aggressive or affiliative strategies. Towl also observed that the reference to biological factors such as genetics, hormones, neurochemistry, and immunity is a unique perspective that "depsychopathologises" bullying.

Humans have evolved to compete for power and status within their societies. In a closed institution such as a prison, behaviors will demonstrate this competitive nature. Survival of the fittest is a prevailing theme in the biodiversity represented on planet earth. It is found in all species of the planet and humans are not apart from the natural response but are a part of the natural forces that prevail. Hence, social issues such as war, poverty, slavery, and interpersonal interactions in the family and the society at-large, can be seen as a human requirement for the pursuit of power, wealth, and status.

Coping Theory

Grennan and Woodhams (2007) introduced coping theory, which refers to how an individual deals with stress and involves cognitive and behavioral strategies. They also noted that research has shown that stress impacts negatively on an individual's psychological welfare and that coping strategies play an important role in the way an individual responds to stressful events. Grennan and Woodham identified two common coping strategies, problem focused and emotion focused coping. They stated that problem focused coping involves cognitive-behavioral efforts to alter a stressful situation by changing the circumstances or by finding ways to solve the problem and is synonymous with "task-oriented coping". It can be argued that task oriented coping strategies may be used by offender victims to prevent bullying through the implementation of tasks such as building alliances with other offenders for protection or enlisting the aid of correctional officers by engaging these officers for future protection. This can be viewed as a method of problem solving.

Grennan and Woodham defined emotion-focused coping as a strategy to regulate emotional distress by changing the meaning of the stressful situation. An example of this can be the coping strategy used by offenders who are the victims of sexual assault bullying. They can alter their perception to accept this form of bullying as a survival strategy. It can be argued that for these inmates, being the "lover" of a sexual bully may prevent victimization from other sexual bullies by engaging in a "committed" relationship with an abuser. Another argument for this strategy can be made on abusive relationships in families.

A third coping strategy identified in the literature by Grennan and Woodham is avoidance coping where efforts are made by the victim to avoid the stressor. For offenders in a prison this may entail attempting to escape through acts of violence that may bring the attention of correctional officers, leading to confinement in a solitary area, thereby allowing the victim to escape the bully, if only for a limited amount of time. Grennan and Woodham termed this strategy as detached coping, which involves cognitive efforts to remove oneself from the stressful event and its associated emotions. They cited a study of Australian male prisoners, which demonstrated that these particular inmates are more likely to adopt emotional or avoidance coping strategies. The research would have to be replicated within penal institutions within the United States to determine if American offenders also use avoidance or emotional coping strategies. This author hypothesizes that American offenders would engage more in task-oriented coping strategies such as attempting to avoid victimization by visiting violence or the commission of murder against the offender bully. American victim/bullies may appear more aggressive than their original bullies because they may feel that they have something to prove and therefor, avoid future victimization. On the other hand, Grennan and Woodham cited a study of young male prisoners, age 18-25, and their response to problems specific to them. The noted that the findings discovered that "approach" coping, a problem –focused coping style, was used more often than "avoidance" strategies. This can be viewed as a key point because bullying and victimization are personal issues and are unique to each individual. Grennan and Woodham cited another study that assessed the coping strategies of prisoners and although they did not classify the prisoner's coping strategies into types, it was discovered that the prisoner's coping skills were poor and ineffective. This is why many individuals are incarcerated. They displayed their inability to cope effectively with the social situations in their societies. Consequently, their lack of coping skills in the society-at-large can also be demonstrated in the penal institution.

The No Blame/Participant Approach

The no blame/participant roles approach discusses bullying by involving observers and those who collude by failing to intervene (Sutton and Smith, 1999). Sutton and Smith noted that these approaches were researched with children whose ages ranged 12 to 13 and 7 to 10 years of age. Their findings revealed that a majority of children reported negative or neutral attitudes towards bullying. This research supported the earlier discussed need for research to determine how young children perceived bullying as viewed through popular animation media. The research question on this can be; are young children desensitized to bullying from an early age because of watching popular shows that glorify the roles of bullies. This researcher hypothesizes that children who watch popular media shows can become desensitized to bullying allowing them to glorify or demonstrate neutrality of this event. This hypothesis can be a subject of future research on children's perspective of bullying. This research can also be completed on inmates in a correctional facility. The hypothesis for prison bullying is that inmates can glorify bullying through the viewing of cinematic productions and television programs they are allowed to watch in a prison or that they watched prior to their incarceration.

Theory of Mind

Sutton, Smith, and Swettenham (1999) discussed the study of social cognitive abilities titled the theory of mind, which is defined as the ability of individuals to attribute mental states to themselves and others in order to explain and predict behavior. They also noted that research investigated the role theory of mind plays in the development of pro-social behaviors but only recently has it been considered in relation to social maladjustment and anti-social behavior. Bullying is defined as, the systematic abuse of power and this inequality of power implies dominance, which is associated with social skills and manipulation of belief (Sutton et al, 1999).

The theory of mind appears to have validity in determining a bully's ability to gain popularity from their anti-social behavior. The ability to influence others in viewing their behaviors as normal can provide a bully with an inordinate amount of power. This power can also be validated by authority figures such as teachers and correctional officers. In a correctional setting, correction officers are seen as the ultimate power. Validation of bullying in a prison, for example, can take the form of failure by correctional officers to intervene in the victimization of another inmate because they may not happen to like that particular person.

Developmental and Environmental Models

Ireland (2005) noted that developmental models of aggression suggest direct forms of aggression are used more by younger age groups. Additionally, they argued that as age increases so does an individual's use of more subtle and indirect forms of aggression and that this form of aggression does not replace the direct approach but complements their aggressive repertoire. This theory segued the child bully into the adult bully by suggesting that as the child bully ages they learn how to make their attacks covert so that they escape the adult sanctions for their behavior, which they probably avoided as a child. Ireland also discussed the environmental model, which explains why indirect bullying is prevalent in certain environments such as prisons. In such institutions, aggression may lead to penalties if noticed by correctional officers (Ireland, 2005). Bullies must learn to perfect their craft, therefor; the most skilled bully can evade observation by caretakers and can be held in even higher esteem by their admirers or those that fear them for their aggressive tendencies. It can be argued that the best bully in a prison may have perfected their craft from an early age, leading to the hypothesis that bullies are made, not born.

Exploitation of the Weak by the Strong

Wood, Moir, and James (2009) posited that prisons provide a climate where the strong can exploit the weak to create their own hierarchies. They continued by noting that this is a social system in which the utmost importance is given the notion of survival of the fittest where those with greater access to power and resources are likely to be viewed as the fittest. This paradigm appears to be very indicative of the hierarchies noticed in the workplace. It is very revealing of prisons in that inmates with the ability to befriend correctional officers can receive privileges and resources not provided to other inmates. This can lead to a perspective of power by other inmates who will seek out the privileged inmate for favors or protection. For example, inmates who have an understanding of criminal justice and law can enjoy a heightened status as jail house lawyers. Wood et al stated that bullying might become the prime means of establishing and maintaining these hierarchies since it is a form of an asymmetrical power relationship itself. They provided an example of this by noting that bullying may become a facilitator of gang recruitment as prisoners may bully others to become a member of a high status group with aspirations to a higher social status. This behavior can also be seen as promoting the joining of gangs in a prison for protection from bullies who

20ar the unity and strength of prison gangs. The aforementioned is supported by Baumeister and Leary (1995) Need to Belong theory, which as previously mentioned, possibly supports highly organized units such as the military, law enforcement, militias, and also, as stated above, prison gangs, who can also be viewed as being highly organized.

Discussion

As stated previously, the definition of bullying provided by Ireland and Qualter (2008) stated that an individual is being bullied when they are the victim of direct and/or indirect aggression that occurs on a weekly basis. Grennan and Woodham (2007) also used the above definition of bullying. However, the term "weekly basis" may require a more in-depth definition. This was evidenced by Ireland (2001) who stated that bullying could be perceived as a repetitive behavior that occurs on a regular basis. It can also be noted that bullying may be defined as taking place not just on a weekly basis but occurs in a manner that transcends time and dates. This assumption is based on Sutton and Smith (1999) who noted that bullying is collective in its nature based on the social relationships in the group. They went on to note that bullies receive encouragement and support from onlookers who may cheer the bully on. With this type of encouragement, especially among children, a bullies' attitude can be enforced and may allow others to join the bullies in their aggressive assaults. This same behavior can be noted among bullies in other arenas such as the workplace, prisons, politics, families, peer relations, and inmate populations. Therefore, it can be posited that bullying is a characteristic of humanity. A study of human behavior over the centuries may demonstrate that bullying has occurred among humans throughout history, from the hunter gatherers and continuing to the present. This view is supported by Towl (2006) who noted that the biopsychosocial and ecological interaction model focuses on evolutionary functions and cultural regulators. Towl went on to note that the above model emphasizes the potentially adaptive nature of aggression and its role as a strategic solution to the challenges of social competition. Additionally, he stated that this model accounts for the value of evolutionary theory and outlines the influence of group living on social interactions and the influence of ecology in the recruitment and success of aggressive or affiliative strategies. Humans must learn to live together. However, humans have evolved a need to have power, thereby, employing tactics that require bullying to achieve power and status above others or to remove power and status from others. Hence, it can be argued that humans are a part of nature and not apart from nature, as bullying is also represented by other creatures existing on this planet. The motives for the bullying behavior may be different but the results are the same; one takes the dominant role and the other becomes the submissive in the interaction. This is supported by Ojala and Nesdale (2004) who posited that most forms of bullying could be considered a subset of aggressive competitive behaviors designed to enhance the prestige and status of one's group. They went on to note that recent findings demonstrated the similarity of status in victims and bullies, which suggested the possibility that the majority of bullying takes place between children who are the members of rejected groups. How this translates to adults was not mentioned by the aforementioned authors. Interestingly, Ireland and Monaghan (2006) noted through their study of perpetrator and victim characteristics that the extent to which offenders considered bullying to be related to an imbalance of power was unclear. They stated that only 26 percent of offenders reported that bullies were always more powerful and stronger and that the majority of offenders, 77 percent reported that a single act of aggression could be considered bullying. Additionally, they also noted that one quarter of offenders, especially young and juvenile offenders, stated the term bullying was "childish".

Current events, such as school shootings, can be studied to determine if the perpetrators of these acts were bullied and decided to take extreme measures against the bullies and their associates. Unfortunately, perpetrators of these acts tend to commit suicide or are killed by law enforcement officers and cannot be interviewed regarding their motivation, but interviews of family and peers may provide a limited insight into their cognitive perceptions. This perspective is based on Wood, Moir, and James (2009) who stated that we exist in a social system in which the concept of survival of the fittest is encouraged and those with access to power and resources are likely to be evaluated as fittest. This theory is greatly evident in the interaction of humans throughout history, i.e. war, poverty, slavery, and interpersonal interaction in society and in family groups. The above position is supported by Baumeister and Leary ((1995) who noted that a need to belong is a fundamental human motivation and that this need can provide a point of departure for understanding and integrating the existing literature regarding human interpersonal behavior. This perspective was explored further in the Theory section of this chapter.

Regarding bullying in prisons, inmates, if incarcerated justly, demonstrate anti-social behaviors that led to their incarceration. It can be argued that inmates are bullies to begin with or victims of social bullying, which led to their acting out in a criminal manner. It can also be argued that bullying in prisons may demonstrate an attempt to have power in a powerless situation.

In conclusion, this section recapped some of the theories pertinent to demonstrating how bullying can be noted throughout the human species. Bullying can be found in all aspects of global societies. Bullying can be on a political level in which leaders can bully their constituents leading to conformity of political views or revolution to protest those same political paradigms. Bullying in the workplace has been and is currently being researched in regards to violence in the workplace. "Going postal" has become a catch-phrase and relates to what is viewed as the original case of workplace violence in which a postal worker shot his supervisor and several other workers before ending his own life. Military bullying has been categorized as sexual harassment of subordinates by their commanding officers or others in a position of power within the organization. School bullying is now the focus of intense research because of school related violence in the last few years. Some examples of this are Columbine, Colorado (US), Virginia Tech shooting (Virginia, US), and the most recent in Littleton, Colorado, (US). An interesting study would be the research on why these incidents appear to be more prevalent in the State of Colorado within the United States.

Conclusion

This chapter reviewed bullying in prisons and explored the possibility that bullying may be a matter of the human condition rather than a specific individual process. To note if this perspective is valid will require an eclectic research of the issue as it relates to humanity. Prisons are closed institutions being able to maintain their functioning regardless of issues faced by the civilian population. In such an institution, bullying can serve the purpose of building relationships and alliances, and gaining a higher status based on fear and the absence of reprisal because of that fear. It may be necessary to view prison bullying as a condition of human behavior rather than a separate entity. The pervasive nature of bullying in human society can be viewed as the ultimate pursuit of control in a human society in which control of one's life and fate is relative in nature. Therefore, prison bullying is just another aspect of pursuing the ultimate state of control in an environment in which control is noted to be absent among inmates and could relatively be placed solely on the correctional officers, who represent the ultimate authority.

Also discussed was the idea that bullying research needs to be re-established in the United States to determine if the paradigms discussed by European researchers can translate to American culture. If bullying is a condition of humanity, the findings of the researchers cited in this chapter could be relevant to any society and any institution.

References

Baumeister, R. F., and Leary, M. R. (1995). The need to belong: desire for interpersonal attachments as a fundamental human motivation. *Psychological Bulletin. 117*(3), 497–529.

Cicchetti, D. V. (1998). Good science and good peer reviewing: are they related? *Journal of Clinical and Experimental Neuropsychology. 20*(3), 428–431.

Farmer, T. W., Estell, D. B., Bishop, J. L., O'Neal, K. K., and Cairns, B. D. (2003). Rejected bullies or popular leaders? The social relations of aggressive subtypes of rural African American early adolescents. *Developmental Psychology. 39*(6), 992–1004.

Grennan, S., and Woodhams, J. (2007, October). The impact of bullying and coping strategies on the psychological distress of young offenders. *Psychology, Crime & Law. 13*(5), 487–504.

Hawker, D. S. J., and Boulton, M. J. (2000). Twenty years' research on peer victimization and psychosocial maladjustment: a meta-analytic review of cross-sectional studies. *Journal of Child Psychology and Psychiatry. 41*(4), 441–455.

Hunte, R. S. (2010). Learning to Change: does life skills training lead to reduced incident reports among inmates in a medium/minimum correctional facility? Ann Arbor, MI: ProQuest LLC. UMI 3397769.

Ireland, J. L. (2001). Distinguishing the perpetrators and victims of bullying behavior in a prison environment: A study of male and female adult prisoners. *Legal and Criminological Psychology. 6,* 229–246.

Ireland, J. L. (2005). *Bullying among prisoners: Innovations in theory and research.* Cullompton, Devon, UK: Willan Publishing.

Ireland, J. L., and Archer, J. (2004). The association between measures of aggression and bullying among juvenile and young offenders. *Aggressive Behavior. 30,* 29–42.

Ireland, J. L., and Ireland, C. A. (2008). Intra-group Aggression among prisoners: bullying intensity and exploration of victim-perpetrator mutuality. *Aggressive Behavior. 34,* 76–87.

Ireland, J. L., and Monaghan, R. (2006). Behaviors indicative of bullying among young and juvenile male offenders: a study of perpetrator and victim characteristics. *Aggressive Behavior. 32,* 172–180.

Ireland, J. L., Archer, J., and Power, C. L. (2007). Characteristics of male and female prisoners involved in bullying behavior. *Aggressive Behavior. 33,* 220–229.

Ireland, J. L., Qualter, P. (2008, January). Bullying and Social and emotional loneliness in a sample of adult male prisoners. *International Journal of Law and Psychiatry. 31*(1), 19–29.

Lord, R. G., and Brown, D. J. (2004). *Leadership processes and follower self-identity.* Mahwah, NJ: Lawrence Erlbaum Associates Publishers.

Macionis, J. J. (2011). *Society: The Basics* (11th ed.). Upper Saddle River, NJ: Pearson Education, Inc.

Monks, C. P., Smith, P. K., Naylor, P., Barter, C., Ireland, J. L., and Coyne, I. (2009). Bullying in different contexts: Commonalities, differences and the role of theory. *Aggression and Violent Behavior. 14,* 146–156.

Mutchnik, R. J., and Fawcett, M. R. Violence in Juvenile corrections: Correlates of victimization in group homes. *International Journal of Offender Therapy and Comparative Criminology. 34*(1), 43–56.

Ojala, K., and Drew, N. (2004). Bullying and Social identity: The Effects of group norms and distinctiveness threat on attitudes towards bullying. *British Journal of Development Psychology. 22,* 19–35.

Patrick, S. (1998). Differences in inmate-inmate and inmate-staff altercations: examples from a medium security prison. *Social Science Journal. 35*(2), 253.

Sutton, J., and Smith, P. K. (1999). Bullying as a group process: an adaptation of the participant role approach. *Aggressive Behavior. 25,* 97–111.

Sutton, J., Smith, P. K., and Swettenham, J. (1999). Social cognition and bullying: Social inadequacy or skilled manipulation? *British Journal of Developmental Psychology. 17,* 435–450.

Tarver, M. L. (2001, December). Rehabilitation strategies for diverse inmate
    populations: Considerations for recreational therapists, counselors and
    educators. *Jce. 52*(4) 167–171.
Tewksbury, R. (2006). *Behind bars: Readings on prison culture.* Upper Saddle
    River, NJ: Pearson Education, Inc.
Towl, G. J. (2006). *Psychological research in prisons* (HM Prison Service (ed.).
    Malden, MA: Blackwell Publishing.
Wood, J., Moir, A., and James, M. (2009, July). Prisoners' gang related activity: the
    importance of bullying and moral disengagement. *Psychology, Crime & Law.*
    15(6), 569–581.

Chapter Seven

Is Bullying the Same as it Has Always Been? Are We Making Too Much of Typical Childhood Behaviors?

Rosalind Duplechain
Barbara Braun
Ashraf Esmail
Felecia M. Bigard

Introduction

Many people think that bullying today is no different than bullying in previous decades: "boys will be boys" and "sticks and stones may break my bones, but words will never hurt me". Even the notion that girls gossip and are catty, although a newer addition to our understanding of bullying, is downplayed, minimized.
Is bullying the same as it has always been? Are we making too much of typical childhood behaviors?

Current Bullying Statistics

The most recent report on U.S. school safety is for the 2007–08 school year is a joint report put out by three agencies: National Center for Education Statistics (NCES); the Institute of Education Sciences (IES), in the U.S. Department of Education; and the Bureau of Justice Statistics (BJS) in the U.S. Department of Justice (Robers, Zhang, & Truman, 2010c). According to this joint report, about 55.7 million children and adolescents attended K–12 schools in 2007–08 (Robers, Zhang, & Truman, 2010d). During this school year, 25.3 percent of the public school principals reported bullying as a problem for their school (4 percent less than was reported in the 1999–2000 school year; Robers, Zhang, & Truman, 2010d). Further, it reports that 31.7 percent of 12- to 18-year-old students reported being bullied at school during the 2007–08 school year (Robers, Zhang, & Truman, 2010d). Of those students who reported being bullied in the school year, 78.9 percent were bullied inside the school and 22.7 percent were bullied on school grounds (Robers, Zhang, & Truman, 2010i). More important, of those students who reported being bullied during the school year, 62.6 percent reported being bullied once or twice during the school year, 20.7 percent reported being bullied once or twice a month, 10.1 percent reported being bullied once or twice a week, and 6.6 percent reported being bullied almost daily (Robers, Zhang, & Truman, 2010e). Only 36.1 percent of these students reported notifying an adult about these experiences (Robers, Zhang, & Truman, 2010e). Also, of those students who reported being bullied during the school year, 11 percent reported being pushed, shoved, tripped, or spat on and 19 percent reported a subsequent injury; and 5.8 percent reported being threatened with harm (Robers, Zhang, & Truman, 2010h). Additionally, bullying seems to be a bigger problem in middle school. According to NCES (2010),

Forty-four percent of middle schools compared to 21 percent of primary schools reported that student bullying occurred at least once a week. Also, a higher percentage of middle schools than high schools reported daily or weekly occurrences of student bullying. (Robers, Zhang, & Truman, 2010b. p. 1)

Cyber-bullying was also explored in this joint report. Three and seven tenths percent (3.7 percent) of the students in this sample reported being cyber-bullied. Of these students, 72.7 percent reported being bullied once or twice in the school year, 20.7 percent reported once or twice a month, and 5.1 percent reported once or twice a week (Robers, Zhang, & Truman, 2010e). No data were provided for reporting almost every day. Of these students, 30 percent reported notifying an adult about their experiences (Robers, Zhang, & Truman, 2010e). Also, of these students 1.6 percent reported that hurtful information was placed on the internet (Robers, Zhang, & Truman, 2010h).

Bullying Behavior Linked to Suicide

There are numerous cases in the U.S. where bullying behavior has been linked to suicide. Here are several examples: Ryan Patrick Halligan (age 14) in 2003, Megan Meier in 2006, and Phoebe Prince (age 15), Asher Brown (age 13), Billy Lucas (age 15), and Tyler Clementi (age 18) in 2010.

Simple internet searches of their names will substantiate the role of bullying in their suicides and will likely provide lists of other children and adolescents as well. Additionally, in review of 37 studies, Kim and Leventhal (2008) examined the link between bullying behavior and suicidal thoughts and action for children and adolescents from 16 countries including the United States. Authors concluded that while there is no definitive evidence, close examination of these studies suggests that "any participation in bullying increases the risk of suicidal ideations and/or behaviors in a broad spectrum of youth" (p. 133) and recommended that intervention efforts include a screening instrument to assess the potential for suicide.

Bullying Behavior Linked to Murder/School Shootings

Since August 1, 1966 to February 21, 2011, there have been some 106 school shootings in the United States. By decades, there was one in the 1960s, two in the 1970s, nine in the 1980s, twenty-nine in the 1990s, forty-eight in the 2000s, and seventeen as of February 21, 2011 (http://en.wikipedia.org/wiki/School_shooting).

The increase of school shootings since the 1980s, especially the Columbine school shooting, has captured national attention. As a result, in 2004, the United States Secret Service and United States Department of Education compiled a joint report on school safety (http://www2.ed.gov/admins/lead/safety/preventingattacks report. pdf). Focusing on a twenty-five year period (1974 until the time of the report, June 2000), the joint report puts the number of school shootings in perspective.

The Department of Education reports that nearly 60 million children attend the nation's 119,000+ schools. The combined efforts of the Secret Service and the Department of Education identified 37 incidents of targeted school-based attacks, committed by 41 individuals over a 25-year period. (United States Secret Service and United States Department of Education, 2004, p. 7)

More simply stated, "the odds that a child would die in school—by homicide or suicide—are, fortunately, no greater than 1 in 1 million" (United States Secret Service and United States Department of Education, 2004, p. 6). Focusing on the 37 of the highest profiled shootings, the report identified "10 key findings," six of which have some relevance to the link between bullying and murder/school shootings:

- Incidents of targeted violence at school rarely were sudden, impulsive acts.
- Prior to most incidents, other people knew about the attacker's idea and/or plan to attack.
- Most attackers did not threaten their targets directly prior to advancing the attack.
- Most attackers engaged in some behavior prior to the incident that caused others concern or indicated a need for help.
- Most attackers had difficulty coping with significant losses or personal failures. Moreover, many had considered or attempted suicide.
- Most attackers had access to and had used weapons prior to the attack.

The most significant finding to the link between bullying and murder/school shootings was: "many [70 percent] attackers felt bullied, persecuted, or injured by others prior to the attack" (United States Secret Service and United States Department of Education, 2004, pp. 11–12).

Roberts (2006), a school violence researcher, counselor, clinician, and teacher for more than 25 years, studied the same 37 high-profiled shootings. He concluded the following: "By my count, clearly 11 of those 37 incidents are directly attributable to victims of bullying and teasing retaliating against their actual or perceived aggressors" (p. 45).

Other Effects of Bullying Behavior

Other negative effects of bullying behavior have also been documented: school achievement, mental health, and psycho-social well-being. In terms of achievement, there are at least two studies which suggest that children who are bullied underachieve in school. For example, Williams and Peguero (2011) surveyed 9,590 students, from 580 schools and found that, even when controlling statistically for former grades and family background, the schools with higher reports of bullying behavior had lower test scores. More specifically, students who were bullied in the tenth grade demonstrated a lower grade point average (GPA) in the twelfth grade. While true of all students who were bullied, this study found the higher achieving black and Latino students had the lowest scores. Additionally, of this sample of students, 40 percent reported being bullied. The relationship between bullying behavior and underachievement was also found in a study conducted by Kochenderfer-Ladd and Wardrop (2001).

In terms of mental health, there are also studies which suggest an adverse relationship between bullying behavior and mental health functioning. For example, Schreier, Wolke, Thomas, Horwood, Hollis, Gunnell, and colleagues (2009) found that victims of bullying often experience mental health concerns. Researchers interviewed 6,437 twelve year olds at an assessment clinic in Bristol, England, "where parents had participated since pregnancy and their children completed a range of physical and psychological annual assessments since age 7 years" (p. 527). Results demonstrated that the risk of psychotic symptoms for these twelve year olds was two times higher for victims who were bullied at ages 8 and/or 10 years. This relationship held true even when researchers controlled statistically for other prior psychopathology, family adversity, or child's IQ. The relationship between bullying and psychotic symptoms was even stronger when bullying was chronic or severe.

Concerns about other mental health issues were also found. In a study conducted by Kochenderfer-Ladd & Wardrop (2001), researchers concluded that victims of bullying develop mental health concerns like anxiety, depression, and low self-esteem.

In terms of psycho-social well-being, research is revealing that the bullying experience adversely effects the psycho-social functioning of the victim as well as the bully. In 2004, Nansel, Craig, Overpeck, Saluja, and Ruan (2004) surveyed 113, 200 public and private school students, from 25 countries to determine the consistency of the relationship between bullying and psychosocial adjustment. The average ages of participants were middle school age (11.5, 13.5, and 15.5 years old). Results revealed that bullying varied across countries, ranging from 9 percent to 54 percent of the youth. However, across all countries, involvement in bullying was associated with poorer psychosocial adjustment. More specifically, in all or nearly all countries, victims consistently reported poorer relationships with classmates. Researchers concluded that bullying is an international issue with psychosocial implications.

The study by Nansel and her colleagues (2004) also contributed additional findings to the understanding of the bullying experience which suggest that bullying has adverse effects on both the victim and the bully. Bullies in this study reported greater alcohol use and weapon carrying.

There is also evidence of effects based on sub-groups of children. For example, researchers have found that female victims of bullying have a significantly higher risk for later psychiatric hospitalization and psychiatric medication use. This finding held true even when researchers took into account the girls' psychiatric symptoms at age 8 (Sourander, Ronning, Brunstein-Klomek, Gyllenberg, et al., 2009).

Another sub-sample showing adverse effects involves a group of gifted students. Peterson, Duncan, & Canady (2009) studied 432 students from 11 states in the U.S. who were classified as gifted, then interviewed 57 of them. Researchers found that, in response to their being bullied, that both boys (37 percent) and girls (23 percent) reported harboring violent thoughts, about 11 percent of them reported using violence (striking a peer) to respond to the problem, and 16 percent reported bullying others.

In conclusion, many people incorrectly think that bullying today is no different than bullying in previous decades. The truth is, however, that today's bullies are capable of going beyond fist fights, stealing lunch money, and idle gossip, and the effect does not stop at hurt feelings and admonitions by parents to stand up for one's self. Today, bullies can multiply shame and increase humiliation by electronically reaching the entire school and beyond. They, and their victims, can get access to lethal weaponry (United States Secret Service & United States Department of Education, 2004). Today, victims commit suicide. Today, victims not only decide to stand up for himself or herself; bullying behaviors can lead victims to commit mass murder. Today's experience with bullying is quite different!

The prevalence of bullying and the seriousness of its consequences to the lives of our children compel us to take a closer look. What do we know about bullying? What is bullying? Is today's bullying behavior different from the behavior of previous decades? If so, what is the nature of that difference?

Bullying

The standard definition of bullying is, influenced greatly by Olweus, the father of the bullying movement, "aggressive behavior that (a) is intended to cause distress or harm, (b) exists in a relationship in which there is an imbalance of power or strength [due to cognitive or physical differences], and (c) is repeated over time" (Limber & Small, 2003 as cited in Scaglione & Scaglione, 2006, p. 4). Scaglione and Scaglione (2006) offer a slight variation on this long-time accepted definition: (1) a deliberate act, (2) hurtful to another, and (3) repeated over time. However, they believe that the motivation of the aggressor decides whether "an imbalance of power or strength or an intention to harm another" is involved (Scaglione & Scaglione, 2006, pp. 5–6).

Scaglione and Scaglione (2006) caution schools not to "broaden" the term of bullying and using it as "an umbrella for all aggressive behaviors by children" (Scaglione & Scaglione, 2006, p. 5). "An aggressive child who easily "blows up" at others and has difficulty getting along with peers may be labeled a bully, when in reality his issue may be anger management" (Scaglione & Scaglione, 2006, p. 5). Thus, any behavior that does not meet all three of their criteria is not bullying behavior. Albeit, it may be inappropriate behavior (e.g., violence, aggression, etc) but it is not bullying. Moreover, it may even be normal conflicts of pushing and shoving, yelling, teasing, fighting, but it is not bullying (Roberts, 2006).

Types of Bullies—The Person

Scaglione and Scaglione (2006) make one more noteworthy contribution that is pertinent to this discussion. They distinguish bullies by their motivation. Accordingly, there are two types of bullies: a pure bully and a bully-victim.

A pure bully is anyone who bullies others. Pure bullies tend to be both popular and respected by peers (Caravita, DiBlasio, & Salmivalli, 2009; Scaglione & Scaglione, 2006). They tend to bully in order to gain, or maintain, power and control (Salmivalli & Peets, 2008; Scaglione & Scaglione, 2006).

A bully-victim is anyone who bullies others and who is also a victim of bullying. Bully-victims tend to be angry, aggressive, and impulsive (Salmivalli & Nieminen, 2002; Scaglione & Scaglione, 2006). "Their motivation stems from their experience as victims . . . They . . . act out of anger and revenge for being victimized themselves" (Scaglione & Scaglione, 2006, p. 34).

Victims

There are three types of victims: pure/passive, provocative, or vicarious. Pure/ passive victims are those victims who are targeted for being different (Scaglione & Scaglione, 2006). Provocative victims are those who are thought to "invite attach" (Scaglione & Scaglione, 2006, p. 36). Vicarious victims are those who are witnesses who are in close proximity to the bullying (Roberts, 2006).

> The impact of observing the attack was traumatizing for this individual, so much so that the individual gets "sick" the next day and stays home. He is afraid to return to school and feels as if he cannot tell anyone—not his parents, not his teachers,

not his friends—what he observed for fear that he will be the next victim of the bully (Roberts, 2006, p. 35).

According to the joint report of the Secret Service and the Department of Education, 70 percent of the school shooters were victims who "had a grievance against at least one of their targets prior to the attack" (United States Secret Service & United States Department of Education, 2004, p. 16). Authors defined "grievance" as "a belief that some other person or organization is directly or indirectly responsible for injury or harm to self and/or someone whom the subject cares about" (United States Secret Service & United States Department of Education, 2004, p. 16).

Victims are selected by bullies (Roberts, 2006; Salmivalli, 2010; Scaglione & Scaglione, 2006). The bully—motivated by prestige, power, and control—selects victims who validate their sense of dominance. As such, these bullies tend to pick their victims based on two criteria (Roberts, 2006, p. 22):

- First, they are 'different" for some reason by "Kid World" standards.
- Second, they have little or no power to negotiate their status among the group or groups who do have power.

First, students may be different due to their social economic status, special needs (e.g., physical, mental, etc), sexual identity, social skills, newness to the school, cognitive ability (either extreme), degree of attractiveness (either extreme), the perception of any weakness, a minority status (e.g., race, ethnicity, religious affiliation, etc), weight—to name a few ways in which students could stand out. Second, the lack of power and status "sends the message" to the bully that "'no one will help this one' if attacked" (Roberts, 2006, p. 31).

The bully—motivated by revenge—selects victims in order to get back at the bully (Scaglione & Scaglione, 2006), and perhaps to gain some sense of power and control (Dubreuil, Andreadis, & Martinez-Ramundo, 2010).

The Others—The Bystanders

Aside from the bully and the victim, there are bystanders. These bystanders consist of several possible sub-groups (http://olweus.org/public/bullying.page):

Supporters of the Bully

- The followers—These students do not play a lead role in the bullying but they do actively participate in the bullying.
- The passive bullies—These students actively participate in the bullying by watching, calling attention to the "event", laughing, and so on.
  The passive supporters—These students like the bully and passively participate in the bullying by being present during the bullying but they do not show any observable support.

- Disengaged Onlookers—These students do not take sides (neither pro-bully nor pro-victim) but they are present during the bullying.

Supporters of the Victim

- The possible defenders—These students do not like the bully and they think they should help the victim but do nothing.
- The defenders—These students do not like the bully and they do try to help the victim.

Types of Bullying Behavior—The Acts

There are several types of bullying behaviors:
- Verbal bullying including derogatory comments and bad names
- Bullying through social exclusion or isolation
- Physical bullying such as hitting, kicking, shoving, and spitting
- Bullying through lies and false rumors
- Having money or other things taken or damaged by students who bully
- Being threatened or being forced to do things by students who bully
- Racial bullying
- Sexual bullying
- Cyberbullying (via cell phone or Internet) (http://olweus.org/public/bullying.page).

Additionally, although both males and females engage in bullying behavior, there are some gender differences in terms of bullying behaviors (Crick, Bigbee, & Howes, 1996). Generally speaking, boys tend to engage in direct forms of aggression. These direct forms of aggression can be physical and/or verbal. On the other hand, girls tend to engage in "relational bullying behaviors (Crick & Bigbee, 1998) such as malicious gossip and/or group ostracism (Lagerspetz, Bjorkqvist, & Peltonen, 1988).

Comparing Today's Bullying Behavior to the Behavior of Previous Decades

According to Garrity, Jens, Porter, Sager, and Short-Camilli (1996 as cited in Roberts, 2006), bullying behaviors occur on a continuum (see Table 7.1). "Left unchecked, aggressive behaviors escalate to increasing levels of interpersonal friction and potential violence between the agents and targets of bullying" (Roberts, 2006, p. 16).

Table 7.1: The Continuum of Bullying Behavior

Mild	Moderate	Severe
Dirty jokes	Public exclusion (shunning)	Inflicting total isolation from peer group(s)
Name-calling	Demeaning acts (both public & private	Regular and routine intimidating behaviors
Taunting	Graffiti (minor & major)	Regular and routine extortion
Gossiping	Vandalism (minor)	Vandalism and property damage (major)
Threats to reveal secrets	Intimidating phone-calls	Efforts to "mob" or "gang up" on targets
Public Embarassment & humiliation	Ethnic, racial or religious slurs	Threats with weapons
Graffiti (minor)	Regular, intentional petty thefts	Inflicting bodily harm
Spitting	Verbal or proximity intimidation	
Pushing & shoving (minor)	Blatant extortion	
	Clearly intentional physical violence	
	Threats of harm to or coercion of family or friends	

Scrutiny of the continuum of bully behaviors shows how society has moved beyond the typical notions of bullying: playground brawls, stealing lunch money, name calling, and "mean girls." Of special concern are the following bullying behaviors: proximity intimidation, threats of harm to family or friends, intentional physical violence, efforts to "mob" or "gang up" on targets, threats with weapons, and inflicting bodily harm. These behaviors are serious threats to one's well-being.

Can Bullying Behavior Rise to the Level of a Traumatic Event?

According to DSM IV-TR, *the Diagnostic and Statistical Manual of Mental Disorders* (4th ed., text rev.; DSM-IV-TR; American Psychiatric Association, 2000), a traumatic event is a serious threat to one's physical or psychological well-being. The person has had a (a) "direct personal experience" with "an event that involves actual or threatened death or serious injury, or other threat to one's physical integrity; or (b) witnessed "an event that involves death, injury, or a threat to one's physical integrity of another person; or (c) learned "about unexpected or violent death, serious harm, or threat of death or injury experienced by a family member or other close associate" (DSM-IV-TR, 2000, p. 463). For a list of specific traumatic events, see Table 7.2.

Table 7.2: Examples of Traumatic Events listed in DSM-IV-TR (2000)

Possible Events	Direct Experiences a	Experiences Experienced b	Experiences Learned About c
military combat	X		
violent assault—sexual • assault d • physical attack • robbery • mugging	X	X	X
• being kidnapped • being taken hostage • terrorist attack • torture • incarceration as a prisoner of war or in a concentration camp	X X X X X		
natural/man-made disasters	X	X	
severe auto or any other kind of accidents	X	X	X
being diagnosed with a life-threatening disease	X		
war		X	
unexpectedly witnessing a dead body or body parts		X	
serious injury experienced by family member or close friend			X
sudden unexpected death of a family member or close friend			X
one's child has a life-threatening disease			X

Note. "The severity, duration, and proximity of an individual's exposure to the traumatic event are the most important factors affecting the likelihood of developing this disorder [PTSD symptoms]" (DSM-IV-TR, 2000, p. 466).

a "Traumatic events that are experienced directly include, but are not limited to" (DSM-IV-TR, 2000, p. 463).

b "Witnessed events include, but are not limited to" (DSM-IV-TR, 2000, p. 464).

c "Events experienced by others that are learned about include, but are not limited to" (DSM-IV-TR, 2000, p. 464).

d "For children, sexually traumatic events may include developmentally inappropriate sexual experiences without threatened or actual violence or injury" (DSM-IV-TR, 2000, p. 464).

This being said, it can be argued that any bullying behavior that can be characterized as a serious threat to one's well-being, is a traumatic event. The continuum of bullying behavior demonstrates that these behaviors are not typical childhood behaviors. Today's bullying behaviors are quite different than previous decades! The nature of bullying behavior has changed.

Moreover, the effects of bullying behavior are quite similar to the effects of traumatic exposure. When school-aged children are exposed to traumatic events, such as violence or abuse and neglect, they have been shown to experience PTSD (Overstreet, Dempsey, Graham, & Moely, 1999). According to the DSM-IV-TR (2000), PTSD can lead to three distressing concerns: re-experiencing the traumatic event in one's mind, persistent avoidance of anything that even remotely resembles the traumatic event, and increase arousal.

PTSD causes the victim to repeatedly relive the traumatic events in a number of ways. One, the victim could experience recurrent and intrusive thoughts—bad memories—of the event that may manifest as persistent talk about the event or some aspect of the event or as a persistent theme in play experiences. Two, the victim may experience a number of dreams with a frightening theme. Three, the victim may act or feel as if the event were recurring. Four, the victim may experience "intense psychological distress at exposure to internal or external cues that symbolize or resemble an aspect of the traumatic event" (DSM-IV-TR, 2000, p. 468). The person may experience a physiological reaction to "exposure to internal or external curse that symbolize or resemble an aspect of the traumatic event" (DSM-IV-TR, 2000, p. 468).

PTSD causes the victim to avoid anything that even remotely reminds him or her of the traumatic event. This avoidance may manifest as the victim trying to avoid "thoughts, feelings or conversations" or "activities, places, or people that arouse recollections" of the event (DSM-IV-TR, 2000, p. 468). This avoidance my also manifest as the victim's inability to remember elements of the traumatic event, disinterest in important activities, detachment from others, limited range of expressed emotion, or "sense of a foreshortened future" (p. 468).

PTSD causes the victim to live in a state of increased arousal. Increased arousal may manifest in several patterns of new behavior. One, the victim may have "difficulty falling or staying asleep" (DSM-IV-TR, 2000, p. 468). Two, the victim may be irritable or erupt in anger. Three, the victim may have difficulty concentrating. Four, the victim may be hyper-vigilant or easily startled (DSM-IV-TR, 2000).

In addition to PTSD, school-aged children who are exposed to traumatic events, such as violence or abuse and neglect, have been shown to suffer from many other types of mental health problems such as anxiety (Pynoos, Fredrick, Nader, Arroyo, Steinberg, Eth, Nunez, & Fairbanks, 1987), social problems (Dyson, 1990; Gorman-

Smith & Tolan, 1998), delinquency (Dyson, 1990), aggression (Garbarino, 1995), depression (Gorman-Smith & Tolan, 1998), and thought problems (Pynoos et al., 1987). Still other studies on traumatic events have shown an adverse effect on school achievement: the trauma of violence exposure (Delaney-black, Covington, Ondersma, Nordstrom-Klee, Templin, et al., 2002; Duplechain, 2004; Schwartz & Gorman, 2003) and the trauma of abuse and neglect (Eckenrode, Laird, & Doris, 1993; Gregory & Beveridge, 1984).

Comparisons of the effects of traumatic events to the effects of bullying behavior illustrate that some children who are being bullied are actually traumatized. Victims who are angry and aggressive may lash out at others and victims who are depressed may either attempt or commit suicide. These are not the types of effects for which the remedy is simply to "Walk it off!" or "Stand up for yourself!" These are deep and lasting hurts. When hurt this deeply, standing up for one's self seems to require a grand act of payback.

Today's bullying behaviors are quite different than previous decades. The serious life-threatening nature of some bullying behavior tells us so. The extreme reactions to the hurt of bullying behaviors tell us so.

Implications of Bullying Behavior

Bullying behavior has implications for schools, for school counselors and mental health therapists and providers, and for research.

Implications for Schools

A few previously stated statistics are of relevance. According to NCES (2010), during the 2007–08 school year,
- a little over 25 percent of the public school principals reported bullying as a problem for their school (Robers, Zhang, & Truman, 2010d).
- of the 12-to 18 year old students who reported being bullied in during this school year (31.7 percent; Robers, Zhang, & Truman, 2010i):
    - 79 percent were bullied inside the school
    - 23 percent were bullied outside on school grounds
- about 7 percent of these 12-to 18 year old student who were bullied reported avoiding school activities and nearly 6 percent of them "avoided one or more places in school" for of fear of attack or harm (Robers, Zhang, & Truman, 2010g).   .
- bullying behavior seems to be peak during middle school (Robers, Zhang, & Truman, 2010b).

These statistics have implications for Maslow's Hierarchy of Needs. Children cannot achieve at their highest potential if they do not feel safe.

Moreover, middle school students are potentially most at risk. At the time that they are facing major developmental changes, may are also changing schools, and consequently may find themselves more vulnerable to both being bullied and bullying others.

Schools must be willing to address bullying. They need to be aware of these implications and work and plan to prevent bullying and to intervene.

Implications for School Counselors and Mental Health Therapist/Providers

There are a number of implications for school counselors and mental health therapists and providers. One, counselors and providers need to take into account that bullying may be a significant contributing factor, maybe even a primary triggering factor, to mental health issues.

For example, a counselor disclosed the following situation:

A new student in a middle school who was feeling different, isolated, had not developed supports in either the school or his neighborhood, and had some deficiencies in reading social cues, was bullied over a two month time period in numerous ways (e.g., bookbag was taken, student was called names, pushed, hit, and knocked down) by the same group of students. Victim student notified teachers who did not intervene or intervened ineffectually. Victim student, desperate to stop the bullying, stated that he made a last-resort verbal threat to bring a weapon to school the next day to harm those bullying him if they did not stop. Bullies told teachers of threat. Victim student was then seen as the aggressor and charges were brought against victim student who was sent to an alternative school.

Two, counselors and providers need to take into account that children who are bullied may retaliate with bullying behaviors. For example, a counselor disclosed the following situation:

A shy, student in a middle school was bullied with negative taunts about her overweight appearance which distressed her. Taunts escalated to include rumors that she was being sexually active, causing her increased distress. Victim student stated that in retaliation she then told lies about others.

Three, as indicated by the examples above, there is a rise in bullying behaviors in middle school (ages 11–13 years; Robers, Zhang, & Truman, 2010b). This rise may be due to students being in a new, larger environment. Children who have been in grade school with the same peers from Kindergarten through 4th or 5th grade are now interacting with a new pool of peers. All the social and emotional supports from grade school are gone. At the same time that students are experiencing these external changes (i.e., making the social change to a new school with new peers, and taking on a more academically challenging curriculum), they are simultaneously experiencing an internal major developmental shift, affecting them physically and emotionally. As students are adjusting to these changes and stressors, they may be more vulnerable to being both bullied by others, and possibly, more likely to bully others.

Implications for Research

There are a number of scales associated with bully behavior (Bosworth, Espelage, & Simon, 1999: Crick & Grotpeter, 1995; Orpinas & Frankowski, 2001). However, only those scales which were designed to specifically measure the construct of bully behavior were analyzed for the purpose of this discussion. These scales include:

- Adolescent Peer Relations Instrument (Prada, 2000)
- Bullying-Behavior Scale (BBS; Austin & Joseph, 1996)
- Bullying Prevalence Questionnaire (BPQ; Rigby & Slee, 1993)
- Illinois Bully Scale (Espelage & Holt, 2001)
- School Crime Supplement (SCS) to the National Crime Victimization Survey (DeVoe & Kaffenberger, 2007)

When reviewing these scales and similar scales found in studies within the bullying literature (Gottheil & Dubow, 2001; Sanchez, Robertson, Lewis, Rosenbluth, Bohman, & Casey, 2001; Smith, 1997), four observations were striking. However, because the list of scales and studies is not exhaustive, and possibly not representative of body of literature, the authors offer these observations tentatively. These observations are:

1. Most scales measured some aspect of frequency of bullying behaviors
   a.   Frequency of each item on the scale (Austin & Joseph, 1996, Espelage & Holt, 2001; Parada, 2000)
   b.   Frequency of all items taken together (U.S. Department of Justice, Bureau of Justice Statistics, 2007)
2. Several of the items on these scales are vague.
3. The continuum of bullying behavior (Garrity, Porter, Sager, Short-Camilli, 1996) was rarely represented in the scales.
4. More important, the serious life threatening bully behaviors were rarely specified by the items found on these scales.

Measuring frequency of bullying behaviors is important. Frequency goes to the heart of the meaning of bullying: (1) a deliberate act, (2) hurtful to another, and (3) repeated over time (Scaglione & Scaglione, 2006, pp. 5–6). While a frequency count of all items taken together can address the repetition criterion, a total bully score (and victimization score) for each student strikes these authors as a bonus (see Austin & Joseph, 1996; Espelage & Holt, 2001; and Parada, 2000). Theoretically, these scores have the potential to tell schools and families whether specific students are more at-risk than others (as bullies and as victims). In turn, schools with limited resources could at least target those students who are deemed more in need of intervention.

Scrutiny of the items on each scale will reveal items which are vague, leaving the reader to wonder what specifically came to mind when the student completed the survey. For example:

- What exactly is meant by a fight? Is it physical or verbal?

- What exactly is meant by "do mean things"? What "things" exactly? Does this extend, in the student's mind, to something being said about him/her or is it actually physical meanness?
- To what degree is someone being excluded? Garrity and colleagues (1996) distinguishes "shunning" from "total isolation from peer groups."
- Do some names hurt more than others? Garrity and colleagues (1996) suggest that there is "name-calling" and there are "ethnic, racial, or religious slurs."
- What distinguishes the severity of vandalism? Is it the monetary amount of the item that was destroyed, is it the sentiment of the item, or is it the intent behind the act?

Of the scales and studies cited in this discussion, many have focused on the typical behaviors that most people consider bullying: picking on others, name calling, taking things, hitting, beating, doing mean things, fighting back, pushing or shoving, making fun of or teasing, making mean jokes about others (Espelage & Holt, 2001; Gottheil & Dubow, 2001; Sanchez, Robertson, Lewis, Rosenbluth, Bohman, & Casey, 2001; Smith, 1997). Some have gone a little beyond typical descriptions citing behaviors such as: exclusion or ostracism; rumors; harassment; threats to hit, hurt, or harm; and encouraging arguments or conflicts (Espelage & Holt, 2001). All of which, typical or not, fit in what Garrity and colleagues (Garrity, Porter, Sager, Short-Camilli, 1996) would likely deem as mild or moderately severe bullying behaviors. Few of the scales and studies noted in this discussion have specifically captured the serious life-threatening behaviors and the frequency of such behaviors (Table 7.3).

Table 7.3: Comparison of Bully Behavior Scales to Continuum of Bullying Behavior

	Mild	Moderate	Severe
Austin & Joseph, 1996	laugh at, name calling, push, pick on, tease	hit	
DeVoe & Kaffenberger, 2007	Made fun of, name calling, push, shove, trip others, spread rumors, put hurtful information on internet, unwanted contact on the internet	Spit on others, destroyed property, excluded others on purpose, insulted others, made others do things they did not want to do, threatened harm	
Espelage & Holt, 2001	do mean things, encourage others to fight, harass, spread rumors, start arguments, start conflicts, tease, upset others for the fun of it	exclude, fight, threats of physical harm	
Gottheil & Dubow, 2001	do mean things, name calling, pick on, push, take things, yell at	fight, hit, hurt others,	

Table 7.3: Comparison of Bully Behavior Scales to Continuum of Bullying Behavior (Continued)

	Mild	Moderate	Severe
Prada, 2000	get others in trouble, make rude remarks, mean looks, name calling, push, shove, swear at others, tease, tell jokes about others	crash into students on purpose, excluded others on purpose, fight, got others to start rumors about a student, got others to ignore a student, hit, punch, slap, threats of physical harm	
Rigby & Slee, 1993	make fun of, name calling, pick on, push, tease, scare others, show others "I'm boss," upset others	exclude, fight, hit	
Sanchez, Robertson, et al., 2001	making fun of, name calling, pushing, shooting the finger, tell mean jokes	hit, take things,	crowd/ corner
Smith, 1997	lie about others, name calling, get others in trouble, shout at, tease, trip others, swear at others	exclude, hit, hurt, threats of harm	gang up on

Note. Each item on a scale was compared to the continuum of bullying behaviors posited by Garrity, Porter, Sager, Short-Camilli, (1996). Unless specified by the item on the scale, the bullying behavior was placed in the lesser level of severity. For example, "destroyed property" could fall in either the moderate or the severe level of the continuum. Because the severity of property destruction was not specified on the student survey, destroyed property was placed in the moderate level.

If this observation is true of the most of the scales and studies in this body of literature, this may explain why many people think that today's bullying behavior is no different than bullying in previous decades. This could also explain why the serious nature, the traumatic nature, of some bullying behaviors has not been recognized by the general public, by educators, and administrators alike. Without the recognition that bullying can and does include serious, life-threatening behaviors, it is unlikely that adults in a position to act and with a societal mandate to act will do so. Further, without this recognition, it is unlikely that schools, school counselors/therapists will have the necessary information to plan for appropriate interventions. Researchers can help bring about this recognition; they can help spread the word: Today's bullying behaviors are not the behaviors of yesterday. Today's bullies can resort to serious life threatening behaviors. They can, as stated earlier, multiply shame and increase humiliation with a few strokes on an electronic device. Today's victims commit suicide. With access to lethal weaponry, today's victims commit mass murder. Today's experience with bullying is quite different!

References

American Psychiatric Association. (2000). *Diagnostic and Statistical manual of mental disorders* (4th ed., text rev.). Washington, DC: Author.

Austin, S., and Joseph, S. (1996), Assessment of Bully/victim problems in 8–11 year-olds. *British Journal of Educational Psychology, 66,* 447–456.

Bosworth, K., Espelage, D. L., & Simon, T. R. (1999). Factors associated with bullying behavior in middle school students. *Journal of Early Adolescence, 19,* 341–362.

Caravita, S., DiBlasio, P., and Salmivalli, C. (2009). Unique and interactive effects of empathy and social status on involvement in bullying. *Social Development, 18,* 140–163.

Crick, N. R., and Grotpeter, J. K. (1995). Relational aggression, gender, and social psychological adjustment. *Child Development, 66,* 710–722.

Crick, N. R., and Bigbee, M. A. (1998). Relational and overt forms of peer victimization: A multi-informant approach. *Journal of Consulting and Clinical Psychology, 66*(2), 337–347.

Crick, N. R., Bigbee, M. A., and Howes, C. (1996). Gender differences in children's normative beliefs about aggression: How do I hurt thee? Let me count the ways. *Child Development, 67,* 1003–1014.

Delaney-Black, V., Covington, C., Ondersma, S., Nordstrom-Klee, B., Templin, T., Ager, J., Janisse, J., and Sokol, R. (2002). Violence exposure, trauma, and IQ and/or reading deficits among urban children. *Archives of Pediatrics and Adolescent Medicine, 156,* 280–285.

DeVoe, J.F., and Kaffenberger, S. (2007). *School Crime Supplement to the National Crime Victimization Survey* (NCES 2011–002). National Center for Education Statistics, Institute of Education Sciences, U.S. Department of Education, and Bureau of Justice Statistics, Office of Justice Programs, U.S. Department of Justice. Washington, DC. Retrieved November 5, 2011, from http://nces.ed.gov/programs/crime/student_questionnaires.asp.

Dubreuil, J., Andreadis, C., and Martinez-Ramundo, D. (2010, Oct. 13). From school bully to role model. *ABC News.* http://abcnews. go.com/2020/TheLaw/reformed-bullies-tolerance-stop/story?id=11873884.

Duplechain, R. (2004). Developing a model for educators of students who are exposed to traumatic events. *Mid-western Educational Researcher, 17*(2), pp. 2–11.

Dyson, J. (1990). The effect of family violence on children's academic performance and behavior. *Journal of the National Medical Association, 82*(1), 17–22.

Eckenrode, J., Laird, M., and Doris, J. (1993). School performance and disciplinary problems among abused and neglected children. *Developmental Psychology, 29*(1), 53–62.

Espelage, D. L., and Holt, M. K. (2001). Bullying and victimization during early adolescence: Peer influences and psychosocial correlates. *Journal of Emotional Abuse, 2,* 123–142.

Family mourns death of bullied, gay CA teen. (October 2, 2010). *California News.* http://abclocal.go.com/kabc/story?section=news/state&id=7702360.

Fifth Gay Teen Suicide Sparks Debate. (2010, October 3). *KABC-TV/DT News.* http://abcnews.go.com/US/gay-teen-suicide-sparks-debate/story?id=11788128.

Garbarino, J. (1995). The American war zone: What children can tell us about living with violence. *Developmental and Behavioral Pediatrics, 16,* 431–435.

Garrity, C., Jens, K., Porter, W., Sager, N., and Short-Camilli, C. (1996, Fall). Bully-proofing our school: A comprehensive approach. *School Safety,* 20–23.

Gorman-Smith, D., and Tolan, P. (1998). The role of exposure to community violence and developmental problems among inner-city youth. *Development and Psychopathology, 10,* 101–116.

Gottheil, N. F., and Dubow, E. F. (2001). Tripartite beliefs models of bully and victim behavior. In R. A. Geffner, M. Loring, and C. Young (Eds.). *Bullying behavior: Current issues, research, and interventions.* New York: The Haworth Press.

Gregory, H., and Beveridge, M. (1984). The Social and educational adjustment of abused children. *Child Abuse and Neglect, 8,* 525–531.

Hensel, K. (2010, September 16). Teen suicide victim hangs himself from barn rafters. *WishTV.com.* http://www.wishtv.com/dpp/news/local/east_central/teen-suicide-victim-hangs-himself-from-barn-rafters.

James, R. (2010, October 1). U.S. gay community reeling from 'epidemic' of suicides among teenagers taunted over sexuality. *Dailymail.co.uk.* Retrieved from http://www.dailymail.co.uk/news/article-1316782/US-gay-community-reeling-epidemic-suicides-teenagers.html?ITO=1490

Kim, Y. S., and Leventhal, B. (2008). Bullying and suicide: A review. *International Journal of Adolescent Medicine and Health, 20*(2), 133–154.

Kochenderfer-Ladd, B., and Wardrop, J. L. (2001). Chronicity and instability of children's peer victimization experiences as predictors of loneliness and social satisfaction trajectories. *Child Development, 72,* 134–151

Lagerspetz, K. M. J., Bjorkqvist, K., and Peltonen, T. (1988). Is indirect aggression typical of females? Gender differences in aggressiveness in 11-to 12-year-old children. *Aggressive Behavior, 14,* 403–414.

Nansel, T. R., Craig, W., Overpeck, M. D., Saluja, G., Ruan, W. J. (2004). Health behaviour in school-aged children bullying analyses working group: cross-national consistency in the relationship between bullying behaviors and psychosocial adjustment. *Archives of Pediatrics & Adolescent Medicine, 158,* 730–736.

O'Hare, P. (2010, September 27). Parents: Bullying drove Cy-Fair 8th-grader to suicide. *Houston Chronicle.* Retrieved from http://www.chron.com/life/mom-houston/article/Parents-Bullying-drove-Cy-Fair-8th-grader-to-1698827.php.

Olweus Bullying Prevention Program. (2011). Types of bullying. Retrieved from http://olweus.org/public/bullying.page.

Olweus Bullying Prevention Program. (2011). The bullying circle. http://olweus.org/public/bullying.page.

Orpinas, P. and Frankowski, R. (2011). Aggression scale: A self-report measure of aggressive behavior for young adolescents. *Journal of Early Adolescence, 21*, 50–67.

Overstreet, S., Dempsey, M., Graham, D., and Moely, B. (1999). Resiliency in the face of violence: An examination of protective factors. *Journal of Clinical Child Psychology, 28*, 151–159.

Peterson, J. S., Duncan, N., and Canady, K. (2009). A longitudinal study of negative life events, stress, and school experiences of gifted youth. Gifted Child Quarterly, 53, 34–49.

Parada, R. (2000). *Adolescent Peer Relations Instrument: A theoretical and empirical basis for the measurement of participant roles in bullying and victimization of adolescence.* Penrith South, DC, Australia: Publication Unit, Research Centre, University of Western Sydney.

Pynoos, R., Fredrick, C., Nader, K., Arroyo, W., Steinberg, A., Eth, A., Nunez, F., and Fairbanks, L. (1987). Life threat and posttraumatic stress in school-age children. *Archives of General Psychology, 44*, 1057–1063.

Robers, S., Zhang, J., and Truman, J. (2010a). Bullying at School and Cyber-Bullying Anywhere: Results from the 2007–08 *Indicators for School Crime and Safety.* (NCES 2011–002). National Center for Education Statistics, Institute of Education Sciences, U.S. Department of Education; and Bureau of Justice Statistics, and U.S. Department of Justice. Washington, DC. Retrieved October 14, 2011, http:// nces.ed.gov/programs/crimeindicators/crime indicators2010/ ind_11.asp.

Robers, S., Zhang, J., and Truman, J. (2010b). Discipline Problems Reported by Public Schools: Results from 2007–08 *Indicators for School Crime and Safety.* (NCES 2011–002). National Center for Education Statistics, Institute of Education Sciences, U.S. Department of Education; and Bureau of Justice Statistics, and U.S. Department of Justice. Washington, DC. Retrieved October 14, 2011, from http://nces.ed.gov/programs/crimeindicators/crimeindicators 2010/ind_07.asp.

Robers, S., Zhang, J., and Truman, J. (2010c). Executive Summary: Results from the 2007–08 *Indicators for School Crime and Safety.* (NCES 2011–002). National Center for Education Statistics, Institute of Education Sciences, U.S. Department of Education; and Bureau of Justice Statistics, and U.S. Department of Justice. Washington, DC. Retrieved October 14, 2011, from http://nces.ed.gov /programs/crimeindicators/crimeindicators2010/index.asp.

Robers, S., Zhang, J., and Truman, J. (2010d). Key Findings: Results from the 2007–08 *Indicators for School Crime and Safety.* (NCES 2011–002). National Center for Education Statistics, Institute of Education Sciences, U.S. Department of Education; and Bureau of Justice Statistics, and U.S. Department of Justice. Washington, DC. Retrieved October 14, 2011, from http://nces.ed.gov/ programs/crimeindicators/crimeindicators2010/key.asp.

Robers, S., Zhang, J., and Truman, J. (2010e). Percentage distribution of students ages 12–18 who reported being bullied at school and cyber-bullied anywhere by the frequency of bullying at school during the school year, percentage of students who notified an adult, and selected student and school characteristics: Results from the 2007–08 *Indicators for School Crime and Safety*. (NCES 2011–002). National Center for Education Statistics, Institute of Education Sciences, U.S. Department of Education; and Bureau of Justice Statistics, and U.S. Department of Justice. Washington, DC. Retrieved October 14, 2011, from http://nces.ed.gov/programs/crimeindicators/crimeindicators 2010/tables/table_11_3.asp.

Robers, S., Zhang, J., and Truman, J. (2010f). Percentage of public schools reporting selected discipline problems that occurred at school, by frequency and school characteristics: Results from 2007–08 *Indicators for School Crime and Safety*. (NCES 2011–002). National Center for Education Statistics, Institute of Education Sciences, U.S. Department of Education; and Bureau of Justice Statistics, and U.S. Department of Justice. Washington, DC. Retrieved November 3, 2011, from http://nces.ed.gov/programs/crimeindicators/crime indicators2010/tables/table_07_1.asp.

Robers, S., Zhang, J., and Truman, J. (2010f). Percentage of students ages 12–18 who reported avoiding school activities or one or more places in school because of fear of attack or harm: Various years, 1995–2007: Results from 2007–08 *Indicators for School Crime and Safety*. (NCES 2011–002). National Center for Education Statistics, Institute of Education Sciences, U.S. Department of Education; and Bureau of Justice Statistics, and U.S. Department of Justice. Washington, DC. Retrieved November 3, 2011, from http://nces.ed. gov/programs/crimeindicators/crimeindicators2010/tables/table_18_1.asp

Robers, S., Zhang, J., and Truman, J. (2010g). Percentage of students ages 12–18 who reported being bullied at school and cyber-bullied anywhere during the school year, by selected bullying problems and selected student and school characteristics: Results from 2007–08 *Indicators for School Crime and Safety*. (NCES 2011–002). National Center for Education Statistics, Institute of Education Sciences, U.S. Department of Education; and Bureau of Justice Statistics, and U.S. Department of Justice. Washington, DC. Retrieved November 3, 2011, from http://nces.ed.gov/programs/crimeindicators/crime indicators2010/tables/table_11_1.asp.

Robers, S., Zhang, J., and Truman, J. (2010h). Percentage of students ages 12–18 who reported being bullied at school during the school year, by location of bullying and selected student and school characteristics: Results from 2007–08 *Indicators for School Crime and Safety*. (NCES 2011–002). National Center for Education Statistics, Institute of Education Sciences, U.S. Department of Education; and Bureau of Justice Statistics, and U.S. Department of Justice. Washington, DC. Retrieved October 14, 2011, from http://nces.ed.gov/ programs/crimeindicators/crimeindicators2010/tables/table_11_2.asp.

Roberts, W. B. (2006). *Bullying from both sides*. Thousand Oaks, CA: Corwin Press.

Salmivalli, C. (2010). Bullying and the peer group: A review. *Aggression and Violent Behavior, 15*, 112–120.

Salmivalli, C., and Nieminen, E. (2002). Proactive and reactive aggression in bullies, victims, and bully–victims. *Aggressive Behavior, 28,* 30–44.

Salmivalli, C., and Peets, K. (2008). Bullies, victims, and bully–victim relationships. In K. Rubin, W. Bukowski and B. Laursen (Eds.), *Handbook of peer interactions, relationships, and groups* (pp. 322–340). New York: Guilford Press.

Sanchez, E., Robertson, T. R., Lewis, C. M., Rosenbluth, B., Bohman, T., and Casey, D. M. (2001). Bullying and victimization during early adolescence: Peer influences and psychosocial correlates. In Robert A. Geffner, Marti Loring, and Corinna Young (Eds.). *Bullying behavior: Current issues, research, and interventions.* New York: The Haworth Press.

Scaglione, J., and Scaglione, A. R. (2006). *Bully-proofing children: A practical, hands-on guide to stop bullying.* Latham, MD: Rowman & Littlefield Education.

School shooting. *Wikipedia.* Retrieved October 15, 2011, from http://en.wikipedia.org/ wiki/ School_shooting.

Schreier, A., Wolke, D., Thomas, K., Horwood, J., Hollis, C., Gunnell, D., Lewis, G., Thompson, A., Zammit, S., Duffy, L., Salvi, G., and Harrison, G. (2009). Prospective study of peer victimization in childhood and psychotic symptoms in a nonclinical population at age 12 years. *Archives of General Psychiatry, 66*(5), 527–536.

Schwartz, D., and Gorman, A.H. (2003). Community violence exposure and children's academic functioning. *Journal of Educational Psychology, 95*(1), 163–173.

Smith, G. (1997). The "Safer Schools-Safer Cities" Bullying Project. In D. Tattum and G. Herbert (Eds.), *Bullying: Home, school and community.* London: WC (Great Britain): David Fulton Publishers.

Sourander, A., Ronning, J., Brunstein-Klomek, A., Gyllenberg, D., Kumpulainen, K., Niemela, S., Helenius, H., Sillanmaki, L., Ristkari, T., Tamminen, T., Moilanen, I., Piha, J., and Almqvist, F. (2009). Childhood bullying behavior and later psychiatric hospital and psychopharmacologic treatment: Findings from the Finnish 1981 Birth Cohort Study. *Archives of General Psychiatry, 66* (9), 1005–1012. DOI: 10.1001/archgenpsychiatry.2009.122.

United States Secret Service and United States Department of Education (2004). *The final report and findings of the safe school initiative: Implications for the prevention of school attacks in the United States.* Washington, DC: Authors.

Williams, L. M., and Peguero, A. A. (2011, August). The impact of school bullying on racial/ethnic achievement. Paper presented at the meeting *American Sociological Association,* Los Vegas, NV. Abstract retrieved from http://www.nagc.org/uploadedFiles/News_Room/Press_Releases/Bullying_Press_Release.pdf.

Chapter Eight

The Importance of Play in Creating Social Awareness to Support a Bully-Free Environment

Maryanne Hunter Longo
Ashraf Esmail
Alice Duhon-Ross

Introduction

The Importance of Play

Ask an Early Childhood Educator what is missing in today's ECE classrooms, and the answer you most often will hear is simply, play. Our early educators are being held accountable for academic skills and mastering concepts that are standardized and nationally assessed. Kindergarten has changed radically in the last two decades in ways that few Americans are aware of. Children now spend far more time being taught and tested on literacy and math skills than they do learning through play and exploration, exercising their bodies, and using their imaginations (Miller & Almon, 2009).

Many of our pre-k and kindergarten students are now required to take standardized assessments to evaluate school entry levels. Authentic learning through developmentally appropriate activities is often being replaced with paper and pencil skill development. Kindergarten has changed radically from 1989 to 2009 from a play setting to one of prescriptive curricula and standardized tests, causing behavioral problems (Miller & Almon, 2009).

Early educators still consider play a very important best practice in classroom environments. Many educators maintain that play is the key factor in promoting children's development in learning. However, an ongoing debate focuses on a teacher's role in children's play. Some researchers suggest that, when teachers engage in play with children, it limits children's cognitive skills and they tend not to interact. In contrast, other researchers maintain that teachers should actively engage in playful activities with children that promote growth and development (Bodrova & Leong, 2005).

Although play has been a well-established curriculum component in early childhood education, the increasing emphasis on accountability appears to have led to a corresponding decline in the general understanding of the important contribution that high-quality play—especially pretend play—can make to children's cognitive development in the early years (Bergen, 2002).

Preparation for entrance into elementary school influences school districts to require early educators to simulate a first grade environment in our kindergartens and even in our pre-k classrooms. At face value, this direction may seem to be a positive step in improving the academic standards of schools across the nation. However, it is having the opposite effect on the overall well-being of the early learner. It is actually detrimental to the development of the whole child. The healthy, early learner is an active learner who uses her imagination to foster healthy brain development critical to overall healthy growth and development.

This push for academic development has the domino effect of reducing the freedom of choice in kindergarten and pre-k environments to dedicated skill development through teacher directed activities. No longer are children encouraged to interact with their environment and their classmates in authentic learning that allows children the freedom to choose to imagine in a life-skills (housekeeping) center or create in an art center, explore in a science center, or enjoy non-directed interaction with other children.

> When you asked me what I did in school today and I say, 'I just played.' Please don't misunderstand me. For you see, I am learning as I play. I am learning to enjoy and be successful in my work. Today I am a child and my work is play (Wadley, 1974).

We need to recognize and remember that the early childhood classroom plays a significant role in all areas of development, social, physical and cognitive development. The development of each of these areas is critical to the appropriate development of the whole child.

Children exhibiting high levels of peer play interaction were found to demonstrate more competent emotional-regulation, initiation, self-determination, and receptive vocabulary skills. Assessments of positive engagement in play early in the year were associated with lower levels of aggressive, shy, and withdrawn adjustment problems at the end of the year. Children who successfully interacted with peers early in the year evidenced greater cognitive, social, and movement/coordination outcomes. Disruptive and disconnected peer play behaviors were associated with negative emotional and behavioral outcomes (Fantuzzo, Sekino, Cohen, 2004).

The concept of play can be very challenging for preschool teachers as many early educators are questioned by parents and community about the true purpose of active play. Clearly, play is fundamental for children to construct knowledge during the early stages of development. In order to provide quality education, the early educator must engage in playful activities with children in a fun and interactive approach to learning.

Our schools are abandoning social learning for academic skill development. Not because it is appropriate, but because schools are under pressure to perform beyond developmentally appropriate levels across the nation. Schools continue to lose federal funding due to unrealistic literacy and math levels required for all students regardless of socio-economic status or cultural diversity. In light of federal regulations and challenges of implementing the No Child Left Behind (NCLB) Act of 2001, all students are required to be reading at a proficient level by 2014 (United States Department of Education, 2002). NCLB legislation is presently being reviewed and potential reform is being addressed.

The National Association for the Education of Young Children (NAEYC) is the largest nonprofit association in the United States representing early childhood education teachers, paraeducators, center directors, trainers, college educators, families of young children, policy makers, and advocates. NAEYC is dedicated to improving the well-being of all young children, with particular focus on the quality of educational and developmental services for all children from birth through age eight. NAEYC is committed to becoming an increasingly high-performing and inclusive organization (NAEYC, 2011). NAEYC's position statement suggests:

> Kindergarten teachers and administrators guard the integrity of effective, developmentally appropriate programs for young children... they do not yield to pressure for acceleration of narrowly focused skill-based curricula or the enforcement of academic standards derived without regard for what is known about young children's development and learning (National Association of Young Children (NAEYC, 2001).

As the achievement gap continues to widen, our youngest learners are being asked to help close the divide by meeting unrealistic requirements. Young learners are being expected to be able to sit in place for teacher directed activities for the majority of the day. Recess, if allowed and weather permitting, is the rare opportunity to participate in unstructured activities. Passing standardized tests in reading and math are now becoming the norm in our early childhood classrooms.

Are we focusing on the early learners to close the achievement gap? A number of factors have contributed to growing state and national interest in promoting early learning and development as one way of preventing school readiness gaps. Groundbreaking research documents the importance of early experiences on brain development, and educators, policy makers, and the public now have a deeper understanding of how best to foster young children's learning (Daily, Burkhauser, & Halle, 2010). Yet, school readiness is more than academics. Research consistently demonstrates that children's positive well-being encompasses successful development in areas such as their physical, social-emotional, cognitive, and language development. Though cognitive development and literacy skills are most frequently associated with school readiness, research suggests that physical, behavioral, and social-emotional factors are equally important. Even aspects such as temperament, aggressive behaviors, and a child's ability to relate to others are associated with their readiness for school (Daily et al., 2010).

Kindergarten students are being assessed on content areas they might never have experienced. Do these scores tell the educator how to effectively reach the young learner? While more and more states are adopting preschool learning standards, few teachers are helping children to develop social skills (Logue, 2007). The growing expectations are controversial, with some experts saying the new kindergarten squeezes out forms of spontaneous play (building with blocks, for instance, or playing make-believe) that are vital to a child's long-term academic success (Schoenberg, 2010).

Striking evidence that missed opportunities for interactions with peers is resulting in the alarming increase in the amount of bullying that is dominating school environments. From the minor "she hit me" to the physical attacks during recess, bullying is becoming epidemic in our schools. Socialization and peer interactions are missing in our universal quest for increased academic achievement. Seeing the early learner as the answer to the achievement gap existing across our nation is not the answer. There is no time for allowing the early learner to interact with her peers through hands on learning activities and developmentally appropriate activities that increase brain-based learning and foster social interaction (National Scientific Council on the Developing Child, 2004).

Experiences are built into our bodies (for better or for worse) and significant adversity early in life can produce physiological disruptions or embedded biological "memories" that persist far into adulthood and lead to lifelong impairments in both physical and mental health (Center on the Developing Child at Harvard University, 2010).

Extensive research is being conducted and has been authenticated on the increase in episodes of bullying in schools throughout the nation. Urban or suburban, upper, middle or low socio-economic levels, diverse or homogenized, neighborhood schools are all feeling the pressure of seeking outbreaks solutions for of bullying throughout the grades (Logue, 2007).

Benefits of Social Interaction

Children and animals that do not play when they are young may grow into anxious, socially maladjusted adults (Wolfgang, 2007).

If you are a proponent of play you know that when children play they are presented with many opportunities through which they will develop and enhance social and emotional health. As children experience appropriate social and emotional growth they easily adjust to their environment. Play offers children a multitude of opportunities to interact within existing environments fostering recognition of self, understanding the complexities of nature and satisfying an innate need to explore their world. Characteristics of cooperation, negotiation, facilitation and healthy competition are explored during play (Alliance for Childhood, n.d.).

Frederick Froebel who is considered "Father of the Kindergarten," believed that play is the foundation for growth and development in the kindergarten environment. Many theorists of his day were vehemently opposed to play in the environment because they thought it was "unworthy" for the human mind (Snider, 2009). However, Froebel argued that "play is the highest phase of a child's development of human development at this period; for it is self-active representation of the inner-representation of the inner from the inner necessity and impulse" (Kilpatrick, W.H., 1916). Froebel suggests that play is a time when children are engaging in cultural experiences and playful activities that often imitate the adult. "These activities were a means of expressing their perception of adult vocations" (Slatterly,1987). According to Froebel:

> Play is the purest, most spiritual activity of man at this stage, and at the same time, typical of human life as a whole- of the inner hidden natural life in man and all things. It gives, therefore, joy freedom, contentment, inner and outer rest, peace with the world. In holds the sources of all that is good (p. 55).

A best practice is a focus by teachers on age-appropriate activities. The National Association for the Education of Young Children (NAEYC, 2009) has worked diligently to ensure that the early childhood field evolves through developmentally appropriate practices (DAP), which is believed to be key to long-term academic success (Follari, 2011). The NAEYC embraces the theory of DAP based on the work of psychologist, Jean Piaget (1896–1980).

Piaget's view of how children's minds work and develop has been enormously influential, particularly in educational theory. His particular insight was the role of maturation (simply growing up) in children's increasing capacity to understand their world: they cannot undertake certain tasks until they are psychologically mature enough to do so. He proposed that children's thinking does not develop entirely smoothly: instead, there are certain points at which it "takes off" and moves into completely new areas and capabilities. He saw these transitions as taking place at about 18 months, 7 years and 11 or 12 years (Piaget, 1921). This has been taken to mean that before these ages, children are not capable (no matter how bright) of understanding things in certain ways and has been used as the basis for scheduling the school curriculum. Piaget's conclusions are still being debated, today.

Although the NAEYC has changed its DAP statement since its inception, the original statement focused on "the use of a child-initiated, play-based, integrated curriculum that reflected both age and individual appropriateness" (Follari, 2011). In 2009, a revision to the DAP statement emphatically states that teachers are required to use teaching strategies that incorporate the following DAP goals:

1. Skillfully balancing child-initiated activities and direct instruction.
2. Recognizing universals and individuality in children's development.
3. Providing routines, boundaries, and limits and allowing children to make choices.
4. Supporting children's need to work in groups and alone on individual tasks.
5. Preparing children for successful lifelong learning by fostering the foundational skills and attitudes they need to be successful in school and beyond (especially literacy and mathematics) (Follari, 2011).

It is critical that teachers establish effective relationships with children. Yet, establishing relationships takes time and should be developed in non-threatening activities, such as play, in order to determine age-appropriate activities that are meaningful and based on children's developmental levels.

How many times have you heard adults suggest that today's children do not know how to play? "We had a stick and a ball and would play for hours with the kids on the block. We made up our own rules and regulated our teams." Is the idea that today's children do not know how to play their fault? Children are either in school where imaginative play is not encouraged or at home with a technically enhanced device with little or no interaction with another child. When are children encouraged to play for play's sake? Spiegel, (2008) suggests that "old fashioned play builds serious skills."

From day one, children are eager and determined to understand how the world works. They do this through play, using all the "tools" they have at their disposal. Watch your child at play, and you will see the kind of concentration, passion, and creative excitement that artists and scientists bring to their projects (zerotothree.org).

Research Supports the Benefits of Social Interaction

In their first years of life, children rapidly develop social and emotional capacities that prepare them to be self-confident, trusting, empathic, intellectually inquisitive, competent in using language to communicate, and capable of relating well to others. Sometimes called early childhood mental health, or infant mental health, healthy social and emotional development refers to a child's developing capacity to experience, manage, and express the full range of positive and negative emotions, and develop close, satisfying relationships with other children and adults and actively learn by exploring their environment. Social and emotional development is the foundation that guides a child into adulthood. Positive, early experiences can build a strong foundation or a fragile one, and can affect the way children react and respond to the world around them for the rest of their lives. Cost-benefit analyses confirm that nurturing young children's social, emotional and behavioral skills through quality early educational experiences produces an economic return to society (Center on the Developing Child at Harvard University, 2010).

Social and emotional development in early childhood is firmly tied to every other area of growth and development—physical growth and health, communication and language development, and cognitive skills, as well as the child's early relationships. If young children do not achieve early social and emotional milestones that are linked to positive early childhood mental health, they will not do well in the early school years and subsequently, are at higher risk for school failure, juvenile delinquency, and a variety of other problems later in life. Cost-benefit analyses confirm that nurturing young children's social, emotional and behavioral skills through quality early educational experiences produces an economic return to society (National Scientific Council on the Developing Child, 2004).

Cohen, Onunaku, Clothier, and Poppe (2005) suggest that ensuring that young children arrive at school ready to learn has become a national priority. State policy-makers have an opportunity to have a significant and lasting effect on young children's development by enacting policies that support healthy, social-emotional development of young children from birth to age five. Social and emotional development extends beyond the realm of education to reach human services, health, economic development, and environmental policies (Cohen, et al., 2005).

Social Learning Theory

Albert Bandura (1977) developed the modern version of social learning theory (SLT). Bandura felt that the key to learning and development stems from social interactions, observation, and modeling. He believed that the learning process involves "reciprocal determinism" which means that the environment and a person's behavior are interactive (Bandura, A. (1977).

Bandura explored the concept of an individual's personality, which consists of the interaction between the environment, behavior, and emotions (Betz & Borgen, 2010). The SLT of today consists of four stages: attentive behavior of others whether human or mediated models by listening and seeing; processing and reviewing the behavior model; reproducing the modeled behavior; and making a decision of accepting and using the behavior model (Kunkel, Hummert, & Dennis, 2006). Children learn through social interactions by observing and expanding on the knowledge of others.

Bandura's social learning theory has become perhaps the most influential theory of learning and development, today. Although his theory is rooted in traditional learning theory, he believed that direct reinforcement of skill development could not account for all types of learning. He added a social element, believing that people can learn new information and behaviors by observing others.

An important aspect of social learning theory is that although behaviorists believe that learning lead to a permanent change in behavior, observational learning demonstrates that people can learn new information without demonstrating new behaviors. Bandura's social learning theory continues to influence other psychologists and has had a significant effect in education. Other classroom strategies such as encouraging children and building self-efficacy are also rooted in social learning theory. Teachers and parents need to recognize the importance of modeling appropriate behaviors in order to have a positive effect on future social interactions.

> Our society is pretty fast-paced, and I think we're groomed since we're little that more is better, and we can get caught up in that too much. Some people need to slow down to enjoy a better quality of life, providing balance as a factor for family, and for all aspects of life. I would suggest that they be cognizant of how much they're taking on, and just allow some time to reflect and just be (G. Moller, 2011).

Emotional Intelligence (EI) is an important indicator of future behavior and a learning characteristic that can be assessed. Young children cannot often express themselves clearly on how they are feeling or if they understand why they are feeling certain emotions. Constructing an emotional intelligence test to appropriately gain indicators of EI would support the educator's ability to identify potential emotional needs of her students. Mavrovelli, Petrides, Shove and White-head's (2008) study investigated the construct of trait emotional intelligence with emphasis on measurement in children. The Trait Emotional Intelligence Questionnaire-Child Form (TEI-Que-CF was created out of a need to fill the gap in emotional intelligence research which was primarily conducted on adult and college student populations. The results determined a propensity for emotional concerns and even significant potential for negative behaviors (Mavrovelli, et.al., 2008).

There are many emotional intelligence resources, such as the Emotional Intelligence Quiz (Institute for Health and Human Potential, n.d.) and Handle with Care: Emotional Intelligence Activity Book (Jensen, Rideout & Freedman, 2006), which can appropriately determine a child's emotional intelligence and health. Such emotional assessments are important for educational psychologists and teachers' use in supporting and defending their concerns about perceived bullying behaviors.

Bullying: An Epidemic?

Bullying is a very serious problem that can have dramatic affects on student achievement both socially and academically. Bullying is often remembered as a larger child picking on a smaller child, physically or mentally. This is no longer the interpretation of today's bully. Victimization takes many forms in our schools. Bullying can be direct or indirect. Direct bullying involves anti-social behaviors such as teasing, threatening, hitting, and stealing. Indirect bullying is forcing the intentional isolation of the victim. Direct or indirect bullying both causes the victim to become a social outcast preferring to isolate himself against further abuse (Rodkin, 2011).

Bullying can be defined as repeated and systematic harassment and attacks on others. Bullying can be perpetrated by individuals or groups. Bullying takes many forms, and can include may different behaviors, such as:

- physical violence and attacks
- verbal taunts, name-calling and put-downs
- threats and intimidation
- extortion or stealing of money and possessions
- exclusion from the peer group
- Racially or ethnically-based verbal abuse and gender-based put-downs are also found in the bullying situation (Sudermann & Schieck, 1996).

What kind of power does a bully really have? Children and youth (and some adults) use bullying to acquire resources and—here is where peers come into the picture—to demonstrate to an audience that they can dominate (Pellegrini et al. 2010). The success of bullies in attaining resources and recognition depends on factors that include the characteristics of the bully, the relationship that exists between bullies and those whom they target for harassment, and the reactions of classmates who witness bullying. Do schoolmates embarrass the harassed and stroke the bully's ego? Do they ignore the bullying in front of them? Does somebody intervene to support the victim and help stop the bullying?

Of course, peer culture in elementary, middle, and high school exists under the watchful eyes of responsible adults: teachers, principals, bus drivers, school staff, and parents. So. how peers and adults act in response to or in anticipation of bullying is crucial (Rodkin, 2011).

Research suggests that bullies often receive physical punishment in the home thereby perceiving that hitting back is an appropriate way to handle problems. The bully is often thought to come from a home environment where parental involvement and nurturing attitudes are frequently lacking. However, there is supporting evidence that peer pressure can and does create bullies who come from homes where no physical, mental or emotional abuse occurs.

Students who are victims of bullying are typically anxious, insecure, cautious, and suffer from low self-esteem, rarely defending themselves or retaliating when confronted by students who bully them. A strong correlation appears to exist between bullying other students during the school years and experiencing legal or criminal troubles as adults, while being bullied leads to depression and low self-esteem.

Parents are often unaware of the bullying problem and talk about it with their children only to a limited extent, and school personnel may view bullying as a harmless rite of passage that is best ignored unless verbal and psychological intimidation crosses the line into physical assault or theft. Effective interventions at the school, class, and individual levels may include the following components: (1) an initial questionnaire distributed to students and adults; (2) a parental awareness campaign conducted during parent-teacher conference days, through parent newsletters, and at PTA meetings; and (3) teachers working with students at the class level to develop class rules against bullying. Other components of effective anti-bullying programs include individualized interventions with the bullies and victims, the implementation of cooperative learning activities to reduce social isolation, and increasing adult supervision at key times (Department of Health and Human Services).

The U.S. Census Bureau states that one in every seven children reports being bullied in school. In an average classroom of 20 children, there are most likely at least three children who are either victims or bullies (United States Census Bureau, 2010). In a Committee for Children (2003) survey, 78 percent of children reported having been bullied "in the past month." A total of 31 percent of girls in grades 8 to 11 reported harassment often, almost on a daily basis; 18 percent of boys reported similar problems of self-isolation in response to bullying, one-third reported plans for getting back at their intimidators (National School Safety Center, 2003).

The National Association for the Education of Young Children (NAEYC), the nation's largest professional organization of early childhood educators, is committed to actions that address two major goals:

1.   To decrease the extent of violence in all forms in children's lives by advocating for public policies and actions at the national level; and
2.   To enhance the ability of educators to help children cope with violence, promote children's resilience, and assist families by improving professional practice in early childhood programs (NAEYC, 1993).

Bullying is Abuse!

Bullying and harassment are widespread problems with significant adverse consequences for students. Bullying and harassment directly interferes with student learning and achievement, while threatening the safety and well-being of millions of students each year. The U.S. Department of Education has concluded that bullying and harassment affects nearly one in every three American school children in grades six through ten and another confirms that harassment in schools is experienced by a majority of students. Bullying can result in long-term social, academic, psychological and physical consequences, including decreased interest in school, increased absences and decreased concentration levels for students. State departments of education have data from surveys as well as articles readily available to the general public (Department of Health and Human Services, 2010).

Creating a Bully Free Environment

How would you begin to develop a bully free environment? Most teachers want and expect to achieve a happy learning environment in which children feel welcome and safe. Bullying expert Carol S. McMullen (2007) says we must look at it as a "bully-proofing puzzle," in which each developmental piece--problem-solving, recognizing and using personal strengths, and building interpersonal skills--is a crucial part of strengthening community. McMullen adds that we can't confront bullying on our own: "Everyone in the school community needs to know the language, expectations about behavior, and consequences of bullying" (McMullen, 2007).

Research reports that a child is bullied every seven minutes. If we want our students to feel safe, how do we accomplish this ever-growing problem? McMullen says to be our own cheerleader. Positive self-talk is an empowering strategy. Encourage children to repeat their strengths over and over to increase confidence and self-worth. Also, have a strategy to use on the bully, such as Bill Cosby's *The Meanest Thing to Say* story; "Just say, "SO!" If you basically ignore the words and say 'So' whenever a bully is trying to verbally abuse, the bully soon tires.

Jackson (2010) also addresses another simple option which is to move away from a bullying situation. Encourage your students to simply turn and go elsewhere. Explain that if the bully steps in front of you, pivot and quickly walk away in another direction. If the bully follows, continue to walk away until the bully gives up or you get to a safer area. This strategy works best if you are dealing with just one person. We need to encourage children always to ask an adult for help!

Case Study: Kara, Middle School Student

Kara is a gifted eight grade enrolled in a public magnet middle school. All of her core subjects are taken in accelerated classes with the exception of her electives. She is taking a computer class with number of rowdy athletics. The teacher of this class resigned from the school only after a month the school term began. The current teacher tries a different seating chart to break up team members from sitting together who are causing the most commotion. Kara returned home in tears one afternoon and confided in her mother that she was were being teased and harassed for over three months since the beginning of school. She begged her mother not to report this to the school because she did not want to appear as a tattle tale. Kara's mother called the teacher the next day and shared with her what Kara had mentioned to her and asked her not to mention it to Kara because she was very embarrassed about reporting this to anyone at school. The teacher was very supportive and agreed to move Kara and a couple of other students so that this would not appear to be an obvious move. The teacher also mentioned to Kara's mother that she had noticed some of the students were joking around, but that none of the students complained to her and she did not think that there was a problem.

The teacher went on a leave of absence and Kara was teased to the point of tears again and this time Kara asked her mother if she could move to another school. When Kara's parents went to the school administrators and attempted to transfer their daughter to another school, the assistant principle ask to give them to give him an opportunity resolved this issue. The assistance principle and the teacher identified other students that they felt may have also been bullied in that class. They contact the parents of the students and scheduled private meetings with the parents and the students. The parents admitted that they did not know that their children were being bullied. The assistant principal assured the students that they would not be identified, which allowed them to share more about their personal experiences in that class. The assistant principle, teacher, and coach worked together to identified two athletics that were bullying a number of students which included boys and girls. The school officials contacted the parents of the athletics and included them in the intervention. The athletics were required to make a public apology in front of the entire class. The school counselor, teachers and parents were also successful of getting this class to begin a after-school peer mentoring group. This process reduced the number student referrals to the office and it reduced the number of students reporting being bullied for the remainder of the year. Kara felt very empowered when due to her actions a number of students admitted to going through the same type of incidents and together they conquered their fears and became trustful of their parents and school administrators.

Parental Intervention

Kara's parents played a key role in identifying the bullying acts that Kara was subjected to in her class. The school officials siege this opportunity by including all parents of the students involved. This case study demonstrates the effectiveness of parents and the importance of parental training on how to witness changes in the children's behavior due to bullying. Parents may be trained on topics such as (a) establishing social norms that reward nonviolence and reduce the stigma of backing down within the community, (b) teaching parent communication skills, and (c) helping them change family norms from pro-bullying behaviors, such as retaliation, to respect for intelligent, nonviolent interactions (Bradshaw, et al, 2009).

Conflict Resolution

Could you be raising a bully? Parents need to be aware of how they react to situations in the home that can lead to approval and acceptance of bullying. Remind parents that they should not encourage a younger child to "get even" with their older sibling, even if the young child was physically hurt. This is a strong teachable moment. The older child needs to be made aware of the fact that he/she is actually abusing their sibling. The sibling must be part of the resolution. Discussion of what took place, how could it have been ignored, and why was there a physical outburst needs to be encouraged and parents should require such a conversation whenever physical or verbal abuse takes place in the home.

Conflicts are seen as inevitable in classrooms. It is almost impossible to have significant numbers of children in one room and not encounter differences of opinion. The idea is not to allow the difference of opinion to escalate. Learning to resolve conflicts is essential for children in our schools. There are many strategies that teachers can initiate to resolve conflicts. Learning how to apologize is a significant step in taking responsibility for one's actions. Recognizing that you are accountable for your actions is another significant step in developing resolution. Encouraging students to think before they act is being accountable for your actions. Another way to teach conflict resolution is to role play. Creating scenarios that allow students to play the roles of adversaries without resorting to fists is often cathartic and proves that they can find solutions to their disagreements beyond fighting.

Research suggests that there are many strategies to help educators and parents address bullying. DiCarlo and Vagianos, 2009 address five things educators can do to limit bullying. One is to simply ask students about and discuss bullying on a regular basis. It can be as easy as placing an anonymous drop-box somewhere so students can relay information to you. Another way is to ask students about their relationships with their peers. Find out who their friends are, who they don't like, and who they think is popular or unpopular. The third way is to form democratic classrooms and climates. Assign roles for students to observe activities when bullying may take place. Being informed about anti-bullying and teaching how to handle conflicts are a few other strategies teachers can use (DiCarlo & Vagianos, 2009).

Another significant anti-bullying strategy is using children's stories to promote a peaceful classroom. There are many components of a successful program, focusing on using children's stories is one strategy for creating a peaceful and caring classroom environments that are conducive to learning (Morris, Taylor & Wilson. 2000). There are many published children's books on the concept of bullying. In addition to using the following seven examples of effective literature to promote understanding you should encourage children to share their own stories through art, discussion, music and any outlet that will promote children's ability to cope with and extinguish bullying in their lives. Some of these are:

- *Incredible Me!* by Kathi Appelt (HarperCollins, 2003). Grades 1-3.
- *Bravemole* by Lynne Jonell (Putnam, 2002). Grades 1-3.
- *Bully* by Judith Caseley (Greenwillow Books, 2001). Grades 1-3.
- *Nobody Knew What to Do* by Becky Ray McCain (Albert Whitman, 2001). Grades 1-3.
- *Mean, Mean Maureen Green* by Judy Cox (Holiday House, 1999). Grades 1-3.
- *The Meanest Thing to Say* by Bill Cosby (Scholastic, 1997). Grades 1-2.
- *The Hundred Dresses* by Eleanor Estes (Harcourt Brace, 1972). Grades 2-3.

There are many programs designed to help schools and other institutions prevent bullying. It is a hot topic in professional development and educational conferences. Hopefully, research will help to diminish and potentially alleviate the scope of the problem in the future.

The Safe Schools Improvement Act

The Safe Schools Improvement Act addresses federal policy recommendations (outlined in the publication *Bridging the Gap in Federal Law*). Members of the National Safe Schools Partnership have signed on to these recommendations to promote school safety and improve student achievement for all students, through legislation that will comprehensively address the issues of bullying and harassment.

The Safe Schools Improvement Act will strengthen the Safe and Drug Free Schools and Communities Act to ensure that:

- Schools and districts have comprehensive and effective student conduct policies that include clear prohibitions regarding bullying and harassment;
- Schools and districts focus on effective prevention strategies and professional development designed to help school personnel meaningfully address issues associated with bullying and harassment;
- States and districts maintain and report data regarding incidents of bullying and harassment in order to inform the development of effective federal, state, and local policies that address these issues (National Safe Schools Partnership, www.glsen.org).

The School Safe Climate Act

School Safe Climate Act of South Carolina defines bullying as a gesture, an electronic communication, or a written, verbal, physical, or sexual act that can be viewed as something that could have an impact on students and cause harm to a student physically or emotionally or damaging a student's property, or placing a student in reasonable fear of personal harm or property damage; or insulting or demeaning a student or group of students causing substantial disruption in, or substantial interference with, the orderly operation of the school. Various data has been collected recently as it pertains to bully of school age children (Safe School Climate Act, 2006).

Most school systems have developed and initiated various strategies for dealing with bullies. Some of the practical strategies for dealing with bullying include discipline policies, code of conduct for students and teachers, and monitoring of school climate. It is important to be committed to understand what is going on and make adjustments to policies and the school environment.

Conclusion

Building safe climates for our students should be an educational priority. Learning cannot take place in fear. Early learners must be made to feel comfortable in their environment. They cannot be pushed prematurely into learning skills that are not developmentally appropriate and should never fear being bullied. Learning to play together is a pathway to diminishing bullying opportunities.

Teaching Tolerance is dedicated to reducing prejudice, improving intergroup relations and supporting equitable school experiences for our nation's children. Tolerance is respect, acceptance and appreciation of the rich diversity of our world's cultures, our forms of expression and ways of being human. Tolerance is harmony (Teaching Tolerance, 2011).

We must teach our children to be tolerant of others, to respect differences, to celebrate understanding and to contribute to society through life-long learning.

References

Alliance for Childhood. (n.d.). *Play resource list*. College Park, MD: Author. http://www.allianceforchildhood.org/play_resources.

Bergen, D. (2002). The Role of pretend play in children's cognitive development [Abstract]. http://ecrp.uiuc.edu/v4n1/bergen.html?ref=casinobettingaction.info.

Betz, N., and Borgen, F. 2011. Integrating self through personality, interests, and self-efficacy. *Integrating Self.* Retrieved from http://www.inspiracenter.com/docs/Chapter9.pdf.

Bodrova, E., and Leong D. (2005). The importance of play, why children need to play. *Early Childhood Today*, 20 (3), 6–7.

Bradshaw, C. P., Sawyer, A. L., and O'Brennan, L. M. (2009). A social disorganization perspective on bullying-related attitudes and behaviors: The influence of school context. *American Journal of Community Psychology*, 43, 204–220. doi: 10.1007/s10464-009-9240-1.

Braithwaite, D. O., and Baxter, L. A., Eds. (2005). *Engaging theories in family communication: Multiple perspectives*. Thousand Oaks, CA: Sage.

Center on the Developing Child at Harvard University. (2010). The foundations of lifelong health are built in early childhood. Center on the Developing Child website: http://developingchild.harvard.edu/library/reports_andworking_papers/foundations-of-lifelong-health/.

Cohen, J., Onunaku, N., Clothier, S., and Poppe, J. (2005). *Helping young children succeed: strategies to promote early childhood social and emotional development*. (Research and Policy Report). Washington, D.C.: National Conference of State Legislatures.

Daily, S., Burkhauser, M., and Halle, T. (2010). A review of school readiness practices in the states: early learning guidelines and assessments. *Child Trends: Early Childhood Highlights, 1*(3), 1–12. http://www.childtrends.org/Files//Child_Trends-2010_06_18_ECH_SchoolReadiness.pdf.

Early Childhood Research and Practice. Department of Health and Human Services, (2010). http://www.hhs.gov.

DiCarlo, C.F., and Vagianos, L., (2009). Using child preferences to increase play across interest . . . early childhood classrooms. Young Exceptional Children. September yec.sagepub.com/content/12/4/31.full.pdf.

Fantuzzo, J., Sekino, Y., and Cohen, H. L. (2004). *An examination of the contributions of interactive peer play to salient classroom competencies for urban Head Start*. onlinelibrary.wiley.com/doi/10.1002/pits.10162/abstract.

Follari, L., (2011) Foundations and Best Practices in Early Childhood Education. www.coursesmart.com/.../lissanna-m-follari/dp/9780137034505.

Froebel, F. (1898) *Mother-Play and nursery songs: poetry, music and pictures for the noble culture of child life, with notes to mothers*. Whitefish, MT: Kessinger Publishing, LL.C

Institute for Health and Human Potential. Emotional Intelligence Quiz, http://www.ihhp.com/quiz.php. Retrieved May 26, 2010.

Institute for Health and Human Potential. mindmedia.com/Detailed/The_ Institute_for_Health_and_Human_Potential_4663.html. Retrieved May 26, 2010..

Jackson, E., (2010). Conflict resolution in the classroom. http://www. lessonplanet.com/article/teacher-education/conflict-resolution-in-the-classroom.

Jensen, A.L., Rideout, M.C., and Freedman, P.E., (2006). Handle with care: Emotional intelligence. http://www.ipacweb.org/conf/02/brock.pdf.

Kilpatrick, W. H. (1916). *Froebel's Kindergarden Principles critically examined*, New York : Macmillan.

Kirschenmann, J., and Farley, J. (2011, October 9). 'Slow Family' Movement focuses on fewer outside activities. http://usatoday30.usatoday.com/news/ health/wellness/story/2011-10-09/Slow-family-movement-focuses-on-fewer-o utside-activities/50712288/1.

Kunkel, A., Hummert, M. L., and Dennis, M. R. (2005). Social learning: modeling and communication in the family context. In D. O. Braithwaite and L. A. Baxter (Eds.), *Engaging Theories in Family Communication: Multiple Perspectives* (pp. 260-275). Thousand Oaks, CA: Sage.

Logue, M. (2007). Early Childhood Learning Standards: Tools for Promoting social and academic success in kindergarten. *Children and Schools, 29* (1), 35–43.

Mavrovelli, S., Petrides, K., Shove, C., and Whitehead, A. (2008). Validation of the construct of trait emotional intelligence in children. *European Child and Adolescent Psychiatry*, 17, 516–526.

McMullen, C. (2007). Safe classroom community where all children thrive. Creating a bully-free classroom. www.flipkart.com/books/0439590248.

Miller, E., and Almon, J. (2009). Crisis in the kindergarten: Why children need to play in school. *Education Digest*, 75(1), 42.

Moller, G., (2011) Associate Professor in the Department of Educational Leadership and Foundations in the College of Education and Allied Professions at Western Carolina www.eyeoneducation.com/Authors/Gayle-Moller.

National Association for the Education of Young Children. (2001). STILL unacceptable trends in kindergarten entry and placement: A position Statement Developed by the National Association of Early Childhood Specialists in State Departments of Education. http://www.naeyc.org/files/naeyc/file/positions/ Psunacc.pdf.

National Association for the Education of Young Children. (2009). Developmentally appropriate practice in early childhood programs serving children from birth through age 8. http://laureate.ecollege.com/ec/courses /56611/CRS-CW-4894979/educ6005_readings/naeyc_dap_position_ statement.pdf.

National Association for the Education of Young Children. (2001). STILL unacceptable trends in kindergarten entry and placement: A position statement developed by the National Association of Early Childhood Specialists in State Departments of Education. http://www.naeyc.org/files/naeyc/file/positions/ Psunacc.pdf.

The National Institute for Play. (2009). Play science—The patterns of play. Carmel Valley, CA: Author. http://www.nifplay.org/states_play.html.

National Safe Schools Partnership, GLSEN. http://www.cfchildren.org/Portals/0/Advcy/NSSP%20List%203%2027%2013.pdf.

National Scientific Council on the Developing Child. (2004). Children's emotional development is built into the architecture of their brains (Working Paper No. 2). Retrieved from Center on the Developing Child, Harvard University website: http://developingchild.harvard.edu/library/reports_and_working_papers/working_papers/wp2.

National Scientific Council on the Developing Child. (2004). Young children develop in an environment of relationships (Working Paper No. 1). Waltham, MA: Author. Retrieved from Center on the Developing Child, Harvard University website: http://developingchild.harvard.edu/library/reports_and_working_papers/working_papers/wp1/.

Pellegrini, A., (2005). *Recess: Its role in education and development.* University of Minnesota. Lawrence Erlbaum Associates. Inc.

Rodkin, P.C. (2011). Bullying-and the power of peers. *Educational Leadership*, 69, 10–16. from https://web.ebscohost.com.ezp.waldenulibrary.org/.

The Safe and Drug-Free Schools and Communities Act (SDFSCA) (1994). Elementary and Secondary Education Act (ESEA) (Title IV, §§ 4114116, 20 U.S.C. 7117116) http://www.ojjdp.gov/pubs/gun_violence/sect08-i.html.

The Safe School Climate Act, South Carolina General Assembly 'Safe School Climate Act' to Prevent School Harassment, Intimidation, or Bullying Findings Section 1. http://www.cga.ct.gov/COC/PDFs/bullying/101907_bullying_SC_law.pdf.

Satterly, D. (1987). Piaget and education in R L Gregory (Ed.) *The Oxford companion to the mind.* http://www.learningandteaching.info/learning/piaget.htm#ixzz1dXvfeJ2F.

Scott, Elizabeth, M.S.,(2011). Conflict resolution skills for healthy relationships. http://www.ehow.com/info_7937622_conflict-resolutions-classroom.html#ixzz1dY7b1i4U.

Snider, D.J. (2009) Life of Frederick Froebel, Founder of the Kindergarden, BiblioBazaar. www.archive.org/stream/lifeoffrederickf00snidrich/lifeoffrederickf00snidrich_djvu.txt.

Spiegel, A. (2008, February 21). Old-fashioned play builds serious skills. NPR Morning Edition, http://www.npr.org/templates/story/story.php?sto=ryId19212514.

StopBullying.Gov. What is Bullying. (n.d.). The Department of Health and Human Services. http://www.stopbullying.gov/topics/what_is_bullying/index. html.

Teaching Tolerance. (2011). A Project of the Southern Poverty Law Center. (1991). http://www.tolerance.org/?source=redirect&url=teachingtolerance.

United States Census Bureau. (2010). 2010 resident population. http://www.census.gov.

United States Department of Education. (2001). Executive summary: No Child Left Behind Act. http://www.ed.gov/nclb/overview/intro/execsumm.html

United States Department of Education. (2002). No Child Left Behind Act of 2001, Pub. L. No. 107-110, 115 STAT. 1425. http://www2.ed.gov/policy/elsec/leg/esea02/107-110.pdf.

Wadley, A. (1974) *Just Playing*, http://www.anitawadley.com/Site/ Poem.html March 16, 2010. thetoyroomchildcare.com/program.html

Warner, L. (2008). 'You're it!' Thoughts on play and learning in schools. Horace, 24(2), 1-6. (EJ849821)

Wolfgang, C. (2001). *Solving discipline and classroom management problems.* New York: John Wiley & Sons.

Zero to Three: National Center for Infants, Toddlers, and Families (2010). Infant-toddler Policy Agenda. Retrieved May 26, 2010, from http://www.zerotothree.org/.

Chapter Nine

Bullying: Recognizing the Warning Signs

Camacia Smith-Ross
Ashraf Esmail
Adnan Omar
Kathy Franklin

Introduction

Bullying is a common feature of every day life. We see it in the workplace, in the home, in the club and the sports field, but most commonly of all at school, where children learn as much about how to behave towards others as they do about their lessons in class. Unfortunately, some children learn only too well how to dominate others by foul means rather than by fair, and sadly begin to enjoy doing so, setting a pattern for how they will behave as adults.

Bullying can be defined as a repeated negative interpersonal relationship characterized by an imbalance of power targeted at a person that is perceived to be weaker or more vulnerable, without apparent provocation (Morrison, 2009). It is a persistent unwelcome behavior, mostly using unwarranted or invalid criticism, nit-picking, fault-finding, exclusion, isolation, being singled out and treated differently, being shouted at, humiliated, excessive monitoring, having verbal and written warnings imposed, and much more.

Most adolescents and teens are very comfortable using technology, and technology has become an important part of their social lives. While using technology can be fun and essential for learning useful skills, it can also be used for cyberbullying, referring to the use of technology, like cell phones and the Internet, to bully or harass another person. Cyberbullying affects many adolescents and teens on a daily basis with over half of adolescents and teens having been victims of online bullying, and about the same number having engaged in cyberbullying. This form of bullying can be very emotionally damaging to teens, and can have legal consequences for teens and parents.

The frequency of bullying in public schools has grown over the years and has contributed to fearful school environments for school aged children. Aggression and antisocial behavior in American schools are persistent and represent a very visible problem, particularly as youngsters make the transition from childhood in primary school to adolescence in secondary school (National Center for Educational Statistics, 2010). It has been recorded that much of the aggression in schools during this period involves individuals bullying their peers (Bosworth & Simon 2000). When bullying is not addressed, lifelong impacts are prevalent. Bullying among school children is a long-standing problem that detrimentally affects a substantial number of students (Nordah, e.g., 2008). It is noted that in many cases of school violence, the student felt bullied, persecuted, or injured by others prior to the attack.

Bullying is on the rise in recent years and apart from the schools and professional environments it effects are visible in almost every sector of life. This has triggered enormous concern from school and public authorities on the mechanism and procedures to put in place to quickly identify this devastating phenomena and curtail its detrimental effects. When it comes to bullying, most of the legislative responses require the State's Department to develop policies and procedures to prevent bullying (Fried & Fried, 2003). This has brought increased spotlight on the issue as state law makers and school authorities attempt to understand the forms of bullying, their progression ,effects on the victims and methods to limit these effects.

Literature Review

Bullying is a purposeful act and is often aimed at those who are weaker, friendless and who differ from the norm in some way. The bullies are usually aware of what they are doing and know that their actions will marginalize their victim. Motivation for bullying varies but the outcome is similar. In their book, *No it's not OK*, Tania Roxborogh and Kim Stephenson discuss five forms of bullying:

1. Physical bullying: Kicking, hitting, punching, pushing, tripping, threatening gestures, breaking belongings, Cornering the victim.
2. Emotional bullying: Name calling, verbal abuse, stalking a person, spreading rumors, blackmail and extortion, theft of belongings, hiding belongings, exclusion.
3. Sexual bullying: Unwanted touching, making obscene gestures to the person, telling lewd jokes or stories about the person, circulating inappropriate photos that may have been taken without permission.
4. Cyberbullying: Large volumes of abusive texts or emails; hate messages on Facebook, Bebo or other similar site, Inappropriate circulation of photographs.
5. Racial bullying; Exclusion because of skin color, language or appearance, mocking cultures, stereotypical classifications, discrimination because of religious differences (Roxbobogh & Stephenson, 2007).

Most people do not realize that bullying is a progression. Recognizing the progression of bullying is important for parents, caregivers and teachers. Any warning signs should be attended to and the child given the opportunity to share in private what has been happening to him or her. There are five typical stages that bullying goes through as it develops from minor annoyances to ongoing and intense harassment among children (Stephenson, 2007).

Phase 1: Bullies Watch and Wait

Bullies typically choose someone who is smaller and weaker than themselves. A bully will watch a potential victim for a period of time, assessing his or her weaknesses and whether he or she is likely to fight back.

Phase 2: Bullies Test out the Waters with Their Victims

After observing their victim for a while, bullies may interact with them and gauge the response.

Phase 3: The Bullying Steps up a Notch

By this stage the child will realize that the bullying is purposeful and upsetting. He or she may ask a teacher or parent for help but is often given glib advice about standing up for himself or herself. The bully watches what is going on and if the way remains clear, he will step up the harassment.

Phase 4: The Bullying Gathers Momentum

If the victim is resigned to the bullying, the perpetrators will take advantage of this and begin to bully more and more.

Phase 5: Bullying is Fully Established.

By the time bullying is fully established, the child will be living in torment. The bullies will harass him or her at school, in the classroom, in the playground and on the way home.

Purpose of Bullying

The purpose of bullying is to hide inadequacy. Bullies project their inadequacy on to others:
- To avoid facing up to their inadequacy and doing something about it;
- To avoid accepting responsibility for their behavior and the effect it has on others, and
- To reduce their fear of being seen for what they are, namely a weak, inadequate and often incompetent individual.

Although general characteristics tend to be displayed by bullies, bullying is really a continuum of behaviors. In other words, no one characteristic will define bullying, but rather, a combination of several traits and characteristics shape the inappropriate behavior. Bullies often engage in a "shopping manner" to target students who will become their preferred victims. They look for students who can warrant self-gratification by showing distress, who relinquish tangible resources, and who are less likely to retaliate or report them. Students who bully have been identified with showing extreme levels of insensitivity, lacking appropriate anger management skills, possessing beliefs that support random violent and impulsive acts of violence. Some of the most prevalent signs of bullying displayed by the aggressor includes but is not limited to the following:

- Are aggressive with others (including parents and teachers)
- Frequently hit or push other children
- Are physically strong and socially dominant
- Have a positive view of aggression
- Have trouble following rules
- Show little empathy for others
- Are emotionally immature
- Are irresponsible
- Show inadequate social skills (also true for bully/victims)
- Seek attention (think fear equals respect)
- Are often contemptuous of both children and adults
- Are often academically below average
- Cannot and will not accept responsibility for their actions

Just like any bullying, cyberbullying is a very serious issue and bullying statistics show that cyberbullying is a big problem among teens. Cyberbullying can be very damaging to adolescents and teens. It can lead to anxiety, depression and even suicide. Also, once things are circulated on the Internet, they may never disappear, resurfacing at later times to renew the pain of cyberbullying.

Cyberbullying can take many forms:

- Sending mean messages or threats to a person's email account or cell phone
- Spreading rumors online or through texts
- Posting hurtful or threatening messages on social networking sites or web pages
- Stealing a person's account information to break into their account and send damaging messages
- Pretending to be someone else online to hurt another person
- Taking unflattering pictures of a person and spreading them through cell phones or the Internet
- Sexting, or circulating sexually suggestive pictures or messages about a person
Cyberbullying can come through many types of technology:
- Emails
- Instant messages sent over the Internet
- Chat rooms, where teens talk to each other online
- Text messages sent to a teen's cell phone
- Web sites
- Blogs, or web logs, which are public online journals

- Interactions through online games
- Social networking sites, like Facebook and MySpace, where individuals have a page about themselves where others can post messages
- Twitter, which sends short messages to a teen's online account and cell phone

Many cyberbullies think that bullying others online is funny. Cyberbullies may not realize its consequences for themselves. The things teens post online now may reflect badly on them later when they apply for college or a job. Cyberbullies can lose their cell phone or online accounts for cyberbullying. Also, cyberbullies and their parents may face legal charges for cyberbullying, and if the cyberbullying was sexual in nature or involved sexting, the results can include being registered as a sex offender. Teens may think that if they use a fake name they won't get caught, but there are many ways to track someone who is cyberbullying.

Like bullying in person, cyberbullying can have negative emotional consequences for both the victim and the bully. There are some things that can make cyberbullying more serious:

- Because the bully can't see the victim, and may be hiding behind an online persona, the cyberbully may be much meaner than he or she would be in person.
- Cyberbullies may use fake names or pretend to be someone else, so the victim doesn't know who is attacking him or her, which can be more frightening.
- Cyberbullying can reach a teen through a cell phone or the computer at any time of the day or night, even at home.
- The messages or pictures that the cyberbully posts may stay around for many years, because once something is posted online it may not go away, or may resurface.
- Victims often retaliate to cyberbullies online, which can lead to a battle of hurtful or threatening messages, which is called flaming.
- Cyberbullies may be bullies in the real world as well, though sometimes cyberbullies are teens who are the victims of bullying at school and want to get even with their tormentors. Girls are more likely to be cyberbullies than boys, but both can be cyberbullies or victims. About one in three teens has been the victim of cyberbvullying.

In the United States, bullying tends to drastically increase over the late elementary school years, with peaks in middle school. Sex differences are also important in this discussion of aggression and antisocial behavior in adolescent bullying. Research has constantly found that boys, more than girls, are bullies at all levels of schooling (Pellegrini & Long, 2001). An analysis on sex differences in aggression has shown that males exhibit higher levels of both physical and verbal aggression from childhood through adulthood. This is credited to society being more accepting or tolerant of boys being involved in acts of bullying than their counterparts. This is not to say that bullying doesn't exist among females and their peer groups but; yet more apparent, in social and relational bullying.

As an under-reported problem, there are signs that bullying is on the rise. According to the National Education Association (NEA), in recent years, "bullying has become more lethal and has occurred more frequently" than in the previous two decades (Cohen & Canter, 2003). The National Association of School Psychologists (NASP) has called bullying "the most common form of violence in society." As researchers continuously probe into what goes on among school-aged children around bullying, alarming statistics are surfacing:

- According to the results of a nationwide survey funded by the National Institute of Child Health and Human Development, bullying affects nearly one out of every three U.S. children in grades 6-10 (Nansel, 2001).
- One-third of high school students polled about issues related to school size said their schools had serious problems with bullying (Public Agenda, 2002).
- A review of 1999 data collected by the Federal government on school safety among 12- to 18-year-old students found that approximately 36 percent of students reported seeing hate-related graffiti at school (Addington, 2004).
- Fifty-five percent of 8- to 11-year-olds and 68 percent of 12- to 15-year-olds say bullying is a big problem (Children Now, Kaiser Family Foundation, Nickelodeon, 2004).
- A nationwide survey highlighted by the Centers for Disease Control and Prevention (CDC) found that 6.6 percent of students in grades 9-12 had missed at least one day of school during the 30 days preceding the survey because they felt unsafe at school or on their way to or from school (Grunbaum, 2002).
- A survey by the American Association of University Women found that although students today are likely to be aware of school sexual harassment policies. 8 in 10 students—both boys and girls—said they experienced some type of sexual harassment in school. The results were the same among urban, suburban, or rural schools (American Association of University Women Educational Foundation, 2001).
- According to the National Center for Education Statistics and the U.S. Department of Education, Student bullying is one of the most frequently reported discipline problems at school: 21 percent of elementary schools, 43 percent of middle schools, and 22 percent of high schools reported problems with bullying in 2005-06. Table 9.1 shows the rates of Bullying compared to other School Discipline.

Table 9.1: Percentage Rates of Bullying and Other School Discipline Problems

	Elementary	Middle	Secondary
Student Racial Tension	2	6	5
Student Bullying	21	43	22
Gang Activities	8	32	39
Cult or Extremist Group Activities	1	5	11

Source: Cited in Indicators of School Crime and Safety, Table 7.2: 2007; National Center for Education Statistics, U.S. Department of Education (http://nces.ed.gov/) http://youth violence.edschool.virginia.edu/violence-in-schools/national-statistics.html.

Despite the potential damage of cyberbullying, it is alarmingly common among adolescents and teens. According to cyberbullying statistics from the i-SAFE foundation:

- Over half of adolescents and teens have been bullied online, and about the same number have engaged in cyberbullying.
- More than 1 in 3 young people have experienced cyber threat online.
- Over 25 percent of adolescents and teens have been bullied repeatedly through their cell phones or the Internet.
- Well over half of young people do not tell their parents when cyberbullying occurs. Table 9.2 shows the frequency of teenagers experiencing cyberbullying.

Table 9.2: Frequency of Cyberbullying Among Teenagers and Adults

Experiences Total	Teens 12–17	Adults 18+
Never	11	29
Only once in a while	47	44
Sometimes	29	18
Never	7	12

Source: http://www.growmap.com/cyber-bullying.

The Harford County Examiner reported similarly concerning cyberbullying statistics:

- Around half of teens have been the victims of cyberbullying
- Only 1 in 10 teens tells a parent if they have been a cyberbully victim
- Fewer than 1 in 5 cyberbullying incidents are reported to law enforcement
- 1 in 10 adolescents or teens have had embarrassing or damaging pictures taken of themselves without their permission, often using cell phone cameras
- About 1 in 5 teens have posted or sent sexually suggestive or nude pictures of themselves to others
- Girls are somewhat more likely than boys to be involved in cyberbullying. Table 9.3 shows the rate of cyberbullying by gender.

The Cyberbullying Research Center also did a series of surveys that found these cyberbullying statistics:

- Over 80 percent of teens use a cell phone regularly, making it the most popular form of technology and a common medium for cyberbullying
- About half of young people have experienced some form of cyberbullying, and 10 to 20 percent experience it regularly
- Mean, hurtful comments and spreading rumors are the most common type of cyberbullying
- Girls are at least as likely as boys to be cyberbullies or their victims
- Boys are more likely to be threatened by cyberbullies than girls
- Cyberbullying affects all races

- Cyberbullying victims are more likely to have low self esteem and to consider suicide

Tale 9.3: Cyberbullying By Gender
(Random sample of 10-18 year olds from a large school district in the southern U.S.)

	Male (n=2212)	Female (n=2162)
I have been cyberbullied (lifetime)	16.6	25.1
I have been cyberbullied (previous 30 days)	7.0	79
Someone posted mean or hurtful comments online	10.5	18.2
Someone posted a mean video about me online	3.6	2.34
I have cyberbullied others (lifetime)	17.5	21.3
I have cyberbullied others (previous 30 days)	9.3	7.9
I spread rumors online about others	6.3	7.4
I posted a mean/hurtful picture online	4.6	3.1

Cyberbullying ResearchCenter, www.cyberbullying.us

Bullying can occur directly, indirectly, aggressively or passively. As a result, two very important labels have been identified and defined as the kinds of behaviors that are exhibited by victims who are bullied. It is apparent that the role which is assumed by the victim will determine possible long term outcomes.

The passive victim feels insecure and helpless and appears cautious, sensitive and nervous on the surface. Passive victims are submissive because these victims submit to attacks and insults without retaliation. Passive victims represent roughly 80-85 percent of all victims (Olweus, 1993).

The provocative victim, commonly referred to as bully-victims, is defensive and exhibit irritable hyperactive behavior and a controversial quick temper which frequently gets them into trouble. They are the least liked in their peer group because they do not embrace the idea of being told what to do by a peer or peer group. Recent research has shown that these types of victims should be monitored carefully, as they frequently display not only the social-emotional problems of victims, but also the behavioral anti-social problems of bullies (Olweus,1993).

Provocative victims also were shown to have poorly modulated affect and behavior. Their impulsiveness, hyperactivity, and emotional instability (e.g., emotional outbursts) were very reactive, quite likely a main reason they emerge as likely targets of bullying (Schwartz, 2000). It is becoming increasingly evident that the effects of bullying are far reaching and can end in extremely tragic circumstances. Several surveys of both adults and children show effects of bullying can be quite severe. There are many implications; however, these are the most often repeated responses.

1) Bullying, especially severe bullying can result in children leaving school early and also not wanting to further their education at university or college.

2) Effects of bullying can be seen in tragic emotional consequences for victims of bullies. Again, nearly 50 percent of those surveyed revealed they had considered or thought about committing suicide as a result of bullying. Sadly to say, this group converts thoughts to actions at approximately 20 percent of these victims actually trying to commit suicide. The effects of bullying shows a victim of bullying also has a chance of more than 3 times the normal of suffering depression.

3) There is often no end to bullying for victims. Devastating effects of bullying is the pattern it creates in victims' minds and personalities that can last their whole life. Of those bullied at school, nearly 40 percent of them report being bullied again later in life, be it during further education, work or even socially.

4) Bullying and the effects of bullying is a self esteem killer! Whatever form the bullying takes and also regardless of the content, just about every bullying victim reports that they feel worse about themselves after they have been bullied. Especially in young and developing children, self esteem is critical. Bullies sap this from their victims creating further problems for the victim. Nearly 40 percent of bullied victims have low self esteem compared with less than 1 percent for normal, everyday kids.

5) Victims of bullying have much higher absenteeism levels than that of normal children. Obviously the more time spent away from classes and work not only limits their education and achievement but also takes them out of the necessary social circles, stopping them from making new friends. This lack of a good network is one of the most dangerous effects of bullying.

6) Because victims have not had the chance to effectively devise coping strategies and abilities, one of the key effects of bullying is that they can often find themselves dealing with more struggles later in life as a result. Long term relationships are harder to form and sustain and sadly, the pattern of bullying continues but now in adult life the victim becomes the bully and is more likely to resort to aggression and violence to resolve conflict (Blum, 2010).

Research has demonstrated a number of serious consequences of cyberbullying victimization. (Patchin, 2006) For example, victims have lower self-esteem, increased suicidal ideation, and a variety of emotional responses, retaliating, being scared, frustrated, angry, and depressed. One of the most damaging effects is that a victim begins to avoid friends and activities, often the very intention of the cyber-bully. Cyberbullying campaigns are sometimes so damaging that victims have committed suicide. There are at least four examples in the United States where cyber-bullying has been linked to the suicide of a teenager. The reluctance youth have in telling an authority about instances of cyberbullying has led to fatal outcomes. At least three children between the ages of 12 and 13 have committed suicide due to depression brought on by cyberbullying, according to reports by *USA Today* and the *Baltimore Examiner* (Hinduja, 2009). Table 9.4 shows the reactions of cyberbullying victims.

Table 9.4: Reactions from Victims of Cyberbullying
(Recent victims only)

	Male (n=93)	Female (n=91)
Angry	50.5	56.0
Frustrated	46.2	56.0
Sad	44.1	49.5
Embarrassed	40.9	36.3
Scared	49.5	25.3
Was not bothered	53.8	51.6

Cyberbullying ResearchCenter, www.cyberbullying.us

Bullying Solutions

Bullying can be stopped and bullies can be held accountable but it normally takes adult intervention. Parents (guardians) should be made aware of these behaviors and intervention efforts in other to curtailing school bullying.

Students who bully have been identified with showing extreme levels of insensitivity, lacking appropriate anger management skills, possessing beliefs that support random acts of violence, and impulsiveness. This dominant behavior has been related to children trying to establish themselves in the social hierarchy and a lack of attachment to their primary caregiver/s. Therefore, if parents (guardians) improve in their ability to respond to their children's needs with consistency, warmth and sensitivity, their children may begin to develop more positive representations of and expectations for social interactions (Goldberg, 2000).

Bullying and harassment thrive on silence. Parents can break the silence by listening and talking with their children about strategies for dealing with bullies. Kids can be encouraged to practice looking assertive and confident, to speak firmly and to practice comeback lines that are short and funny. With their parents' help, kids can develop alternate routes to bus or school, avoid places where bullies hang out, sit near the bus driver or walk with friends (Barreto, 2011). Kids should also be encouraged not to give up and to join clubs and other social groups to widen their safe social circle.

Parents can work with teachers and schools by asking for a school conference to address the problem. Parents should keep a detailed record of harassment and the ways in which the school is handling the situation.

Parents should ask if their school already has a bullying prevention committee and if the answer is no—they can work to establish a bullying prevention committee in their school. The most effective of these committees are those with representatives from administration, teachers, school mental health teams and parents. These committees develop programs that look at the total school environment and work to educate everyone to create a network of adult support for children. Such a network is particularly needed in the middle-school years, where children are learning to negotiate a social environment that is no longer primarily overseen by one teacher.

There are many useful public education resources available free of cost on-line (e.g. U.S. Department of Health and Human Services HRSA http://www.Stop bullyingnow.org). In the neighborhood, parents can team up to make their children's routes to school safer and to be on the lookout for harassment.

Teachers can be encouraged to involve students in creating classroom rules against bullying. Teachers should have a serious talk with the bully, explaining such behavior is not acceptable and explaining the negative consequences. Involving the bully's parents in these discussions can be very helpful. Of course, teachers also should listen to the victim's concerns and document episodes of bullying. There are many creative classroom solutions that will ease children's fear of retaliation, including anonymous drop boxes and surveys of bullying and harassment among the student population.

Bullying Prevention Guidelines

- Don't ignore the problem! Leaving kids alone to deal with bullying doesn't make them tougher-it makes them more vulnerable. If in any doubt, assume the child is being bullied and take action from there.
- Look for the signs of harassment because children may be too emotionally overwhelmed or frightened to tell you.
- Work with teachers and schools directly so that everyone can become more aware of the problem.
- Take steps to make the neighborhood safe. Talk to your children about how to protect themselves.
- Seek help from a mental health professional if necessary (Romme, 2010).

Cyberbullying often results in teens being depressed, afraid, or upset, especially when using the computer or cell phone. Teens may not want to tell parents if they are the victim of cyberbullying because their internet or cell phone access is very important to them and they don't want to lose it. Let teens know that they will not be punished for being the victim of cyberbullying so they feel comfortable telling you what is happening.

If a teen is the victim of cyberbullying, parents don't have to take away their cell phone or computer access. Instead:

- Don't retaliate
- Keep a copy of the messages as evidence
- Teach teens to ignore cyberbullies or to respond with short, unemotional messages like "Knock it off."
- Try blocking the email address or phone number of the person sending the messages.
- Tell the parents of cyberbullies what their teens are doing. If they don't do

anything, remind them that they are legally responsible for their teen's actions and you may be able to take them to court if the behavior doesn't stop.

- If the cyberbully is sending messages anonymously or with a fake name, ask your Internet Service Provider to help track the sender so you can tell the person to stop. If the messages are threatening or damaging, ask the police to help.
- Many email providers and social networking sites will shut down an account if you show them evidence that it is being used for cyberbullying. Go to the "contact us" page and send them copies of the messages.
- Teens who are being cyberbullied repeatedly may need to change their phone number and get a new email address.

Teens who have been the victims or perpetrators of cyberbullying may be at increased risk for depression or teen suicide, and may need counseling to overcome the harmful effects of cyberbullying.

Some ways to discourage cyberbullying include:

- Tell kids that cyberbullying is wrong, no matter who started it, and find out if they have ever been the victim or perpetrator
- Have a use contract for the Internet and cell phones that specifically tells kids not to cyberbully or they will lose their technology privileges
- Teach kids to never share their passwords except with parents, and to use passwords that would be hard for another person to figure out
- Encourage teens to never share personal information online - they don't know who they are really talking to, and the information may stay online for a long time.
- Tell teens not to open or accept messages from people they don't know.
- Parents should pay attention to what teens are doing online, which may include keeping the computer in a high-traffic area of the house, setting up your own online accounts and requiring teens to "friend" you so you can see the messages they send and receive, or installing monitoring software on the computer and telling teens that you can see what they do online (you should not secretly spy on teens).
- Encourage kids to speak up if someone they know is being a cyberbully, or is a victim

There are state laws that cover bullying that occurs on school grounds and at school-sponsored activities. Unfortunately, there is no national-mandated and uniform school crime reporting to help schools assess issues and concerns. Only a little more than a dozen states now require crime reporting in grades K-12. One of the reasons that national legislation hasn't been developed is that educators don't like to report problems and deficiencies that may exist on their campuses (School Security Report, 2003).

The National Conference of State Legislatures has compiled a list of State actions that relate to bullying, harassment, and hate crimes. States that have passed formal laws on bullying include California, Colorado, Connecticut, Georgia, Illinois, Louisiana, Mississippi, Nevada, New Hampshire, New Jersey, Oklahoma, Oregon, Vermont, Washington, and West Virginia. Others will soon follow as bullying in schools is at an all time high.

Conclusion

Bullying can have long lasting effects on people. It must therefore be taken seriously and dealt with early on. This brief study presented a comprehensive view of bullying in schools, its consequences and some solutions to curtail these effects. Standardized methods and procedures for dealing with bullying still remain areas of work for law makers but education remains the key to every successful action and powerful movement against this increasingly devastating social problem. Communities leaders, teachers, parents, students must build a consistent, planned program to educate schools and the society in general about the dangers and negative effects of bullying.

References

Addington, L. A., Ruddy, S. A., Miller, A. K., and DeVoe, J. F. (2002). *Are America's schools safe? Students speak out: 1999 School Crime Supplement.* http://www.gpo.gov/fdsys/pkg/ERIC-ED472826/pdf/ERIC-ED472826.pdf.

American Association of University Women Educational Foundation. (2001). *Hostile hallways: Bullying, teasing, and sexual harassment in schools.* New York: Author.

Barreto, Dr. Steven. (2011). Bullying solutions. http://www.lifespan.org/services/childhealth/parenting/bullying.htm.

Bosworth, K., and Long, J.D. (2002). Factors associated with bullying behaviors in middle school students. *Journal of Early Adolescence,* v19, p341–362.

Bullying statistics (2010). Dealing with bullying. http://www.bullyonline.org/workbully/defns.htm.

Children Now, Kaiser Family Foundation, and Nickelodeon. (2001). Talking with kids about tough issues: A national survey of parents and kids (Chart pack). Retrieved October 23, 2011, from http://www.kff.org/mediapartnerships/3105–index.cfm.

Cohn, A., and Canter, A. (2003). Bullying: What schools and parents can do. http://www.naspcenter.org/factsheets/bullying_fs.html.

Cyberbullying Research Center. (2010). Summary of our cyberbullying research from 2004–2010. http://cyberbullying.us/.

Cyberbullying Research Center. (2010). Preventing Cyberbullying: Top Ten Tips for Parents. http://cyberbullying.us/.

Roome, Debbie. (2010). Five stages of bullying. http://debbieroome.suite101.com/the-five-stages-of-bullying-a218193.

Dr. Susan. (2010). Dr. Susan's Guide to Surviving the bully at work. https://www.enterprisesa.com/za/?module=publish&sub_module=display_article&articleid=662&magid=50&magpage=.

Field, Tim. (1999). Those who can, do. Those who can't, bully. http://www.bullyonline.org/workbully/defns.htm.

Fried, S., and Fried, P. (2003). *Bullies, targets, and witnesses: Helping children break the pain chain.* New York: M. Evans and Company.

Goldberg, S. (2000). Attachment and development. London: Arnold (Hodder Headline Group).

Grunbaum J.A., Kann, L., Kinchen, S.A., Williams, B., Ross, J.G., Lowry. R., and Kolbe. L. (2002). Youth risk behavior surveillance—United States, 2001. *Journal of School Health*, October

High, B. (2007). Bullying is an adult problem—there must be an attitude of change. http://www.how-to-stop-bullying.com.

Hinduja, S., and Patchin, J. W. (2009). Bullying beyond the schoolyard: Preventing and responding to cyberbullying. Thousand Oaks, CA: Corwin Press. ISBN 1412966892.

i-SAFE Inc.(2009). "Cyberbullying: Statistics and Tips" http://www.isafe.org/outreach/media/media_cyber_bullying.

Kinchen, S. A., Williams, B., Ross, J. G., Lowry, R., and Kolbe, L. (2002). Youth risk behavior surveillance-United States, 2001. *Morbidity and Mortality Weekly Report*, *51*(SS-04).

Morrison, Charles T. (Apr 2009). What would you do, what if it's you? Strategies to deal with a bully. *Journal of School Health*. Blackwell Publishing. v79, n4: 201–204.

National Association of School Psychologists. (1999). Position statement on early childhood assessment. http://www.nasponline.org/information/pospaper_eca.html .

National Center of Educational Statistics (2010a October). Student victimization at school. Washington, DC: U.S. *Department of Education, Office of Educational Research and Improvements*.

Nordahl, J.K., (Ed.). (2008). *A Review of School-Based Bullying Interventions.* Portland, OR: *Lewis and Clark Graduate School of Education and Counseling.* v18, n1, 16–20.

Olweus, D. (2003). A profile of bullying at school. *Educational Leadership*, *60*(6), 12–17.

Patchin, J. W., and Hinduja, S. (2006). Bullies move beyond the schoolyard: A preliminary look at cyberbullying Youth. *Violence and Juvenile Justice*, 4(2), 148–169.

Pellegrini, A. D., and Long, J.D. (2002). A longitudinal study of bullying, dominance, and victimization during the transition from primary to secondary school. *British Journal of Development Psychology*. v20: 259–280.

Roxborogh, Tania, and Stephenson, Kim. (2007). *No its Not OK*. New York: Penguin Books.

Schwartz, D. (2000). Subtypes of victims and aggressors in children's peer groups. *Journal of Abnormal Child Psychology*.

Student violence in lower grades: Dealing with a growing and difficult problem. (2003). *School Security Report*, *19* (7): 5–8.

Webster, Richard. (2009). "From cyberbullying to sexting: What on your kids' cell?" *Harford County Examiner*.

Willard, Nancy. (2011). Parent's Guide to Cyberbullying and Cyberthreats. Center for Safe and Responsible Internet Use. https://www.researchpress.com/books/495/cyberbullying-and-cyberthreats.

Chapter Ten

K-12 Bullying Through a Generational Lens: Consequences and Interventions

Doris L. Terrell
Raphael L. Terrell
Ashraf Esmail
Taylor C. Terrell

Introduction

Twenty-first century students face many of the challenges of their peers in centuries past, challenges that include diversity, changing demographics, non-conducive learning environments and unacceptable consequences of the socialization process. As members of a group, these students differ in terms of: personalities; likes/dislikes; socioeconomics; cognitive abilities; intellectual aptitudes; physical appearance; race; gender; religion, or its absence; left-brain/right-brain talents; sexual proclivity; home environments; ethnicity; nationality/geography; culture; hygiene; and clothes/shoes, just to name a few differences. Each student is a complex composite of these characteristics, dynamics of their families, and individual idiosyncrasies that inevitably define the individual. While most individuals can point to bullying taking place, there is oftentimes a psychological disconnection between the definition of bullying, and certain acts of physical, verbal, cyber and/or emotional violence, disrespect or just plain bad manners. From observation and inference, it is not possible to understand the proximate circumstances or physiologies that cause an individual to engage in the behavior of bullying; however, it is practical to postulate reasons for such behavior. To this end, it is reasonable to understand bullying from the perspectives of individuals who perceive that they are victims of bullies or have witnessed the egregious acts of bullies.

Definition

A bully is defined as a person who uses strength or power, whether real or seeming, to engage in verbal, physical, mental, emotional, cyber and/or economically harmful acts designed to harm or intimidate or dominate those who are or who are perceived to be weaker (Smith, Cowie, Olafsson, & Liefooghe, 2002). It follows that the act of bullying causes the weaker party to experience a feeling of powerlessness, depression, embarrassment, anger, and confusion, the latter of which may stem from a lack of intervention by direct and/or indirect bystanders. This absence of intervention can also be interpreted as a form of bullying in and of itself.

Reasons for Bullying

Children and teenagers bully others for many reasons. These reasons include:
- The home and community environments of the bully may not be welcoming and caring and include domestic violence as a day-to-day norm along with other negative family issues.
- Bullies enjoy a feeling of power and control over others. This feeling is highlighted by a societal culture that gives more attention to negative behavior while giving short shrift to positive behavior.

There are other words that have the same connotation as bullying; however, society has decided to assign the word bully to children whereas adult bullies are described by different names. While this article expounds on bullies who are members of K-12 aged groups, it is acknowledged that bullies are also members of the age groups from 20 through life. Some subset of K-12 bullies become adults who continue to bully and engage in practices such as harassment, intolerance, robbery, battery, assault homicide.

Bullying: Predator, Victim or Bystander

School-aged children within a K-12 environment are expected to learn and achieve without fears of reprisal or harassment from their peers or school mates. Though this may appear to be a reasonable expectation, statistics indicate that the vast majority of school-aged children can be characterized as a predator/bully, a victim of bullying and/or an innocent bystander who witnesses the act of bullying by others. Approximately 160,000 children miss school every day because of a fear of being bullied by other children (Hart, 2011).

It is estimated by the National Education Association (NEA) that:
- One-third of American schoolchildren in grades six through 10 are affected by bullying; and
- Eighty-three percent of girls and 79 percent of boys report experiencing harassment.

Additionally, data from the National School Safety Center (NSSC)[1] suggest that approximately 2.1 million bullies are resident in K-12 schools and 2.7 million children are victims of bullies, while the number of bystanders, namely those who witness acts of bullying exceeds 50 percent of the K-12 population of 55 million students (NSSC, 2006). Regardless of the category in which a child finds herself or himself, there may be long term or lifelong negative impacts on these children that serve to impede the socialization and learning processes. (Wang, Lannnotti, & Nansel, 2009).

Predators

Bullies, in every sense of the word, are predators. They target children, their peers or others, who seem to be vulnerable and then act to cause harm to them in ways that can be categorized as physical, social, economic, or cyberbullying.

- Physical bullying involves aggressive behavior that may include hitting, punching, shoving, or other more violent acts that can be labeled as criminal acts of violence.
- Social bullying can be far more subtle than physical bullying; however, its affects are equally as severe. This form of bullying involves ostracizing others, i.e., excluding someone from being a member of a team or playing a game; spreading rumors about a person that are false, misleading and/or hurtful; and ignoring a person when they are trying to participate in a discussion or conversation or simply attempting to ask a question.
- Economic bullying includes acts that destroy personal property, e.g., books, clothing, mobile phones, music players, backpacks, shoes, etc., or acts that result in the theft of money.
- Cyberbullying is a consequential product of the widespread use of technology. It includes the use of the internet to communicate hurtful messages and pictures; and the use of internet-based chat rooms to allow individuals, who may or may not know the victim of bullying or those who are instigators of the acts of bullying, to participate in a deluge of messages. These messages may encourage the act of bullying while other messages that may criticize the bullying acts. Also mobile phones are used to transmit hurtful messages, pictures and/or videos. This form of bullying is the more difficult to stop because of constitutional rights to freedom of speech, oftentimes because oftentimes pseudo names are used to hide the real identity of the bully or group of bullies who act in cyberspace.

Regardless of the type of bullying, those who are the predators of these senseless acts cause harm to their victims.

Victims

According to information from the National Center for Education Statistics (NCES), in 2009, about 28 percent of students ages 12–18 reported being bullied at school during the school year. In 2009, a higher percentage of females (20 percent) than males (13 percent) ages 12–18 reported being the subject of rumors, while a lower percentage of females (8 percent) than males (10 percent) reported being pushed, shoved, tripped, or spit on. In addition, a higher percentage of females (6 percent) than males (4 percent) also reported being excluded from activities on purpose. In 2009, approximately 6 percent of students ages 12–18 reported being cyber-bullied anywhere during the school year. Among those students who were bullied at school or cyber-bullied anywhere, there generally were no measurable differences between males and females in the frequency in which they were bullied (NCES, 2011). Victims of bullies experience emotional, physical, economical, and/or mental harm. The apparent consequences of bullying are many and vary in degree. Consequences include: feelings of sadness and/or depression; lowered academic achievement; inability to sleep; not wanting to go to school; loss of appetite or overeating to ease discomfort; headaches; loss of self-confidence; urge to retaliate against others—both bullies and bystanders; and thoughts of committing suicide, which may lead to '*bullycide*', defined as suicide as a result of acts of being bullied.

Bystanders

Bullying occurs in many settings—inside of the classroom, on school grounds, in cyberspace, in the home and in communities. When bullies have an audience there is a tendency for the negative acts to escalate because, on many levels, bullies seek power, attention and the right to declare that they won the physical and/or verbal fight. Bystanders tend not to get involved in halting the act of bullying because they fear retaliation by the bullies and fear having to suffer similar consequences as the bullies such as expulsion from school. Many school regulations do not differentiate between the bully and those who act to stop physical violence. Therefore, many bystanders exercise extreme caution when deciding whether to attempt to halt senseless acts of bullying.

Generational Lens—First Graders, High School Students, K-12 Teachers, and College Professors

Bullies, victims of bullies and bystanders witnessing bullying are each perceived differently depending upon the age, demographics, and character of the individual evaluating a particular situation. The questions that underpin this discussion of perception by others include the following: Why do students bully? How do bullies select their victims? Why do bystanders not attempt to halt acts of bullying? What can be done by teachers and college professors to prevent bullying? There are no universally accepted answers with realized, viable solutions to these questions; however, there are schools of thought regarding the answers to each question. Provided are outward signs that bullying may be taking place; and examples, consequences and intervening strategies regarding acts of bullying as seen through the lens of a first grade student, a high school students, a K-12 teacher, and a college professor.

First Grade

If a *first grade child* does not want to attend school, has nightmares about being bullied, becomes withdrawn, has declining performance in school, has signs of physical altercations, e.g., scratches or bruises, and shows fear when asked about a certain child or classmate, then these outward signs are signals that the child may be a victim of bullying. In contrast, an early childhood bully or one who demonstrates a predilection to becoming a bully may demonstrate aggressive behavior towards adults as well as children; may like violence as seen in the media or as illustrated by others in their home and community environments; may have a need to be in control without a sense of compromise; and may join in the fray when witnessing someone being bullied. These signs signal a need for early intervention to curtail the aggressive behavior before it results in more severe behaviors and their consequences as the child matures.

First Grade Lens

A little boy wanted to play soccer with his schoolmates during recess. In selecting who would be on each team, this little boy was not selected by either team. When the little boy yelled out, *"What about me?"* his schoolmates laughed, ignored him and started to play soccer. Even though teachers and other students were on-lookers, no one bothered to intervene and allow this situation to become a teaching moment on fairness and kindness for all involved. Subsequently, the little boy, who was not selected to play soccer, began to cry and ran off to hide at the back of the playground. The lingering effects of this encounter are not known; however, retrospectively, the on-looking teachers should have felt remorse for not interceding to aid this distraught little boy.

High School

Most *high school students* who are victims of bullying have a more advanced set of thinking processes in comparison to early childhood students. Additionally, more high school students succumb to peer pressure and do not report incidents of violence or bullying. Physical abuse is more common among teenage boys and verbal/emotional abuse is more common among teenage girls. Additionally, girls are more likely to ostracize others as a bullying tactic in contrast to boys who generally do not engage in this type of behavior. High school victims of bullying may experience depression, drug use and inhibited social development, and at the extreme may attempt or commit suicide.

High School Lens

Bullying was experienced by an attractive, popular, high-achieving, 17-year old African American female who plays clarinet in the marching band, plays piano for her church, winner of numerous awards, junior class president, president of several other clubs, member of the National Beta Club and has a handsome, intelligent boyfriend who is the envy of her peers. Who would believe that this high-achieving teenager could be the victim of bullies? She would and her guidance counselor and parents empathized with her situation; however, felt powerless to confront the bullies for fear that they would escalate their bullying acts, retaliate, and cause further negative impacts on the young lady.

The popular teenage girl described above had enviable talents, popularity and intelligence. While on many levels these were positive qualities, the escalating envy and jealousy developing within her closest female peers resulted in torturous acts of verbal and emotional bullying. As a result of this bullying, the young lady dropped out of high school and, throughout her life, was skeptical of and limited her close social interactions with females. Physical abuse can result in visible scars; however, emotional and verbal abuse can have more far-reaching effects as was the result in this situation.

K-12 Teachers

K-12 teachers are taught how to mitigate acts of bullying and when to involve safety officers when the acts of bullying cross a pre-determined demarcation line. Teachers are taught how to halt physical fights; how to teach the principles of fairness and kindness to their students; how to discipline children when their behavior does not meet an established norm; how to report acts of bullying to higher level school administrators; and how to engage the parents or guardians of their students when negative behavior occurs. *Why then is there such a prevalence of bullying in K-12 schools?*

K-12 Teachers Lens

In any given day, 10 percent of the students in the classroom engage in some form of bullying—physical, emotional, verbal, cyber and/or economical. Though bullying exists and serves to disrupt the learning environment within the classroom, teacher evaluations are based on the academic achievement levels of students and these achievement levels are not weighted or offset by the number of bullies in the classroom that disrupt the learning process. It is impracticable to believe that all learning takes place in the classroom and that the learning that occurs outside of the classroom does not weigh heavily on the in-class dynamics. Teachers cannot do it all. The widespread societal proliferation of violence, which is often glamorized in cinema, television and in video games, is viewed as being acceptable behavior. Teachers cannot 'undo' the lessons learned and the behaviors internalized outside of the school environment. Therefore, society's teachers, whether their name is mother, father, business leader, president, preacher, politicians, sports players, movie stars, rappers, etc., must accept the reality that they each must be part of the active solution to curb bullying in K-12 schools.

College Professors

College professors have the heightened responsibility to educate future generations of teachers on ways to address classroom and school bullying while not engaging in acts of bullying themselves. This is an important and difficult responsibility. For reasons that are systemic in design, many college professors have not experienced the level of violence and bullying that exists in twenty-first century K-12 schools. These professors hear and read about the cascading degrees of bullying; however, intervention strategies are best taught by those with the breadth and depth of experiences to answer questions of *'What if. . . ?'* For example, What if a student destroys someone's property? What if a bully posts a picture of a student's oily and food-stained lunch bag on the internet and texts this picture to others? What if a bully makes fun of a student because they do not have a smart phone or computer? What if a bully ostracizes a student because he or she does not have money to buy the latest fad clothing or shoes or to attend the prom? What if bullies make fun of studious students? Professors educated in the twentieth century may not have a working knowledge of these twenty-first century K-12 dilemmas. So how do they teach what they do not know or have not experienced? The current approach is to send teacher candidates into the K-12 classroom to engage in on-the-job training by K-12 teachers; however, the current K-12 teachers were taught by the same professors who have not experienced twenty-first century K-12 students and bullies? A changed paradigm in higher education must be instituted that is designed to mitigate this cycle of teaching and introduce solutions that serve to lessen violence and bullying.

College Professor Lens

In teaching the tenets of classroom management, the following question arises from a teacher candidate: Why is classroom management a separate course and multiculturalism a separate course, and ethics of teaching a separate course? Why can't students be taught how to integrate the principles of the three courses in a capstone format before engaging in a student teaching practicum? The college professor offers the following response: The faculty approved this degree program. Therefore, this is the scope and sequence of material that must be taught. While the response from the college professor heard, it was not well-received by the teacher candidates in the course. Again, the question must be addressed as to what must be done, systemically, to ensure that the principles taught to teacher candidates within institutions of higher education address the needs of twenty-first century K-12 students. Mitigation of bullying while enhancing the self-esteem of bullies must be taught to teacher candidates and not assumed known instinctively by these candidates.

Impact of Media on Bullying

Access to media and technology, whether through the internet, video games, television, cinema or smartphones, is widespread. Students today are immersed in a sea of technology. Whether through television, videos, smartphones, video games, theater movies, computers (Facebook, Twitter, YouTube, etc.), or digital music, students are bombarded with messages that highlight and sensationalize episodes of violence, bullying, or verbal tirades. It is these types of messages that garner the most attention and seem to generate a following, particularly among teenagers, tweens, and even elementary school students. No longer are schools a 'learning zone' they have become a 'proving ground' for students to reenact events that should be foreign in this environment, events that are underpinned by the actions of bullies. It is widely held that children gain knowledge, learn behaviors, and have their value systems significantly shaped and defined by their exposure to media.

From the age of six months, children are exposed to most media sources that display 'near-real-time' information. No longer are depictions of *'reality'* left to the predilections of journalists or news editors. Today, everyone can be a journalist, write a story or take a picture and have this story, with color video and sound, travel around the world in less than 80 seconds. Today's youth can be exposed to the best and the worst circumstances of life with the click of a mouse or the maneuverings of a video game controller or the tap of a smartphone or the viewing of one of the thousands of local, national, international or Internet Provider Television (IPTV) programs. Children and teenagers do not take the time or possess the critical thinking skills needed to understand the consequences of actions but rather they witness the fact that negative behavior garners more attention and receives higher viewership than positive behavior.

Individuals from the fields of education, medicine, law, violence psychology, sociology prevention, and communication have studied the impact of media on children and adolescents for several decades. In a seminal study of the impact of television violence, a volume of articles, edited by Joel Federman, of the Center for Communication and Social Policy at the University of California, Santa Barbara, summarizes the body of work. This study involved more than 300 people, nearly 10,000 hours of videotaped television programming over a three-year period, and the participation of more than 1,600 individuals as study participants in five separate experiments. The project is characterized by many as a landmark in the history of television research in that its analysis of TV content is based on the most representative sample of the television landscape ever collected. While this study was initiated in 1994 and culminated over a decade ago, it findings are meaningful in society today. The National Television Violence Study was commissioned by the National Cable Television Association in direct response to public concern that TV violence has harmful impacts on society. [National Television Violence Study, 1996; Federman, 1997; Federman, 1998]

Teaching the Arts of Communication and Problem Solving

Many episodes of bullying stem from a lack of communication and problem solving skills. These skills, on many levels, are learned behaviors and can be acquired as knowledge threads woven into every aspect of the K-12 curriculum. There is a tendency in K-12 education to compartmentalize knowledge. Science is taught independent of history. Mathematics is taught independent of writing. Problem solving is taught independent of how to play in the sandbox. Additional examples of this type of interdisciplinary pairing can continue indefinitely; however, the basic concept of teaching the skills of communication and problem solving is as follows: Everyone is different and differences are good. Everyone must learn to be accepting of differences while embracing the benefits of these differences. There are ways to channel anger, resentment, hatred, jealousy, and dislike of others into positive directions through the teaching of age-appropriate communication and problem-solving skills. Once these skills are learned and bullying episodes decrease, disciplinary strategies can then be employed to deter further negative behaviors and to build self-esteem.

Understanding the Influence of Discipline on Bullying

Discipline is perceived as an act designed and applied to halt negative behavior. Discipline is also perceived as a negative as it is generally an act that the individual engaged in negative behavior will not and does not like. So then, how does one deter negative behavior with an intervention that is deemed negative? Unfortunately, if the discipline applied is severe enough, or deemed to be severe enough, to not only punish the negative behavior that has occurred, but also deter others, through example, from engaging in the same or similar negative behavior, then is this type of discipline an example of bullying? Children and teenagers are human beings and have the same needs as adults. When teachers herald accolades on students for doing a great job then the students will work to please the teacher even more. When bullies are disciplined by sending them to an in-school detention or expelling them from school for a period of time, then this may encourage negative behavior because an expelled student generally stays at home with all-day access to television, video games, or the internet. To a bully, this type of punishment may not be viewed negatively and may not result in the desired outcome of deterring negative behavior. Using hard-to-find federal middle school data from the U.S. Department of Education, which included over 9,000 middle schools, the findings of Losen and Skiba (2010) indicate that 28.3 percent of black males, on average, were suspended at least once during a school year, nearly three times the 10 percent rate for white males. Black female middle school students were suspended more than four times as often as white females (18 percent vs. 4 percent) (Losen & Skiba, 2010). Not only are these statistics troubling, it sounds an alarm for the need to examine the ways that we prepare teacher candidates to meet the challenges that they will face in the twenty-first century K-12 classroom—urban, rural, suburban, and private.

Parents, teachers and the broader learning community must work collectively to develop discipline strategies that allow children and teenagers to express their anger without harming others; that teach correct, consistent behavior designed to meet a societal norm; and how to empathize with others and, through peer pressure, dissuade acts of bullying and violence. Disciplinary strategies should have an intended outcome of positive behavior.

Intervention Strategies

Adults must lead by example and not expect children, teenagers or college-age teacher candidates to be the torchbearers of tolerance, respect, fairness and civility. Higher education must begin to examine, in concrete and statistically significant ways, the effectiveness of its teaching strategies that are designed to mitigate bullying, deter violence and apply discipline in ways that work to enhance self-esteem not further marginalize it. While in-service teacher professional development is a pro-active way to supplement the repertoire of skills mastered by K-12 teachers, it does not excuse institutions of higher education from their responsibility to teach teachers how to tailor intervention strategies to meet the needs of the demographics of their twenty-first century K-12 classrooms.[2] Examples of intervention strategies include:

- Engage in age-appropriate role playing exercises among peers followed by discussions on feelings, reasons, self-esteem, punishments by principals, teachers, parental or the juvenile court systems;
- Hold discussions on the consequences of bullying;
- Develop age-appropriate punishments for bullying, consequences/ punishments that are visible to peers yet are aimed to encourage character-development, fairness to all;
- Develop and implement age-appropriate programs to foster positive self-esteem;
- Ensure broader development and implementation of age-appropriate programs to discuss 'valuing differences among peers and others;
- Reward changed behavior with positive reinforcements; and
- Find ways to abolish suspensions for non-violent disciplinary offenses and replace these suspensions with disciplinary actions that enhance, in some form, K-12 learning, critical thinking, communication, and problem-solving skills.

Conclusion

Bullying in K-12 schools exists in critical proportions. This article examines bullying through the generational lens of a first grade student, a high school student, a K-12 teacher and a college professor. It captures the reality that bullying must be addressed by incorporating the thinking of those who are bullies, those who are victims of bullies, bystanders who witness bullying, and society's teachers, whether their name is mother, father, guardian, business leader, president, preacher, politicians, sports players, movie stars, rappers, etc., must each accept the reality that they must be part of an active solution to curb bullying in K-12 schools. Without a concerted effort, led by education professors in institutions of higher education, our nation will experience heightened levels of K-12 bullying and school violence.

Notes

1. National School Safety Center (NSSC): The National School Safety Center was established by Presidential mandate in 1984 by Ronald Reagan as a joint program between the United States Departments of Education and Justice. The Center, based in Westlake Village, California, now operates as an independent non-profit organization serving schools and communities worldwide providing training and technical assistance in the areas of safe school planning and school crime prevention.
2. Reflections. "Oftentimes students do not do what they are taught to do, they do what they see, hear and experience in their worlds - homes, communities, states, nation and world." Dr. Doris L. Terrell, PhD (2012).

References

Bullying Statistics. (2009). http://www.bullyingstatistics.org/content/bullycide.html.

Federman, J. (Ed.). (1997). *National Television Violence Study: Vol. 2. Executive summary*. Santa Barbara: University of California, Center for Communication & Social Policy.

Federman, J. (Ed.). (1998). *National Television Violence Study: Vol. 3. Executive summary*. Santa Barbara: University of California, Center for Communication & Social Policy.

Hart, Kevin. (December 12, 2011). Pennsylvania Students Stand Up to Bullying, News Release. http://neatoday.org/2011/12/12/pennsyl vania-schools -stand-up-to-bullying/.

Losen, Daniel J., and Skiba, Russell J. (2010). Suspended Education—Urban Middle Schools in Crisis, The Civil Rights Project, University of California at Los Angeles, 25pp.

National Center for Education Statistics (NCES). (2012). U.S. Department of Education. *Indicators of School Crime and Safety: 2011* Washington, D.C.: NCES.

National Education Association, *Nation's Educators Commit to Bully-free Schools*, News Release. (April 12, 2012). Washington, D.C. http://www.nea.org/home/51562.htm.

National Education Association, Ten Steps to Stop and Prevent Bullies, (December 27, 2012). http://www.nea.org/home/51629.htm.

National School Safety Center, 2006, NSSC Review of School Safety Research.www.schoolsafety.us.

National Television Violence Study, Executive summary, 1994–95. (1996). Studio City, CA: MediaScope, Inc.

Smith, K P., Cowie, H., Olafsson, R. F., and Liefooghe, A. (2002) Definitions of bullying: A comparison of terms used, and age and gender differences, in a Fourteen–Country international comparison. *Child Development*, 73(4), pp.1119–1133.

Terrill, Doris. Personal Reflections. (2012).

Wang, J., Lannnotti, R., and Nansel, T. R. (2009) School bullying among adolescents in the United States: Physical, verbal, relational, and cyber. *Journal of Adolescent Health*, 45(4), pp. 368–375.

Chapter Eleven

Bullying, Gender Equity, Harassment, Drop-Out Anticipation, and Solution: What Would You Do?

Brucetta McClue-Tate
Faye Jones
Ashraf Esmail
Marcus Henderson

Introduction

This study investigated the effects of bullying on African American high school students. This study also determined whether urban students are dropping out due to bullying. This study surveyed and observed a focus study that is directly or indirectly impacted by "bullying."

Statement of the Problem

In the twenty-first century, students are faced with "bullying" more than ever. In addition to that, high school dropout rates are on the rise. A recent U. S. Department of Education study (2012) indicated that 7.4 percent of students in U. S. schools drop out before obtaining a high school diploma (NCES, 2012).

Bullying, Gender Equity, Harassment, Dropout Anticipation, and Solution. What Would You Do? This question can be an alarming bell that one should address and push without thought.

Recently, a study was conducted at an urban high school. Forty-two ninth through twelfth graders participated in a group discussion to understand why bullying takes place. Students were asked a series of questions pertaining to "bullying" and how it affected the decision to drop out of school; possible solutions were also discussed. Students who participated in this study were cognizant of the term "bully," as well as its social manifestations, which student participants believed to begin as early as elementary school. A significant population of students stated that they had experienced the practice of bullying, informing investigators that they would inform their teacher of the practice if they felt their life was in danger; however, student participants also informed investigators that they often used their own individual means to alleviate any bullying practices with which they may have been confronted.

According to participants, gender differences were of no real significance because there were often physical confrontations between different gender groups—girls fighting boys and vice versa. Discussions with student participants highlighted the "no limit" effect—in terms of gender transcendence—on the culture of "bullying" in schools, with girls stating that they would often confront the effects of "bullying" by fighting back (physically) if the need presented itself. According to student participants, peers often harass peers for any of the following "common" reasons: 1) Dislike of another student, 2) The student thinks he/she is more than the other, 3) For no reason at all, and 4) Upbringing and cultural differences. According to Seals and Young (2003), students often harass one another for no reason at all.

Interviews during this study revealed the rising effects of "bullying" on students during a normal school day. Many students move from school to school to avoid the potentially devastating effects of "bullying" (Toldson, 2011; Peguero & Williams, 2011). According to Peguero and Williams, students who are bullied experience a drop in grade point average, most detrimental to African-American and Latino students, who experience a 0.3 point drop in GPA from ninth through12th grade because of "bullying" activity (www.jbhe.com). According to "bullying" data, to avoid the negative effects of "bullying," many students drop out of traditional secondary school academic setting, often enrolling in GED programs later in life. Many studies are conducted to address this growing social issue (Fryer, 2006; Fordham & Ogbu, 1986; Toldson, 2011). In *Breaking Barriers 2: Plotting the Path Away from Juvenile Detention and Toward Academic Success for School-age African American Males*, an analysis of the social ills that plague African-American males, with suggested solutions, Toldson explicates the importance of safety in schools to the successful academic experiences of African-American males, in comparison to their Latino-American and European-American male counterparts (Toldson, 2011).

High school students are often characterized by their peers according to their perceived socio-economic station in life—what they have and where they reside (Fryer, 2006; www.jbhe.com, 2011). These characterizations often imply student success and failure in school, regardless of gender. A study by researchers from the University of Michigan and the University of Wisconsin found that African-American students from affluent neighborhoods have a 96 percent likelihood of graduating high school, compared to a 76 percent likelihood for African-American students from high poverty neighborhoods (www.jbhe.com, 2011). In reference to the culture of "bullying" and scholarly success, Toldson (2011) postulates a similarity of experiences for African-American, Latino-American, and European-American students, ". . . with low achieving students participating in the most bullying activity" (p. 32). According to the Toldson study, "Although black male students reported the lowest overall level of bullying, when compared to white and Latino males, black males were the only racial group where high achievers experience bullying at the same rate as the lowest achievers" (p. 36).

While most student participants, from a high school in the south, agreed that the culture of "bullying" starts at the elementary school level, often originating in the home environment, many also believed that the culture of high school "bullying" could lead to fights, hatred, and even death, as many students take what they may have learned in their home environment to school and into the streets beyond the academic setting. This current study revealed that students feel that principals do not care and that they (the principals) are concerned only about grades. According to Willard (2011), less than half of bullying incidents are even reported at school, and the punitive nature of the punishments for bullying result in only 34 percent of bullying issues being resolved. "If administrators knew that we have major concerns of life on our minds," stated one student, "they would address our fears and the pressures of life" (personal communication). Therefore, the question remains: Is there really a solution that can be derived from a direct connection towards gender and environment? Are the leaders in the schools really listening?

Bullying is a form of aggressive behavior that may manifest as abusive treatment and involve an imbalance of power. This imbalance of power may be social power and/or physical power. The victim of bullying is sometimes referred to as a target.

Bullying consists of three basic types of abuse: emotional, verbal, and physical. It involves a pattern of behavior repeated over time and is an imbalance of power and strength. It ranges from simple one-on-one bullying to more complex bullying, such as cyberbullying, which, according to Willard and Paris (2012), is a problem of great proportions--for students and adults alike. Bullying in school is referred to as peer abuse.

The goal of every school should be to create respectful and safe learning environments. If everyone works toward that end, productive conditions will be created for students, as well as, administrators. Paris (2012) discusses the five R's that make schools effective, safe, and productive: 1)Respond, 2) Research, 3) Record, 4) Report, and 5) Revisit. According to Paris, a secondary school principal, schools who take heed to these five concepts are often more climatically safe for students and teachers, free of bullying dilemmas because of the thorough and proactive stance to the practice of bullying (Paris, 2012). However, can you change a social behavior that has taken place since birth as stated by those students who participated in the discussion? The culture has taught them to fight and defend themselves at an early age.

Purpose of the Study

This study investigated the effects of bullying on African American urban high school students. This study also determined whether urban students are dropping out due to bullying. These research findings are important to administrators, educators, and parents of children with and without disabilities have an interest in finding a solution to bullying in the schools.

Research Questions

- Is there a higher dropout rate in high school in an urban setting due to a high bullying rate among peers?
- Is gender a true independency of the drop-out the rate in school within high unknown bullying rates?
- Is bullying among students a turf issue that dependent on both school and location.
- Does gender impact an absolute direct cause of bullying which results in dropout?

Literature Review

Bullying, harassment, and teasing within the schools have become critical issues nationwide (Bowman, 2001). This is true as it applies to students with disabilities, also. In July, 2000, the United States Department of Education issued an official statement on behalf of the Office for Civil Rights (OCR) and the Office of Special Education and Rehabilitative Services (OSERS) in reference to disability harassment in the schools. The number of complaints to OCR and OSERS has increased with proven situations of disability harassment (U.S. Department of Education, 2000).

There is a very small, but increasing, amount of bullying among children with disabilities. Research indicates that children with disabilities are at greater risk of being teased and physically bullied (Mishna, 2003). These children often include students with learning disabilities, students with Attention Deficit Hyperactivity Disorder (ADHD), students with medical conditions (e.g., muscular dystrophy and spina bifida), overweight children, and even children with articulation and fluency deficits. Labeling and separating students based on their academic or athletic aptitude provides an opportunity for bullying and teasing (Hoover & Salk, 2003).

Bullying can have a serious affect on children, especially those with disabilities. These children are more likely because of bullying to be depressed, have low self-esteem, experience poor appetites, dislike school, and contemplate suicide. Bullies tend to focus on peers who appear vulnerable, such as those who are passive, quiet, sensitive or having an identifiable disability (Khosropour & Walsh,

2001). Additionally, personality characteristics of these individuals are shy, sad, weak, or helpless.

Bullying behavior can become "disability harassment," which is illegal under Section 504 of the Title II of the Americans with Disabilities Act of 1990. According to the United States Department of Education, disability harassment is "intimidation or abusive behavior toward a student based on disability that creates a hostile environment by interfering with or denying a student's participation in or receipt of benefits, services, or opportunities in the institution's program" (U. S. Department of Education, 2000).

Disability harassment can occur in any location of the school, such as the classroom, cafeteria, hallways, on the playground, or school bus. It can even occur during school sponsored events (Education Law Center, 2002). Bullying has different forms including verbal harassment, physical threats, or threatening written statements. One of the most prevalent and dangerous forms of bullying is cyberbullying (Willard & Paris, 2012). According to bullying research, cyberbullying can take place in the form of 1) continuation, 2) retaliation, 3) mutual conflict, and 4) impersonation (Willard & Paris, 2012). Regardless of form, bullying literature informs us of the profound importance of remaining focused, diligent, consistent, and organized in handling cyberbullying and all other forms of bullying (Toldson, 2011; Willard & Paris, 2012).

Presently, 15 states have passed laws addressing bullying among school children. States that have passed formal laws on bullying include California, Colorado, Connecticut, Georgia, Illinois, Louisiana, Mississippi, Nevada, New Hampshire, New Jersey, Oklahoma, Oregon, Vermont, Washington, and West Virginia. Most of these laws have gone into effect since 2001 and were possibly motivated by tragic events occurring at several U.S. high schools (Vossekuil, Fein, Reddy, Borum, & Modzeleski, 2002). The 2001 Louisiana Acts, H.B. 364, Act 230, requires local school boards to adopt policies prohibiting harassment, intimidation and bullying by students and protecting students and employees who report such incidents. It also authorizes local school boards to adopt zero tolerance policies for fighting in schools and requires students expelled for fighting to pay for and attend conflict resolution classes with their parents (www.bullypolice.org/la_law.html, 2001).

When an administrator or faculty member finds out that harassment may have occurred, the staff must promptly investigate the incident and respond appropriately. To end bullying in the school, administrators can distribute surveys to students, school personnel, and parents. Once the data are collected, school personnel can provide supervision, deliver negative consequences to those who bully, teach positive behavior through modeling, coaching, and praise, and take a proactive stance by implementing programs that teach students social skills, conflict resolution, and anger management.

When a parent thinks his/her child is being bullied they should be supportive and encourage the child to describe who was involved and how and where the bullying occurred. Talk with your child's teacher immediately to see if he or she can help to resolve the problem quickly. If the bullying is severe, contact the principal in writing. Ask the school to convene an Individualized Education Program (IEP) or Section 504 meeting to ensure that the school district is meeting the needs of the student's with disabilities. This meeting will allow you to explain what is happening and allow the team to take steps to stop the bullying. Be persistent and talk regularly with your child and school staff to ensure the behavior has ceased .

According to an article by CNN (2009) 6.2 million high school students dropped out of high school in 2007 and by 2010, it was 7.4 (NCES, 2012). Dropout rates are on the incline for a number of reasons and students who participated in the discussion said that they knew of students who did not return to school because they were being bullied or felt they were different from other students. In the discussion, students were asked what would they do if they just had to leave for being harassed, almost all of them stated that they would give it a good fight and they would tell their parents, teachers, and the principal and leaving the school would be the last result.

Finally, bullying can cause health problems for students. Other signs include stomach pain, wanting a pass to leave class, coughing, always ill. The most concern of them all is stress. Stress will cause a student to not perform or achieve academically (*Teen Health*, 2011).

Method

The population of interest for this study was students in an urban setting in the United States between the ages 14 and 21. The population for this study consisted of African American students with the following social concerns or ethical conditions: 1) a history of non-graduating from college, 2) a willingness to bully someone, 3) each student was either on the free or reduced price lunch program, and 4) knew someone who dropped out school. The sampling frame was obtained directly from students in an open discussion forty two students participated. This resulted in a sample school size of 210 students. On average, surveyed participants were 16 years old and live with at least one parent. All students knew the other parent and 100 percent were African American. Twenty young women and 22 young men with at least one family member who has been in trouble with the law were included in the study. While the study sample cannot be considered representative of the original population of interest, generalizability was not a primary goal.

Setting

The study was conducted in an urban high school environment with a high drop-out rate and low test scores. Students populations consist of 250-350 students. The climate included at-risk school with a range of essential needs such as educational resources. The cultural environment provides preventive programs, social counseling, free school lunches, counseling for homeless problems, anger, and more.

Sample

A total of 42 teenagers were surveyed and participated in focus group discussions. Ratio included 20:22 female to male students. All students had equal opportunities to answers the following questions with rebuttals:

1. Have you ever been bullied by someone?
2. Does bullying take place in this school?
3. How did you handle bullying?
4. Did you tell an administrator or faculty member?
5. What is going on at the time?
6. Do you know of anyone who dropped out of school because they were bullied by a peer?
7. Have you ever thought about dropping out if you have been bullied?
8. How can bullying stop?

Surveyed questions were:

1. Are boys and girls bullied the same way?
   - A   Yes
   - B   No
2. How do bullies learn to become aggressive?
   - A   Learn early in families
   - B   Watching others do it
   - C   Being bullied themselves
   - D   All of the above
   - Other _____
3. Bullying violates me as person
   - A   My emotion
   - B   My Ego
   - C   My Me as Person
   - D   All of the above
   - Other _____
4. Bullying gives a person power and leadership among peers
   - A   Yes
   - B   No
   - Comment_____
5. I see a pattern of behavior among bullies
   - A   Poor
   - B   Belong to a Gang
   - C   Need to have rank in the school
   - D   Low performance in school (D or C students)
   - E   Need attention
   - F   All of the above

Comment/Other_____
6.   Bullying leads to drop-out
     A   Yes
     B   No
     Comment:_____
7.   Discussion Focus Group Open Question: What does bullying mean to you and
     how has it affected you at school?
     The Focus Group Study was an open ended discussion for one hour.

Instrument

This study focuses on Qualitative instrument via a focus group. It entailed observations and note taking of individual and group responses (Jansick, 2004). All of
one's senses were included with spontaneous and discerning senses were taken into
consideration when analyzing the response of the participant, (Jansick, 2004). This
study also used a Quantitative method via survey of general questions to ensure the
validity which determines whether the researcher truly measures so show what was
intended to be measure or how the truthfulness of the researcher denotations.

Reliability

The extent to which results are consistent an accurate representation of the total
population under study is referred to as reliability and the results of a study shows
consistency in responses to the questions and discussion of the focus group thereof.
Embodied in the survey and focus group is the idea of reliability or repeatability of
results responded too or observed.
     The degree to which the questions were measured were repeatedly consistence
in responses. This remains the same throughout the focus group discussion which
showed satiability and results of consistency in reactions of participants. A high
degree of stability indicates a high degree of reliability of the response, which
means the results were repeatable and may result in additional studies (Winter,
2000).

Validity

While this research shows truthfulness to drop-out rate can be affective by bullying
it Validity agree upon whether the research truly measures that which it was
intended to measure or how students response where a direct participation of a
bullying event or opinion as to why their peers dropout of high school (Patton,
2001, Winter, 2000). Other causes were mention which will be displayed in the
analysis and results section.

Data Collection Methods

Students were given a series of questions before the focus group discussions. Students were asked to answer the seven questions, and write one or more comments to each question if they choose too. The surveys were collected. The focus group discussion was done right after surveys were collected. The interviewer took notes, listen, and observed body languages (Jansick, 2004).

Analysis

Bullying has a greater influence to those who seem part of that violent cycle and with this study, we viewed it as part of a bully's daily activity from birth. Can you really stop a bully? Bullying was not a direct reason why students drop-out school according to our findings. Students bully each other no matter what, partly because that is what they do to protect themselves whether physically or emotionally. Table 11.1 shows other comments and suggestions written on the questionnaire by participants while Table 11.2 shows the correlation as to why students bully one another and why it may continue unless parents of these communities are trained to change their image. In addition, a preventive intervention program is a must for high schools with high violent rates. Table 11.3 is a transcript of what was discussed in the focus group.

Table 11.1: Other Comments/Suggestions Written on Questionnaire by Participants

a.   No One Cares
b.   A white man's world
c.   Do not live with parents
d.   School work to hard
e.   Too much pressure in school
f.   Do not have the same opportunities
g.   You must fight back to survival the world
h.   I never get anything
i.   Parents do not care
Conversation Terms
•   Stupid
•   Dumb
•   Do not know what you are talking about
•   Government makes more off children

Table 11.2: Correlations as to Why Bullies Exist in High Schools and Gender Relationship If Any

Do boys and girls get bullied the same way?	How do bullies learn to do it?	Bullying violates me as a person?	Bullying gives a person power and leadership among peers?	I see a pattern or behavior among bullies?	Bullying leads to drop outs?
Yes (0) No (42)	Learn early from family Watching others do it Being bullied themselves All of the above (42)	My emotion (1) My ego (5) Me as a person (8) All of the above (28)	Yes (28) No (14)	Poor Belong to a gang Need to have rank in the school Low performance in school (D or C students) Need attention All of the above (42 agreed)	Yes (2) No (40)
Comment/Other	Comment/Other	Comment/Other	Comment/Other	Comment/Other	Comment/Other
Girls are worse than boys	When they come from a violent family, the children tend to be bullies	Step on my turf, mind their own business, give me the right to hurt the person	They are controlled at home and come to school and control; they are controlled in a gang and want to rule the school	Parents, family, and friends want to have control and keep the name going	Drugs, Gangs, children, must work

(#) Denotes responses

Table 11.3: Focus Group Consistent Responses, Concerns and Suggestions:
What Needs to be Done or What Would You Do?

- The need for correction to be consistent and fair for all students
- Teachers and School Leaders should be educated as to why students are not passing and absent from school
- It would be good if we could have gender discussion and select the teacher of choice for those discussion and preventive lessons on bullying
- It would be good to have a confidential method as to how one could tell on another students without identifying ourselves
- How can we be protected after school hours
- If one is unable to think a day of a test how can we get permission to text on another day
- There is no way out of a bullying system if it is gang related; You cannot talk about it
- I have experience a lot of pain and rejection in my life and no one seems to care
- If I do not do what my friends do I will be lonely
- If I come forward I am considered a snitch
- We should put out students who interrupt the class and not use an excuse or say they are special especially if they are bullying other students
- Give the teacher more rights freedom to address bullying rather than ignoring the situation
- Sometimes when I am angry I will bullying because it helps me excerpt my angry
- People are just stupid and the need to be told when they are stupid
- My parents are the cause of me hating. Some of us need new parents: They do not care
- Participate in a lot of school activities such as the band, dance team, clubs, choir, sports, etc.
- Have a Bully Team on campus that includes students
- Focus on mutual understanding because some people do not know there [are] other people who are good [and] that are different from their own upbringing
- Organize groups that would do plays, posters, and film video that will help with preventing "bullying" and create a safe environment
- Use teachable moments in the classroom to help peers develop a sense of similarities and differences in a positive manner
- I am unable to focus in class when someone bully me on a day or a period of time

Results

In our research involving approximately 42 randomly selected high-schoolers from Urban School District in the United States, At Risk Students are victims and offenders when comes to bullying students. The populations is at risk low performing students with a lot of angry build up end to have experience bullying long before they enter high schools. The correlation of the bully and angry had a strong relationship per that data. This survey also showed alone with the discussion how those students who normally bully all the time would eventually drop out of school because of multiple reason which this study did not address. Students' relationship with their parents from birth to extended schools years has attributive to the bullying. Students' relationship continued while controlling for gender, race, and age, though our results suggest female girls were specially tend to have lower levels of self esteem than their peers which brings on added stress and surroundings of pressure. Based on the standardized regression percent of variance explained, the relationship between the student and parent has projected a low self esteem in the child that is stronger than that of just an offensive which contribute to the student who is bullying others. There was a strong correlation because parental upbringing, and peer bullying. There was a strong correlation of sickness, stress and absences among the student bullied. Students rather stay home then deal with the person or person attaching them each day. Thus, eventually some of them never return to school and is consider a dropout. Students that dropout according to this study are due highly to student being tired, age, raise their child, and must work to help the family pay the bills, and 10 percent stated to get a GED. Finally, will in the focus group bullying was displayed multiple times one person wanted to no more than then other. It appears that students had a need to be the leader at all times. Participants called each other names such as "stupid," "dumb," "he or she do not know what they are talking about," other profound cursed words during the discussion. An actual bullying fight occurred during the time of the focus group discussion.

Conclusion

In this study there was evidence that support the argument in the eyes of the students that "bullying" is not the primary issue they face in school. The major issue involved the issue of testing. Schools are more concerned with raising the academic scores on standardized testing rather than nurturing support of students' everyday life issues at hand. Yet, some literature has provided support that attention being paid to "bullying" was not a major concern. Although, the many shootings across the nation that have occurred on various school grounds can possibly be a factor of long-term "bullying" which has a greater influence to those who seem part of that violent cycle. This study did provide evidence that bullying is part of a bullies' daily activity from birth. Yet, we found in this study that there was no direct correlation between "bullying" and student dropout rates. Student dropout was due to lack of interest and failure. Furthermore, this study did show that environment is a factor and that bullies have larger issues than the school system can handle. The results of the study showed that students cannot simply walk away from being bullied without peer back lash. It was determined that student bullies' culture and their parents are both advocating them to protect themselves by encouraging ongoing bullying. It is recommended that preventive programs be developed on school ground and enforced in the first week of school and/or before a student can participate in any school activities. Further research should investigate the impact of silent bullying which study demonstrates may lead to suicide. Furthermore, the results of the study found that bullying does impact the students' ability to learn. Further research should study the impact of academic performance and bullying in Pk-12 schools.

References

Bowman, D. H. (2001). At school, a cruel culture. *Education Week*, 20(27), 1, 16–17.

Bully Police. (2001). (www.bullypolice.org/la_law.html, 2001).

CNN (May 2009). 'High school dropout crisis' continues in U.S., study says, http://articles.cnn.com/2009-05-05/us/dropout.rate.study_1_dropouts-enrollment-graduations?_s=PM:US

Education Law Center (2002). What can you do if your child with a disability is being harassed by other students? (fact sheet). Retrieved September 21, 2011, from www.elc-pa.org.

Fordham, S. and Ogbu, J. (1986). Black students' school success: Coping with the "burden of 'acting white.'" *Urban Review*, 1986, Vol. 18, pp. 176-206

Fryer, R. (2006). "Acting White: The social price paid by the best and brightest minority students." *Eductionnext*, Vol. 6, No. 1. http://educationnext. org/acting white/.

Green, Samuel B., Salkind Neil, J. (2005). Using SPSS For Windows and Macintosh Analyzing and Understanding Data (4th edition) Pearson Prentice Hall. Upper Saddle, New Jersey.

Hatch, Amos J. (2002). Doing Qualitative Research in Education Settings. State University of New York Press. New York, NY.

Hoover, J. H., and Salk, J. (2003). Bullying: Bigger concerns. St. Cloud State University, Department of Special Education.

Jansick, Valerie J. (2004). Stretching Exercises for Qualitative Researchers (2nd Ed). Thousand Oaks, CA Sage Publishing, Inc

The Journal of Blacks in Higher Education. www.jbhe.com.

Khosropour, S. C., & Walsh, J. (April 2001). That's not teasing–that's bullying: A study of fifth graders' conceptualization of bullying and teasing. Paper presented at the Annual Conference of the American Educational Research Association. Seattle, WA.

Mishna, F. (2003). Learning disabilities and bullying: Double jeopardy. Journal of Learning Disabilities, 36(4), 336–347.

National Center for Education Statistics. U.S. Department of Education. (2012). The Condition of Education 2012 (NCES 2012-045), Indicator 33.

Paris, Barbara. (2012). Cited in "Cyberbullying and school: Disruptive, hurtful behaviors the adults can't see." http://www.examiner.com/article/cyber bullying-and-school-disruptive-hurtful-behaviors-the-adults-can-t-see.

Patton, M. Q. (2002). Qualitative evaluation and research methods (3rd ed.). Thousand Oaks, CA: Sage Publications, Inc.

Peguero, Anthony A., and Williams, Lisa M. (2012). "Racial and Ethnic Stereotypes and Bullying Victimization." *Youth & Society*.

Popham, James W. (2000). Modern Educational Measurement *Practical Guidelines for Educational Leaders* 3rd Ed. Boston. A Pearson Educational Company.

Raskauskas, J. & Scott, M. (2011). Modifying Anti-Bullying Programs to Include Students with Disabilities. Teaching Exceptional Children, 44(1), 60–67.

Rogers, Alex (2011). *I'm Only Human After All* (The Empowerment Series Book 1) [Kindle Edition] http://www.amazon.com/Im-Only-Human-After-All/dp/1461051916.

Seals, Dorothy, Young, Jerry (2003) Bullying and victimization: prevalence and relationship to gender, grade level, ethnicity, self-esteem, and depression http://findarticles.com/p/articles/mi_m2248/is_152_38/ai_n6005507/.

Teen Health Retrieved, November 11.11. 2011 "Dealing with Bullying" from http://kidshealth.org/teen/your_mind/problems/bullies.html.

Toldson, I. A. (2011). Breaking Barriers 2: Plotting the Path Away from Juvenile Detention and toward Academic Success for School-age African American males. Washington, D.C.: Congressional Black Caucus Foundation, Inc.

U.S. Department of Education (2000). Prohibited disability harassment: Reminder of responsibilities under Section 504 of the Rehabilitation Act of 1973 and Title II of the Americans with Disabilities Act. Office for Civil Rights. Washington, DC.

Vossekuil, B., Fein, R., Reddy, M., Borum, R., & Modzeleski, W. (2002). *The final report and findings of the safe school initiative: Implications for the prevention of school attacks in the United States*. Washington, DC: U.S. SecretService, National Threat Assessment Center.

Willard, Nancy. (2011). Parent's Guide to Cyberbullying and Cyberthreats. Center for Safe and Responsible Internet Use. https://www.researchpress.com/books/495/cyberbullying-and-cyberthreats.

Willard, Nancy, and Paris, Barbara. (2012). When cyberbullying spills into school. http://www.ssc.coop/cms/lib2/MN06000837/Centricity/Domain/1/Policy%20Priorities%20-%20Cyberbullying.pdf.

Williams, Lisa, and Peguero, Anthony. (2013). "The Impact of School Bullying on Racial/Ethnic Achievement." Paper presented at the annual meeting of the American Sociological Association Annual Meeting, Caesar's Palace, Las Vegas, http://citation.allacademic.com/meta/p519119_index.html.

Winter, G. (2000). A comparative discussion of the notion of validity in qualitative and quantitative research. *The Qualitative Report*, *4*(3&4). http://www.nova.edu/ssss/QR/QR4-3/winter.html.

Chapter Twelve

Cyberbullying from Schoolyard to Cyberspace: An Evolution

Kelly Gray
Ashraf Esmail
Lisa Eargle

Introduction

Everyone remembers times in middle or high school when a girl, boy or group of girls/boys said something mean or rude to you, excluded you from some event or gossip session or even physically attacked you. In each case, those actions made you feel sad, hated, disgusted, angry and displaced from the world, like you were unwanted by everyone. Such actions are those of bullies.

When a person thinks of a bully they see an image from the movies, of that big, strong kid looking menacing at the wimpy kid, who stands quivering, sniveling, waiting to be pummeled in the middle of the school hallway, while all around are the bystanders, laughing, cheering or staring in shock. It seems like an antiquated scenario, yet, it is played out over and over again in schools all around the United States. Today, this antiquated bullying scenario has evolved from the school halls into a virtual existence, enveloping the wonders and benefits of technology such as e-mails, blogs and instant messaging. Cyberspace has become the new playground for bullies and their victims, giving a new face to an old pastime.

No matter the landscape, schoolroom or cyber chat room, incidents of bullying are very real, detrimental events for the victims, their families and the communities in which they live. One only has to go back to Tuesday, April 20, 1999, the day of the Columbine massacre. While the entire set of motives was not clear at the time from the shooters, Dylan Klebold and Eric Harris, one motive was very clear: the shooters had been both bullying victims and bulliers. Klebold and Harris had been victims of continual ridicule and taunts from their high school classmates and eventually turned that ridicule toward their aggressors via the Internet. Websites published by Eric Harris were filled with mocking rhetoric regarding groups of people, classmates and basically the world, followed by ranting threats of physical harm and revenge to said groups. It was one of the first times bully/victim scenarios evolved from the classroom to cyberspace.

Since that April day in 1999, bullying has evolved rapidly and synchronously with technology and networks, i.e., the Internet. Most children from first grade to twelfth grade have access to some electronic device (e.g. computer, phone) in school, at home or both, which connects to the Internet and all the social networking websites (e.g. Facebook), e-mail, blogs and instant message services. Such ubiquitous and instantaneous access to the Internet and all its realms increases the availability and likelihood a bully/victim scenario will occur.

Most, if not all, researchers outside of the United States (e.g. Italy, the United Kingdom, and Sweden) have conducted the bulk of the research into cyberbullying. It is one of the goals of this research to provide some insight into the cyberbullying issue in the United States and how aware or engaged are parents, schools and law enforcement. The second goal of this research is to lessen the technological divide between parents and children of the cyber generation. "Part of the problem in combating cyberbullying, say experts, is that parents and kids relate to technology very differently. Most adults approach computers as practical tools, while for kids the Internet is a lifeline to their peer group" (Keith and Martin, 2005, p. 226). This fear and disconnect can exacerbate the bully/victim scenario. The third goal is to promote further research into this new realm of bullying, as it is likely to increase in number, scope and intensity as technology advances at an exponential pace.

This chapter takes a mixed-method approach to studying bullying. First, we will examine state-level rates of bullying and school violence using secondary data from The American Youth Behavior Survey of High School Students 2009. Questions we hope to address are: (1) what are the overall rates of bullying and violence victimization reported by students across states? (2) Do bullying and violence victimization rates vary by gender and race/ethnicity? (3) How do school characteristics influence bullying and violence victimization rates?

Next, we will also examine results from a survey on sample of teenagers (N=103), ages 14-17, to determine the level of their bullying experience from the traditional in school hallways to the complex in the world of cyberspace. Questions to be hopefully answered viewing this sample of teenagers through a routine activity theory lens:
1) Are victims of traditional bullying more likely to also face continued victimization in cyberspace?
2) Is one more hurtful to the victim than the other?
3) How are school boards and legislators responding to the new issue of cyber-bullying?
4) What can be done by the guardians in a teen's life to ameliorate the incidents and effects of cyberbullying?

5) Where do the boundaries of responsibility for schools, parents and law enforcement begin and end in a cyber-bullying scenario? Can traditional responses be effective? Before such questions can be answered, some definitions are needed.

Definitions

What is bullying? Is it when one girl confronts another calling her ugly, fat and stupid in front of other kids? Is it when a child is excluded from a fun activity or school function because another child or group of children has told all the participants not to include them? Bullying is both scenarios and " . . . defined as a physical, verbal, psychological attack or intimidation that is intended to cause fear, distress or harm to the victim, with a more powerful person oppressing a less powerful one" (Baldry & Farrington, 2000, p.17).

Take the bullying definition above; add the Internet and technological access via phones and computers and you now have what is known as cyberbullying.

Cyberbullying involves the use of information and communication technologies such as e-mail, cell phone and pager text messages, instant messaging (IM), defamatory personal Web sites, and defamatory online personal polling Web sites, to support deliberate, repeated, and hostile behavior by an individual or group, that is intended to harm others (Keith & Martin, 2005, p.1).

Transition from Physical Bullying to Cyberbullying

Traditionally, bullying manifests itself in the physical world such as in the definition above where one child or many children physically and/or verbally abuse another child over a period of time. Most generations recognize traditional bullying, they see it as something everyone goes through; it is just a part of childhood, the norm, something that will pass with time. Society has quickly moved away from this static view of bullying after several high-profile incidents of violence and suicide such as Columbine, the murder of bully Bobby Kent by seven of his friends in 1993 and the recent suicide in Massachusetts of Phoebe Prince, 15, who killed herself after months of bullying from fellow classmates. Present day society has essentially come to understand that bullying is not the norm; it is a vital issue in schools and households everywhere and could mean life or death for their children.

What society has also come to understand is that with the age of technology advancing at an exponential pace, bullying has fluidly moved from the school environment into the home environment. This fluidity occurs instantaneously through the click of a mouse, through home computers, cell phones, tablets or other electronic devices that connect to the Internet. For those homes and families that are not computer-oriented or dependent on computers for many daily activities and social networking, cyberbullying may confine itself to the schoolyard. However, according to the U.S. Census Bureau for 2009, 31.3 percent of households surveyed did not have Internet access at home while 68.7 percent of households had access to the Internet in the home and 76.7 percent access the Internet at some location (U.S. Census, 2009). Statistically then, the likelihood that a child being bullied in the schoolyard receives a reprieve or "cooling off" period from the trauma of the bullying scenario diminishes once they leave school grounds. The evolution of bullying from schoolyard to cyberspace is now in motion.

Who is Responsible?

With the evolution of bullying from schoolyard to cyberspace, the level and point of responsibility to help a victim becomes even more blurred. The breadth and scope of the Internet and social networks has not only expanded the audience to a bully scenario but also further obscured the levels of responsibility by parents, schools and law enforcement to the victims.

Parents, schools and law enforcement face a daunting jurisdictional issue when it comes to traditional bullying or cyberbullying of a student. In the case of cyberbullying, "Cyberspace represents new territory for peer mistreatment, often leaving school administrators with doubts about the boundaries of their jurisdiction" (Strom and Strom, 2005, p. 36). Where do the legal and moral boundaries of the school end and begin? What is the best recourse for parents? When does law enforcement get involved? Is the First Amendment protecting only the bullies? It is a constant dilemma being fought in schools, homes and courtrooms across the United States.

At the heart of the responsibility question lays a simple, yet unanswered question by most American communities; what is the state of bullying in their respective school districts? Has anyone researched and surveyed the school population regarding the existence of bullying? More often than not, the school, as well as parents, has no idea there is a problem with bullying or even that it is occurring on school grounds and on their kids' phones and computers at school. Alternately, some communities, parents and schools know there is a problem but it is such a common problem that it is just accepted as the norm or something that cannot be combatted due to the scope of the problem. "Many experts fear bullying has become so widespread and common, adults are blinded to its extensive harm" (Borba, 1999).

Bullying: Research and Statistics

Research

As cited by Campfield (2008) and Juvonen & Gross (2008), traditional bullying is well documented in the United States and most countries; however, cyberbullying is a phenomenon with few empirical studies. "Research on cyberbullying and victimization in the U.S. is in its infancy. Information about incidences of cyberbullying and victimization are found online and reported in the media more so than in scholarly journals at this point" (Campfield, 2008). As of October 2011, this statement remains true. In doing research for this chapter, only about 10 percent of the articles and scholarly journals focused on cyberbullying, with the remaining 90 percent focused on traditional bullying. There are multitudes of cyberbullying centric websites; however, good portions are based solely in European countries.

Although the disparity in cyberbullying research between Europe and the United States remains fairly significant, the United States is slowly beginning to conduct more empirical research, initiate websites, form organizations and information repositories focused on cyberbullying. With that, it is one of the goals of this chapter to aide in closing this empirical divide.

Statistics

Traditional Bullying

Traditional bullying, stated previously, is what we typically think of when the term bullying is discussed. It is a single child or teen, or perhaps a group of children or teens that repeatedly and over time inflict negative actions on one or more students. Negative actions by Olweus are defined as someone intentionally inflicting, or attempting to inflict, injury or discomfort on another. Such negative actions are divided into three categories: verbal, physical contact, and nonverbal and nonphysical (also known as relational bullying). Technically, the definition of bullying requires more than a single incident of one of these actions; however, a single incident can be deemed bullying if serious enough (Chin, 2011).

According to the website, BullyingStatistics.Org, bullying remains a problem among children and teens with no hint of dissipation anytime soon. Bullying statistics for 2010 reveal that about 160,000 children miss school every day out of fear of being bullied. One in seven students from kindergarten through twelfth grade is either a bully or has been a victim of bullying.

- Over half, 56 percent, of all students have witnessed a bullying incident while at school.
- 71 percent of students report bullying as an ongoing problem.
- The peak years for bullying incidents are in fourth to eighth grade with more than 90 percent reporting they were victims of some kind of bullying.
- There are about 2.7 million students being bullied each year by about 2.1 students taking on the role of the bully (BullyingStatistics.Org., 2010).

Cyberbullying Statistics

According to Feinberg and Robey, "Approximately half of cyberbullying victims are also targets of traditional bullying"(Feinberg & Robey, 2008). Campfield surveyed 219 middle school students and found that 69 percent of participants were involved in cyberbullying and/or victimization. A significant overlap was found among face-to-face (traditional) bullies and victims and cyberbullies and victims

(Campfield, 2008). Essentially, bullying that goes on in the schoolyard does not necessarily cease when a child or teen leaves school grounds. The evolution of social networking and the Internet has broken the traditional bullying-in-the-schoolyard boundaries bringing bullying into the boundless area of cyberspace.

The Cyberbullying Research Center, led by Dr. Sameer Hinduja and Dr. Justin Patchin, has conducted cyber-bullying research and maintained said research on their Center's site since 2002. In February 2010, Drs. Hinduja and Patchin surveyed 4,441 youth between the ages of 10 and 18 from 37 schools in a large school district in the southern United States. The following are some of the results from that survey.

- Approximately 20 percent of the students responding stated they had cyberbullied someone in their lifetimes.
- Posting mean or hurtful comments (12 percent) and spreading rumors online (13 percent) were the most common forms of cyberbullying.
- Girls were most often found to be the victim of cyberbullying (25.8 percent to 16 percent) and the most likely to report it than boys (21.1 percent to 18.3 percent).
- Cell phones remain the most popular technology utilized by teens (83 percent).
- Cyberbullying victims are more likely to consider suicide but the research was still premature (Hinduja & Patchin, 2011).

Judi Wise, President of Web Wise Kids, a non-profit organization aimed at providing online safety information to educators and parents, appeared before Congress to testify to the growing issue of cyberbullying on September 30, 2009. Wise, armed with the research conducted by her organization, testified that:

- 93 percent of youth ages 12-17 are online and 94 percent of their parents are online.
- 80 percent of teens 13-17 use cell phones with most of these devices having built-in cameras.
- Nearly 90 percent of teens 13-19 have a profile on social media sites.
- 43 percent of teens were victims of cyberbullying in 2008
- Youth who create Internet content and use social networking sites are more likely to meet harmful contact.
- 40 percent of teens stated that their parents have no idea of their online activities.
- 64 percent of online teens (ages 12-17) stated they do things online that they don't want their parents to know about, and 79 percent say they are not careful when giving out their personal information online (U.S. Congress, 2010).

Statistically speaking, no matter what form or venue bullying takes place, it is happening more often than society knows or wishes to comprehend. The question becomes does society really not comprehend or realize the depth of the bullying problem as it appears or is society so inundated with bullying knowledge and horrible stories, that one more story or a new venue like cyberbullying just white noise? Whether white noise or not, the reality is there are many victims of cyberbullying out there, living in fear day to day, cringing every time they login in to a computer or answer their cell phone.

Cyberbully Victims

Research on bullying has found that traditional bullying victims were likely to also be victims of cyberbullying. Feinberg and Robey determined that approximately half of cyberbullying victims are also targets of traditional bullying (Feinberg & Robey, 2008). Chin cited two studies from 2007, one by Q Li in which 54 percent of the participants in the study were traditional victims and over a quarter of those victims were also victims of cyberbullying. The other study cited was by Ybarra, Diener-West and Leaf and they found some overlap with victims of both traditional bullying and cyberbullying (Chin, 2011).

From this and other research there appears a fairly seamless transition between traditional and cyberbullying but what is not as definitive in the research is which type of bullying is more psychologically and emotionally damaging to the victim.

Traditional bullying implies the victim can see, touch and hear the bully; the victim generally knows who they are. It also implies that the name calling, rumors, physical violence and other vicious behaviors aimed at the victim are confined to the schoolyard. In the case of cyberbullying, the Internet and social networking sites dissolve this confinement, bringing the name calling, violence, rumors and other vicious behaviors to the victim's home, cell phone and any public area.

With no true, physical boundaries, the effects of cyberbullying may be more harmful to the victim than is known or reported. In cyberspace, bullies have several advantages over their victims and choose cyberspace to commit their heinous acts because of these advantages. According to Jaishankar:

1. Identity flexibility, dissociative anonymity, and lack of deterrence provide for an easier environment to bully someone and disappear without detection.
2. The audience is much more broad and strangers may help in the bullying of the victim.
3. Intermittent ventures and the dynamic spatio-temporal nature of cyberspace allows for many chances to escape.
4. Due to bully's status or position in society (e.g. teacher's child, public figure's child) they may choose cyberspace in order to avoid heightened scrutiny.
5. Free speech protection provides bullies a safer haven in cyberspace (Jaishankar, 2007).

While cyberbullies revel in these advantages in cyberspace, their victims may feel even more isolated and trapped than if they were literally cornered in a school hallway, bathroom or other physical space by the bully. According to Sturgeon, cyber attacks have the potential to cause more harm than the in-your-face version (Sturgeon, 2006). Why may they feel more trapped and isolated than in a traditional bullying scenario is subject to interpretation and more research; however, the following facts and observations from the available research propels the previously-stated supposition.

1. The victim of cyberbullying has no real escape from the torment. The bully can find their victim 24/7 if they wish.
2. The victim is not sure who their bully is. It could be one person or many persons across the Internet or members of a social networking site. If the victim cannot name or see their victim, how can they defend or respond to them?
3. The bully feels a stronger sense of anonymity and fear of getting caught is lessened online, therefore, the bully may be more volatile and aggressive toward the victim.
4. Monitoring and intervention by a parent or guardian against cyberbullies is not as robust as in traditional bullying scenarios (Sturgeon, 2006).

According to Dempsey, Sulkowski, Nichols and Storch:

Adults are rarely present to intervene when cyber victimization occurs, as suggested by the reported discrepancies between children and parents' online monitoring activities. In addition, even if parents are vigilant about monitoring their children's online activities, only 21 percent of cyber victims report being victimized in public domains such as online chat rooms, which allow for some degree of supervision. The remainder of online peer victimization occurs in less supervised forms, including text messages, e-mails, and online bulletin boards (Dempsey, et. al, 2009, p. 963).

Cyberbullying appears, with the few factors stated above, to set the stage for a more harmful experience for the victim or victims. Anonymity, little monitoring by a guardian, an unexpected, unknown audience of bystanders and participants brings a whole new level of fear to the victim and their family not seen in traditional bullying. The whole new level of fear cyberbullying brings not only brings a new level of fear for its victims it also conjures up a new level of criminality and political-legal issues for school administrators and law enforcement.

Law Enforcement and Cyberbullying

Cyber crime, in general, is a criminal conundrum for law enforcement and legislative bodies. Hackers, crackers, and identity thieves are just some of the criminal elements in cyberspace that create havoc for businesses and the average citizen, domestic and abroad. Hiding behind firewalls, encryption, anonymous Internet Protocol (IP) addresses, and a spider web of networks and exponentially advancing technology in the form of computers and cell phones, cyber criminals consistently have the advantage over law enforcement agencies that are generally one step behind, technologically and legally. Furthermore, law enforcement agencies face a lack of cooperation from businesses, citizens, and in this study, educators, school administrators, others within the law enforcement community and legislative bodies when investigating and prosecuting cyber crimes.

The police are steeped heavily in tradition and the physical world. Cyber crimes', including cyberbullying, goes against that tradition in every way. In most cyber crimes there is no tangible suspect, no "real" crime scene, possibly more than one victim and multiple national/international jurisdictions to legally untangle. As cited by Behzat Yucedal:

> Huey's 2002 article argues that challenges to policing cyber crime stem from the nature of cyberspace and from old law enforcement habits in which "the police culture is grounded in a perceptual schema tied to understandings of the policing function as being linked to physical/geographical notions of what constitutes territory to be policed (Yucedal, 2010, pp.17-18).

Cyber crimes are something, although not newly reported or unknown to law enforcement is new to their every day policing efforts, investigations, laws, policies and traditional criminal modus operandi. The learning curve for law enforcement remains an issue in all of the aforementioned areas and this translates into a lack of cohesive, comprehensive cyber crime legislation, particularly regarding cyber-bullying, around the United States.

Current Cyberbullying Legislation

State Legislation

The first piece of anti-bullying legislation was passed by the state of Georgia in 1999. The law covers both traditional and cyberbullying but does not specifically state or use the term cyberbullying, since the term was not created until between the years 2001 and 2003. (In 2001, Bill Beasley, an educator from Canada, coined the term cyberbullying. Attorney, Nancy Willard, also coined the term in 2003.) From 1999 to present, 47 states followed Georgia's lead by enacting anti-bullying legislation with the most recent legislation being established in the states of North Dakota and Hawaii. Three states currently do not have any anti-bullying legislation in place; South Dakota, Michigan and Montana.

The current legislation varies across the states in definition, inclusion of the terms bullying and cyberbullying, responsibility and inclusion of intervention and prevention programs in schools. In some states, the only legislation regarding bullying-like behavior is regulated under Safe School laws. Safe School laws are in place to fight discrimination against certain groups of people such as the lesbian and gay community. Bullying behavior is not specifically defined in Safe School laws and any protection they do provide is for certain groups of people not neces-sarily the average student. Three very different pieces of anti-bullying legislation apply to this study, as the sample of 103 includes teenagers from Texas, Louisiana and Washington, D.C.

- Louisiana passed a bill in 2001 and stated that school boards adopt policies prohibiting harassment, intimidation, and bullying by students; enact zero tolerance policies as needed; provide protection for those students or teachers who report bullying. No specific bullying prevention programs were established and written into the bill and a cyberbullying section was not included.

- In 2005, Texas enacted an initial anti-bullying law. Recent updates to the legislation took place in 2011 with additions of a cyberbullying clause, parental notification and inclusion of "sexting."

- In Washington, D.C., there is currently no anti-bullying law on the books. At present, D.C. has only Safe School laws in place, that protect students from discrimination based on race or sexual orientation. The D.C. City Council is currently considering the passage of the Harassment and Intimidation and Prevention Act, which enumerates anti-bullying policies for school districts statewide. The Act asks for anti-bullying policies that are not based on specific classes of students, are age appropriate and include faculty training programs and curricula for the students to learn about bullying and prevention. Furthermore, a cyberbullying provision will be added to the Act for inclusion in statewide policies.

Federal Legislation

The Federal government has generally taken the ultimate bystander role to bullying law by merely placing a directive to each of the 50 states to create and implement robust, comprehensive anti-bullying laws for their respective states and school districts. In furtherance of this directive and in recognition that cyberbullying is an issue, Congress updated the 2001 Children's Internet Protection Act (CIPA). CIPA requires all schools that receive federal funding through E-rate, a grant program that makes some communication devices affordable for qualifying schools follow set guidelines to filter and limit a child's access to unsuitable materials and content (Fegenbush & Olivier, 2009).

CIPA was updated in 2008 requiring that schools and libraries that receive federal grant money must include in their Internet safety policy an education component for minors about appropriate online behavior, including cyberbullying awareness and response and how to interact properly in social networking sites such as Facebook and MySpace.

In 2010, the Federal government proposed a move away from their traditional bystander role and opted for a more aggressive role in the bullying fight. The Secretary of Education, Arne Duncan, has proposed the inclusion of bullying under federal civil rights violations. Secretary Duncan proposed the Office of Civil Rights would aggressively collect more civil rights data and gather new and better data on harassment from schools to help implement more robust school anti-bullying policies. Essentially, ". . . the federal government will be taking a stronger and more intrusive role into how local school districts report and respond to bullying" (Trump, 2010).

Theoretical Framework and Hypotheses

The purpose of this chapter is to follow in the footsteps of the federal government and take a more aggressive approach to the issue of cyberbullying, especially in its research. By applying the tenets of routine activity theory to the cyberbullying issue, it is the goal of this chapter to: 1) expound upon the limited research available; 2) lessen the technological divide between parents and their children; 3) give a voice to those that face cyberbullies every day; 4) provide insight to parents, educators and legislators to the potential severity of the issue that they may not be aware of and 4) encourage guardians (e.g. parents, school) to intervene and help their children protect themselves from cyberbully attacks.

Routine Activity Theory

Classical criminal theorists such as Bentham and Beccaria believed criminal behavior was an extension of personal choice, rationality and free will. These basic beliefs became the foundation of what would become known as rational choice theory. Rational choice theory posits that each of us is a rational actor that chooses to engage in a behavior, whether delinquent or not, based on a series of cost/benefit analyses (e.g. risks versus benefits) that involve elements such as available target, how well the target is protected, risk of apprehension and personal need.

Cohen and Felson (1979) expounded upon rational choice theory and formulated routine activity theory. Like rational choice theory, routine activity theory relies on a series of cost/benefit analyses conducted by the perpetrator to see if engaging in a criminal/non-criminal act is worth the risks involved. In routine activity theory, the cost/benefit analysis focuses on and requires three elements to improve the likelihood engagement in an act such as a crime will occur; motivated offender, suitable target and absence of capable guardianship. As cited by Yucedal (2010), "When these three elements converge in time and space, crime occurs. Convergence of these three elements creates opportunities for criminal and deviant activities and increases the likelihood of criminal victimization"(Yucedal, 2010, p. 29).

In a school environment, the three elements of rational choice theory constantly converge. Evidence of this lies in the statistics stated previously in which 71 percent of students report bullying as an ongoing problem in their schools and 51 percent have actually witnessed a bullying incident. The statistics show that school is an opportune, routine, target rich environment where rational cost/benefit analysis regularly results in a criminal act.

In the cyberspace environment, the cost/benefit analysis process is lessened because the offender does not have to emphasize weighing the risk of getting caught or there being a guardian to intervene on the Internet. The Internet simply cannot be monitored on a twenty-four hour, seven day a week basis by any one person or group of people. Compounding this lack of guardians in cyberspace is society's ever-increasing dependence on computers and the Internet. Daily life, socialization with friends and family and many routine activities heavily depend on computers and the Internet to function and this includes education. With such a heavy dependence on computers and the Internet in schools and most areas of life, the convergence of motivated offenders to suitable targets without much guardian intervention increases, creating a prime environment on the Internet for cyberbullying victimization.

Research Questions for the State-Level Analyses

With the state-level data analyses, we hope to address the following questions:
1. What are the overall rates of bullying and violence victimization reported by students across states?
2. Do rates of victimization vary widely across locales?
3. Do bullying and violence victimization rates vary by gender and race/ethnicity?
4. How do school characteristics influence bullying and violence victimization rates?

Hypotheses

- Hypothesis 1: A sizeable segment of high school students are victimized.
- Hypothesis 2: There is wide variation in victimization rates across states.
- Hypothesis 3: Female students have higher rates of victimization than male students.
- Hypothesis 4: Minorities have higher rates of victimization than white students.
- Hypothesis 5: School characteristics have a significant impact on victimization rates.

Methodology

Using data from The American Youth Behavior Survey of High School Students 2009 reports on-line, rates of traditional forms of bullying and youth violence are examined for the 50 states. Four items on the survey address bullying and violent incidents within the last year. These items are: (1) Bullied on school property; (2) In a physical fight on school property; (3) Threatened or injured with a weapon on school property one or more times; and (4) Did not go to school because they felt unsafe at school or on the way to or from school. Rates for states on these four items are reported for all students and by the gender (male and female separately) and race/ethnicity (white, black, Hispanic, Asian/Pacific Islander, and American Indian) of students.

Data from the National Center for Educational Statistics, for the school year 2009-2010, is used to obtain information on school characteristics for states. These characteristics are average high school size, average racial/ethnic composition, average poverty rates, and region of the country that a state is located within. Analyses for this part of our research includes obtaining means and standard deviations for each of the variables and Pearson correlations between the bullying/ violence and school characteristics variables. We also perform Ordinary Least Squares regression analyses, where the four different bullying/violence variables are the dependent variables, and the school characteristic variables are the independent variables.

Descriptive Statistics

Results

Using data from The American Youth Behavior Survey of High School Students 2009 reports on-line, rates of traditional forms of bullying and youth violence are examined for the 50 states. Four items on the survey address bullying and violent incidents within the last year. These items are: (1) Bullied on school property; (2) In a physical fight on school property; (3) Threatened or injured with a weapon on school property one or more times; and (4) Did not go to school because they felt unsafe at school or on the way to or from school. The means and standard deviations for these items are reported in Table 12.1.

Results for 34 states are reported for the Bullied item. On average, states have 19.65 percent of students being bullied on school property during the last year. More male students (21.11 percent on average) report being bullied than female students (18.15 percent on average). More white students (20.99 percent on average) report being bullied than Hispanic (19.66 percent) or black students (14.01 percent). Very few states report bullying statistics for Asian or American Indian students, so the percentages reported in Table 12.1 (15.64 and 23.08 percent, respectively) should be viewed with caution. However, these results do suggest that many Asian and American Indian students face bullying on school property.

Results for most states are available for the Did Not Go To School item. On average, states have 5.88 percent of students reporting that they did not go to school at least 1 day because they felt unsafe. Slightly more females (5.84 percent on average) report not going to school than male students (5.80 percent). More Hispanic students (10.12 percent on average) report not going to school than white (4.44 percent) or black students (8.61 percent). A small number of states reported percentages for Asian and American Indian students, so the percentages reported in Table 1 should be regarded with caution. However, the statistics do suggest a sizeable segment of American Indian students (9.24 percent) avoid attending class because of safety concerns.

A majority of states also reported percentages for the Threatened item. On average, states have 7.91 percent of students being threatened or injured with a weapon at school. More females (9.98 percent) report being threatened or injured with a weapon than male students (5.64 percent). More Hispanic students (12.16 percent) and black students (10.22 percent) report being threatened or injured with a weapon than white students (6.61 percent). A small number of states reported

Table 12.1: Means and Standard Deviations for Bullying/Violence Items

Item	Mean	Std Dev	N
Bullied on school property			
All students	19.65	2.82	34
Male students	21.11	3.02	34
Female students	18.15	3.10	34
White students	20.99	2.21	34
Black students	14.01	4.34	25
Hispanic students	19.66	6.42	25
Asian students	15.64	2.84	9
American Indian	23.08	10.23	5
Did not go to school at least 1 day (because felt unsafe at, on the way to or on the way from school)			
All students	5.88	1.69	44
Male students	5.80	1.52	44
Female students	5.84	2.12	44
White students	4.44	1.39	43
Black students	8.61	3.86	32
Hispanic students	10.12	3.92	35
Asian students	5.85	2.47	11
American Indian students	9.24	3.07	7
Threatened or injured with a weapon on school property 1 or more times			
All students	7.91	1.38	42
Male students	5.64	1.08	42
Female students	9.98	1.93	42
White students	6.61	1.36	40
Black students	10.22	3.49	32
Hispanic students	12.16	5.55	33
Asian students	6.61	3.19	12
American Indian students	11.19	7.04	7
In a physical fight on school property 1 or more times			
All students	10.66	1.73	44
Male students	6.98	1.69	44
Female students	14.12	2.44	44
White students	8.89	1.50	44
Black students	16.12	4.43	31
Hispanic students	15.50	5.70	34
Asian students	7.30	1.18	11
American Indian students	13.84	7.27	9

Source: The American Youth Behavior Survey of High School Students 2009, http://www.cdc.gov/mmwr/pdf/ss/ss5905.pdf.

percentages for Asian and American Indian students, so the percentages reported in Table 12.1 should be regarded with caution. However, the statistics do suggest a sizeable segment of American Indian students (11.19 percent) are also confronted with weapons on school campuses.

Most states also report percentages for the Physical Fight item. On average, states have 10.66 percent of all students involved in a physical fight on school campuses. More female students (14.12 percent) were involved in fights than male students (6.98 percent). More black (16.12 percent) and Hispanic students (15.50 percent) were reported being involved in physical fights than white students (8.89 percent). A small number of states reported percentages for Asian and American Indian students, so the percentages reported in Table 1 should be considered with caution. However, the statistics do suggest a sizeable segment of American Indian students (13.84 percent) are involved in physical fights at school.

As predicted in Hypothesis 1, a sizeable segment of students encounter bullying while on school property (almost 20 percent, on average). More physical forms of school violence, as indicated by the Did Not Go To School, Threatened or Injured With A Weapon, and In A Physical Fight, occurs less often than Bullied. As predicted in Hypothesis 2, bullying and school violence rates vary little across locales, as indicated by the small standard deviations shown in Table 12.1.

Limited support is provided by the results for Hypothesis 3, regarding gender patterns. Male students, on average, have higher rates of bullying than female students; however, female students are more likely to encounter physical forms of violence than male students (as indicated by the higher percentages reported for females on the Did Not Go To School, Threatened, and In A Physical Fight items). Limited support is also provided for Hypothesis 4, regarding racial/ethnic rates of victimization. Racial/ethnic minorities do have higher average rates on the physical violence items, whereas whites have higher average rates of bullying victimization.

Table 12.2 reports the means and standard deviations for states on school characteristics. These characteristics are average high school size, average racial/ethnic composition, average poverty rates, and region of the country that a state is located within. The data for these variables comes from the National Center For Educational Statistics (NCES) for the school year 2009-2010. The average size of high schools in states is 792.12 students. On average, 61.13 percent of all students are white, 13.13 percent are black, 15.56 percent are Hispanic, 3.69 percent are Asian and 1.98 percent are American Indian. On average, schools have 17.51 percent of their students living in poverty. Most states (32 percent) are located in the South (according to U.S. Census definitions of region), followed by the West (26 percent) and the Midwest (24 percent).

Table 12.2: Means and Standard Deviations for School Characteristics Variables

Item	Mean	Std Dev	N
Average High School Size	792.12	322.16	50
Percent White Students	61.13	18.20	50
Percent Black Students	13.13	8.95	50
Percent Hispanic Students	15.56	11.65	50
Percent Asian Students	3.69	5.81	50
Percent American Indian Students	1.98	4.11	50
Percent Students In Poverty	17.51	4.56	50
Northeast	.18	NA	50
Midwest	.24	NA	50
South	.32	NA	50
West	.26	NA	50

Source: NCES, http://nces.ed.gov/fastfacts/display.asp?id=49.

Inferential Statistics: Correlations and Regressions

Results

Table 12.3 presents the results of Pearson correlation analyses of bullying/violence variables and school characteristic variables. Among the types of bullying/violence, No School has a positive moderate and statistically significant association with Threatened (.683, p<.01) and In Fight (.572, p<.01). This means students are more likely to not attend school for one or more days when they have been threatened or injured with a weapon, or if they have been involved in a physical fight on school property. Threatened has a negative moderate and statistically significant association with In Fight (-.506, p<.01). This means that students who have been threatened or injured with a weapon are less likely to be involved in a physical fight as well. All other relationships between types of bullying/violence are statistically insignificant (p>.05).

Examining the relationship between the Bullied and school characteristic variables, negative moderate and statistically significant relationships exist between Bullied and Average School Size (-.486, p<.01), Percent Black (-.576, p<.01), Percent Poverty (-.451, p<.01), and South (-.535, p<.01). A positive moderate association exists between Bullied and Percent White (.626, p<.01). All other school characteristics have a statistically insignificant relationship with the Bullied variable.

Table 12.3: Pearson Correlations between Variables

Variable	Bullied	No School	Threatened	In Fight
Bullied	—			
No School	-0.166	—		
Threatened	0.132	0.683**	—	
In Fight	-0.178	0.572**	-0.506**	—
Avg School Size	-0.486**	0.338*	0.044	0.069
Pct. White	0.626**	-0.389**	-0.172	-0.439**
Pct. Black	-0.576**	0.329*	0.282	0.360*
Pct. Hispanic	-0.248	0.141	0.077	0.330*
Pct. Asian	-0.020	0.183	-0.053	-0.087
Pct. Native American	0.151	-0.129	-0.148	0.029
Pct. Poverty	-0.451**	0.255	0.241	0.501**
Northeast	0.020	-0.163 -	0.420**	-0.253
Midwest	0.360*	-0.374*	-0.076	-0.424**
South	-0.535**	0.353*	0.259	0.445
West	0.263	0.133	0.178	0.168

Four school characteristic variables have statistically significant relationships with the No School variable. Percent White (-.389, $p<.01$) and Midwest (-.374, $p<.01$) have negative moderate associations with the No School variable. Average School Size and Percent Black have positive moderate associations with the No School variable (.338 and .329, $p<.01$, respectively).

Only one school characteristic variable, Northeast, has a statistically significant relationship with the Threatened variable. These two factors have a negative moderate association (-.420, $p<.01$) with each other. Five school variables have statistically significant relationships with the In Fight variable. Average School Size, and Northeast have moderate negative associations with In Fight (-.439 and -.424, $p<.01$, respectively). Percent White, Percent Black, and Percent Native American all have positive moderate associations with the In Fight variable (.360, .330, and .501, $p<.01$, respectively).

Ordinary Least Square regression analyses were also performed on the data, with the different bullying/violence variables used as dependent variables and the school characteristic variables used as independent variables. Only two factors produced statistically significant results for any of the models. In the regression model with Bullied (percent of all students) as the dependent variable, Percent Black Students as an independent variable had a negative impact. For a one percent increase in black students, the percent of students bullied decreased by approximately .11 percent ($p<.05$). In the regression model with Threatened (percent of all students) as the dependent variable, West as an independent variable had a positive impact. If a school is located within a state in the West region (relative to other regions), the percent of students threatened or injured with a weapon increases by 2.25 percent.

All other regression results are statistically insignificant; a table displaying these results is not presented here.

While results from the Pearson correlation analyses do provide some support for Hypothesis 5, the results from the OLS regression analyses provide almost no support. Almost one-half of the school characteristic variables have a significant relationship with the bullying/violence variables in the correlation analyses. However, only 2 variables in two different regression models have any significant relationships with the bullying/violence variables, taking into account the effects of the other school characteristic variables. Some of the school characteristic variables do have moderate and statistically significant relationships with one another, such as average high school size and percent white students ($r=-0.607$, $p<.01$), percent white and percent Hispanic students ($r=-0.656$, $p<.01$), and percent black students and South ($r=0.718$, $p<.01$). With these relationships between independent variables, multicolinearity may be affecting the regression results. Multicolinearity inflated the standard errors for regression coefficients, making it less likely that a relationship between an independent and dependent variable would appear as statistically significant.

Research Questions for the Individual-Level Survey of Students

In the light of the limited literature on cyberbullying, this chapter plans to answer many questions regarding cyberbullying, both simple and complex

1. Are victims of traditional bullying also likely to be victimized online?
2. Are teens that use the Internet for extended hours and days more susceptible to victimization?
3. Are females more likely to cyberbully and be victims of cyberbullying than males as has been suggested by conventional wisdom?
4. Does the age of the teen determine more involvement in traditional bullying or cyberbullying or neither?
5. Is cyberbullying more or less prevalent than traditional bullying?

Hypotheses

*   Hypothesis 1: Teenage victims of traditional bullying are more likely to also be victimized online.
*   Hypothesis 2: Teenagers who use the Internet for extended hours and days will likely experience more cyberbullying.
*   Hypothesis 3: Teenage females will likely commit and be victims of cyberbullying more than teenage males.
*   Hypothesis 4: Age will likely not impact teenage involvement in either traditional or cyberbullying.
*   Hypothesis 5: Cyberbullying is likely equally prevalent to traditional bullying incidents.

Methodology

The initial survey methodology attempted for this chapter came in the form of an e-mail survey sent to a few teenagers with the request to forward it on to their contacts of the same age groups, creating a snowball sample. No responses were received using this method so a new methodology was implemented.

The final methodology consisted of the use of a "white paper" survey physically administered to a random sample of (N=103) teenagers, ages 14-17, and living in the El Paso, Texas, New Orleans, Louisiana and Washington, D.C. areas. The survey used was an established 54-question survey created in 2008 by Dr. Delia Campfield, a psychiatrist and author of the dissertation, *Cyberbullying and Victimization Psychosocial Characteristics of Bullies, Victims, and Bully/Victims* (2008). There were two sections to the survey; one dealing with the respondent and their Internet usage/habits and the other section with questions centered on traditional bullying and cyberbullying occurrences experienced by the respondents since the beginning of the school year.

Prior to administration of the surveys, verbal consent was received from the students' teachers and other guardians on site. Respondents were reminded that the survey was anonymous, voluntary and participation could be halted at anytime.

Data

The survey was administered to a random sample of (N=103) high school students, ages 14-17, from the El Paso, Texas, New Orleans, Louisiana and Washington, D.C. areas. The previously vetted survey from Dr. Delia Campfield had 54 questions in total with 25 related to traditional bullying and 29 related to cyberbullying behaviors. Traditional bullying questions referred to those including kids physically attacking one another, physical isolation of a classmate, etc. The cyberbullying questions referred to such behaviors as spreading rumors on the Internet, sending threatening emails or using the "silent treatment" toward someone during an online game or chat. The questions that were traditional bullying-centric were grouped together and classified as TBV. Cyberbullying-centric questions were grouped together and classified as CBV.

If a respondent answered 'Yes' to any of the 54-questions on the survey, it was followed up by two supporting questions to determine frequency and harm felt according to the respondent: 1) Ordinal variable - How many times did it happen? (i.e. 1-2 times a week, everyday) and 2) Ordinal variable – How much did it bother you? (i.e. none, some, very much).

The data was analyzed mainly from a descriptive statistical angle in order to superficially answer the research questions proposed and tentatively confirm or deny the hypotheses posited, as well, to provide a baseline for future research. Descriptive statistics of the sample (N=103) include frequency of Internet usage, the average time spent on the Internet, gender of those most involved in traditional and/or cyberbullying, average age of the respondents, the most common uses of the Internet by the respondents, etc.

Results

Descriptive Statistics

Demographics

The sample of 103 students from El Paso to Washington, D.C. was comprised of 59 percent female respondents, 43 percent male respondents and 1 percent that left the gender question blank. Approximately 78 percent of the total respondents were between the ages of 14-15 years old with the remaining 24 percent between the ages of 16-17 years old. Most of the respondents were Hispanic (73 percent) and this was due to the survey being given to 75 students from the El Paso, Texas area where the population of nearly 700,000 people is predominantly of Hispanic origin.

Internet Usage

As stated previously, the US Census Bureau, in 2009, found that 68 percent of children have access to the Internet in their home and 76 percent of children have access to the Internet at some other location. High access and availability to the Internet were also found in this study with 78 percent of the students surveyed using the Internet everyday (48 percent) or almost everyday (30 percent). On average, students used the Internet for 2-3 hours a day (53 percent) with 11 percent as the exception, using it more than 6 hours a day. The finding that is most telling is that of the 103 students surveyed they used the Internet almost equally for homework and research (83 percent) and chatting on social networking sites such as MySpace and Facebook (86 percent). 49 percent used the Internet for sending and receiving e-mails; 27 percent used the Internet for instant messaging and 28 percent used it for online gaming.

Traditional Bullying

The survey contained 54 questions in total with 25 questions focused on traditional bullying behaviors both from a bully and victim perspective such physical violence, exclusion at parties or other events, calling other students names, saying something offensive to others, etc. The answers relate to behaviors or instance that the respondents' say have taken place since the beginning of the school year (2011).

Questions 11-18, 21, 23, 27-29, 31, 34-37, 39-41, 51, 53-54 and 59-60 were defined as related to traditional bully/victims. The remaining 29 questions relate to the respondents' actions as a traditional or cyberbully. A summary of some of the findings is presented.

Bully Victims

- The first question asked respondents whether other kids had broken or stolen things from them. 22 of those surveyed responded 'yes' that kids had stolen or broken their things. Of the 22, 15 (68 percent) had their things stolen or broken 1-2 times since the school year began; five students (22 percent) responded that it happened a few times a month and 1 student (4 percent) had it happen almost every day.

- 43 total respondents answered 'yes' that kids had something to offend them. 28 students (52 percent) said they were offended 1-2 times since the school year began; 11 students (20 percent) said a few times a month, six students (11 percent) said it happened daily.

- 22 students answered 'yes' that kids had threatened to hurt them or beat them up. 10 students (45 percent) answered 'yes' that kids had threatened to beat them up at least 1-2 times since the school year began; six students (27 percent) said they were threatened a few times a month.

- 39 students responded 'yes' to kids laughing or giggling at them to be mean. 21 students (53 percent) answered 'yes' that kids had laughed at or giggled at them to be mean 1-2 since the school year began; eight students (20 percent) said this happened once a week and four students (10 percent) said they had experienced this a few times a month and four students (10 percent) almost every day.

- 34 students responded 'yes' to kids giving them the "silent treatment." 20 students (58 percent) answered 'yes' that kids had given them the 'silent treatment' at least 1-2 times since the school year began; 11 students (31 percent) stated they received the 'silent treatment' a few times a month or at least once a week. Seven students (9 percent) said it happened to them almost everyday or daily.

- 10 students said 'yes' they had been physically hurt or beaten up. Eight students (80 percent) said 'yes' they had been physically beaten or hurt by another student at least 1-2 times since the school year began.

- 28 students responded 'yes' that someone at school spread rumors about them. 18 students (64 percent) said 'yes' to someone at school spreading rumors about them 1-2 times since the beginning of the school year; seven students (25 percent) said this happened a few times a month.

Bullies

- 28 students responded 'yes' that they had broken or stolen someone's things. 16 students (66 percent) stated 'yes' they had broken or stolen someone else's things at 1-2 times since the beginning of the school year; five students (20 percent) said that they had broken or stolen someone else's things a few times a month.

- 14 students responded 'yes' they had started rumors about someone at school. Nine students (64 percent) stated they had started rumors about someone at school; two students (14 percent) said they had started rumors at once a week about someone.

- 37 students responded 'yes' they acted like they were going to beat someone up in school. 23 students (62 percent) stated they acted they were going to beat someone up in school at least 1-2 times since the beginning of the school year; six students (16 percent) said they acted this way a few times a month and four students (10 percent) said they acted this way daily.
- 27 students responded 'yes' to physically hurting or beating someone up at school. 19 students (70 percent) stated they had physically hurt or beat someone up at school at 1-2 times since the school year started; three students (11 percent) said they had physically hurt someone at least a few times a month and three students (11 percent) said they had done this once a week.
- 28 students responded 'yes' to giving someone the 'silent treatment' to someone at school. 18 students (64 percent) said they had given someone the "silent treatment" at 1-2 times since the beginning of the school year; five students (18 percent) said they did this a few times a month and three students (10 percent) said they ignored someone daily.
- 42 students responded 'yes' to refusing to sit next to someone during lunch at school. 25 students (59 percent) said they had refused to sit next to someone during lunch at school at least 1-2 times since the beginning of the school year; 10 students (24 percent) said they refused to sit next to someone at least once a week or daily.

Cyberbullying Victims/Bullies

As stated previously, 29 questions in the survey focused on cyberbullying related behaviors. The questions looked at both the bully perspective and the victim perspective, just as the traditional bullying questions did. The following are a summary of the cyberbullying results.

Cyberbully Victims

- 22 total students surveyed answered 'yes' to the fact that kids had sent them a hurtful e-mail calling them a bad name or saying something mean. 14 students (63 percent) said kids had sent hurtful emails at least 1-2 times since the beginning of the school year; five students (22 percent) said this happened to them a few times a month and three students (13 percent) said this happened to them once a week.
- 38 students responded 'yes' to kids taking cell phone pictures without their permission. 26 students (68 percent) said that kids had taken a cell phone picture without their permission 1-2 times since the beginning of the school year; six students (15 percent) said this happens a few times a month and five students (13 percent) said it happens once a week.

- 16 students responded 'yes' that kids had threatened to beat them up over the Internet. 11 students (69 percent) said that kids had threatened to beat them up over the Internet 1-2 times since the beginning of the school year; two students (12 percent) said they were threatened once a week.
- 14 students responded 'yes' that someone had started a rumor or lied about them on the Internet. Eight students (54 percent) said that someone had started a rumor or lied about them on the Internet 1-2 times since the beginning of the year; 4 students (27 percent) said this had occurred a few times a month.
- 14 students responded 'yes' that someone had something mean or hurtful on MySpace or other social networking website. Eight students (57 percent) said someone had said something hurtful or mean on MySpace or other social networking website 1-2 times since the beginning of the school year; four students (27 percent) said this has occurred a few times a month.
- 15 students in total responded 'yes' that a student from school sent them something sexual over the Internet since the beginning of the school year. Nine (60 percent) students said they were sent something sexual 1-2 times since the school year began. Four students (26 percent) said this happened a few times a month and two students (13 percent) it happened once a week.

Cyberbullies

- 31 total students responded 'yes' they had called people names on the Internet since the beginning of the school year. 20 students (64 percent) said they had done this 1-2 times since the beginning of the school year; six students (19 percent) said they had done this a few times a month.
- 20 total students responded 'yes' they had taken cell phone pictures of another student without their permission. 12 students (60 percent) said they had done this 1-2 times since the beginning of the school year and four students (20 percent) said they did this once a week.
- 4 total students said they had sent something sexual to another student over the Internet.
- 46 total students responded 'yes' they had given the 'silent treatment' to someone over the Internet. 28 students (60 percent) said they had given the 'silent treatment' to someone 1-2 times since the beginning of the school year. Six students (13 percent) said they did this once a week to someone and four students (8 percent) said they did this daily.
- 22 total students responded 'yes' they had sent a threatening text message to someone. 16 students (72 percent) said they sent threatening messages 1-2 times since the beginning of the school year. Three students (13 percent) said they did this a few times a month and two students (9 percent) said they did this daily.
- 14 total students responded 'yes' they had something hurtful or mean to embarrass someone on the Internet since the beginning of the school year. Eight students (57 percent) said they did this 1-2 times since the beginning of the school year. Two students (14 percent) said they did this daily to someone.

Overall, at least one third of the 104 students who responded to the survey had engaged in or been a victim of both traditional and cyberbullying. Engagement and victimization regarding traditional bullying appeared to be slightly more prevalent than engagement and victimization in cyberbullying, especially in the number of respondents who had things stolen, broken or destroyed by others, being ditched by another student or ditching a student and giving the "silent treatment" to another student. What was telling about the cyberbullying and victimization responses was the number of students who had taken a picture or someone had taken their picture with a cell phone without permission and sending/receiving threatening text messages. The issue here is that taking pictures, while generally an innocuous behavior, can lead to that student's or their victim's exposure to other predators online, exploitation by other students online via websites, chat rooms and social networking sites such as MySpace and Facebook.

With regard to female respondents in this survey, they appeared to be engaged in more cyberbullying behaviors than males and in ones that involve a passive aggressive action such as giving someone the "silent treatment", spreading rumors or not inviting the other person to an event or online game/chat. More in-depth research is needed, however, to determine female affinity to passive aggressive cyberbullying behavior.

The number of hours and days a student spent online appeared to related to the number of and/or likelihood that a student would be a victim of and/or engage in cyberbullying. There were several respondents (>10) that reported no issues with cyberbullying, despite being online everyday, daily and for at least 2-3 hours a day. Again, more research with a larger sample of students is needed to determine the correlation between hours/days online with incidents of cyberbullying.

Limitations

Every research has several layers of limitations that both put the data into question and pose stimulating questions for future research. The following were the limitations in this chapter.

The first limitation to this chapter was the use of a survey research design. Initially, this researcher attempted to obtain the final sample for this chapter by conducting an e-mail survey using a few high school students from the local area. The notion was that these few students would take the survey and forward it to their classmates creating a snowball sample. What resulted from this e-mail survey attempt were no responses. A second attempt at administering the survey was undertaken but this time via "white paper" to a random sample of students in the local area and through colleagues' access to the necessary sample population. The result of N=103 was finally obtained by physically administering the survey.

A survey design is a very common approach used by researchers to understand and explore human activity, particularly their opinions, attitudes and experiences in a moment in time. The problem is that surveys are just a snapshot of a population and their opinions, not necessarily a complete picture. As well, respondents to surveys do not always provide a truthful response to the questions posed due to the sensitive nature of the questions and topic; despite anonymity and assurance their responses are confidential.

A second limitation related to using a survey is social desirability bias. "Social desirability bias occurs when respondents distort answers to make their reports conform to social norms" (Neuman, 2006, p. 285). Many times respondents provide inflated answers to survey questions to make themselves appear better or worse than they really are. Such responses tend to distort the overall survey findings.

Another limitation lies in the generalization of the results. In the case of this chapter, generalizability is limited due to the small sample size and lack of ethnic diversity of the respondents. A large proportion (75 percent) of the students surveyed for this chapter were Hispanic, leaving only 25 percent representing various other ethnicities.

Reliability and Validity Issues

As there are limitations associated to any research, so are there issues with reliability and validity. "Reliability and validity are central issues in all measurement. Both concern connecting measures to constructs. Reliability and validity are salient because constructs are ambiguous, diffuse, and not directly observable" (Neuman, 2006, p. 189). Reliability refers to the dependability and consistency of the measurement a researcher uses across time and populations. If the measurement is incomplete, not vetted or flawed in a significant way, then the results will be erratic, unstable and inconsistent.

In the case of this chapter, descriptive statistics were used to understand and visualize the prevalence, frequency and normality of the issue of cyberbullying and traditional bullying for the sample (N=103). The problem with using descriptive statistics on a data set, according to the Texas State Auditor's Methodology Manual (1995), is that the data can be misinterpreted, misused and incomplete, be of limited use when samples and populations are small, fail to fully specify the extent to which non-normal data are a problem and offer little information about cause and effects (Texas State Auditor, 1995, p. 11).

Validity

Validity refers to the truthfulness or correctness of the measurement tool used in a particular research. Essentially, validity asks whether the measurement tool used in a particular piece of research measures what it is supposed to measure.

The measurement tool used in this chapter was a survey previously created and used in research. Dr. Delia Campfield originally created the survey used in this chapter for use in her 2008 dissertation on cyberbullying. In Campfield's dissertation, she stated there was a measurement error found in the response choices of once a week and a few times a month. They responses were ordered incorrectly in that a few times a month is actually less than once a week. These responses are similar enough that they could have been combined into one response choice (Campfield, 2008).

Future Research

According to Fegenbush and Olivier's literature review on cyberbullying in 2009, "bullying as a phenomenon was not well researched until recent years" (Fegenbush & Olivier, 2009, p. 11). The first bullying research began with Dr. Dan Olweus pioneering research in 1973 conducted in Sweden. Olweus's comprehensive bullying research, *Aggression in the Schools: Bullies and Whipping Boys* published in 1978 did not reach the shores of America until 2001 amid a rash of school shootings such as Columbine and Paducah.

In response to the rash of school shootings, research began in the US but with little progression. As cited in Fegenbush & Olivier's 2009 literature review, "In 2001, Nansel, Overpeck, Pilla, Ruan, Simons-Morton, and Scheidt noted that while aggression among U.S. youth was increasing, such as the incident at Columbine, there was no obtainable national data on the pervasiveness of school-aged bullying" (Fegenbush & Olivier, 2009, p. 12).

Today, traditional bullying research has gained momentum in the U.S.; cyberbullying research remains limited in scope. The limited research on cyberbullying can be explained by a few core tenets: 1) the concept is very new; 2) technological advancement continually surpasses finished research creating continuing intelligence gaps; 3) cyberbullying is not well defined legally or socially (e.g. harassment, stalking); 4) under reporting is high from victims, schools and law enforcement and 5) social norm of "kids will be kids" and "bullying is part of young life" remains strong in communities across the US.

It is the hope that this research prompts educators, parents, law enforcement and researchers to embrace the issue of bullying, as something not solely confined to school walls. Technology advancement, the Internet and society's ever-increasing dependence on computers and technology to function in everyday life has broken down the barriers of traditional bullying, left the school walls and found a virtual home in cyberspace. According to Campfield (2008), "The likelihood of being involved in cyberbullying and victimization is amplified because of the widespread use of the Internet and cell phones among youth as well as the ability for youth to be online/cell phone without adult supervision"(Campfield, 2008, p. 128). Just as the physical barriers of bullying have dissipated with technology, giving way to cyberbullying, so should barriers in researching it more efficiently and successfully in the US.

Future research into cyberbullying should include several factors that were not included in this chapter such as the effect or correlation of socio-economic factors on cyberbullying behaviors (e.g. family income, exposure to family violence, overall child's social network, family involvement in everyday welfare); the impact of law enforcement/legislation/school's response in cyberbullying cases on future reporting; the impact of parents involvement in Internet/cell phone usage of their children and overall coping skills presented by respondents to stress, anger, depression and life obstacles and how that may influence engaging in or becoming a victim of cyberbullying.

References

The American Youth Behavior Survey of High School Students 2009 http://www. cdc.gov/mmwr/pdf/ss/ss5905.pdf.

Baldry, A.C. and Farrington, D.P. (1999) Types of bullying among Italian school children. *Journal of Adolescence*, 22, 423–426.

Baldrey, A., and Farrington, D. (2000). Bullies and delinquents: Personal characteristics and parental styles. *Journal of Community and Applied Social Psychology*. 10, 17–31.

Bentham, J., and Beccaria, C. http://en.wikipedia.org/wiki/Classical_school. Retrieved August 30, 2013.

Borba, M. (1999). Parents do make a difference: How to raise kids with solid character, strong minds and caring hearts. San Francisco, CA: Jossey-Bass.

Bullying Statistics. (2009). http://www.bullyingstatistics.org/content/bully cide.html.

Campfield, D. C. (2008). *Cyber Bullying and Victimization: Psychosocial Characteristics of Bullies, Victims, and Bully/Victims.* University of Montana, Department of Psychology. Ann Arbor: UMI.

Chin, M. A. (2011). *Prevalence, Gender Differences, and Mental Health Problems Associated with Traditional and Cyber bullying.* University of Hawaii at Hilo. Ann Arbor: UMI.

Cohen, L., and Felsen, M., (1979). Social change and crime rate trends: A routine activity approach. *American Sociological Review.* Available on-line at https:// www.d.umn.edu/~bmork/2306/readings/cohenfelson.htm.

Dempsey, A., Sulkowski, M. L., Nichols, R., & Storch, E. A. (2009, December 01). Differences Between Peer Victimization in Cyber and Physical Settings and Associated Psychosocial Adjustment in Early Adolescence. *Psychology in the Schools , 46* (10), 962-974.

Fegenbush, B., & Olivier, D. (2009). Cyberbullying: A Literature Review. *Annual Meeting of the Louisiana Education Research Association* (pp. 1–70). Lafayette: University of Louisiana at Lafayette.

Feinberg, T., & Robey, N. (2008 September). Cyber bullying. *ED Digest* , pp. 10–14.

Felson, M., & Cohen, L. E. (1979). Social Change and Crime Rate Trends: A Routine Activity Approach. *American Sociological Review* , 588–608.

Hinduja, S., & Patchin, J. (2011–October). *Cyber Bullying Research Center.* Cyber Bullying Research Center: http://www.cyberbullying.us

Jaishankar, K. (2007). Establishing a Theory of Cyber Crimes. *International Journal of Cyber Criminology , 1* (2), 7–9.

Juvonen, J., and Gross, E. (2008). Extending the school grounds?—bullying experiences in cyberspace. *Journal of School Health.* Sep;78(9):496-505.

Keith, S. and Martin, M. (2005). Cyber-bullying: Creating a culture of respect in a cyber world. *Reclaiming Children and Youth.* 15:4: pp. 224-228.

Neuman, W. L. (2006). *Social Research Methods.* Boston, MA: Pearson Education, Inc.

Olweus, Dan. Olweus Bullying Prevention Programme: design and implementation issues in Norway. (2004). In *Bullying in Schools: How Successful Can Interventions Be?* Edited by Peter Smith, Debra Pepler, and Ken Rigby. Cambridge, UK: Cambridge Univeresity Press, pp. 13–36.

Smith, P., Pepler, D., and Rigby, K. (Eds.) (2004). *Bullying in Schools: How Successful Can Interventions Be?* Cambridge, UK: Cambridge Univeresity Press.

Strom, P. S., and Strom, R. D. (2005). When teens turn cyberbullies. *Education Digest: Essential.* Readings Condensed for Quick Review, 71 (4), 35-41.

Sturgeon, J. (2006, September). *District Administration.* Retrieved August 25, 011, from DistrictAdministration.com: www.DistrictAdministration.com.

Texas State Auditor. (1995). *Methodology Manual.* Austin: Texas State Auditor.

Trump, K. (2010 13–August). *School Security Blog.* Retrieved 2011 07–November from http://www.schoolsecurity.blog.com/2010/08/radical-policy-shift-targets-bullying-as-federal-civil-rights-issue.

U.S. Census Bureau. (2009). www.census.gov.

U. S. Congress. (2010). *Cyberbullying and Other Online Safety Issues for Children.* U.S. House of Representatives, Subcommittee on Crime, Terrorism, and Homeland Security. Washington: U.S. Government Printing Office.

Yucedal, B. (2010). *Victimization in Cyberspace: An application of routine activity and lifestlye exposure theories.* Kent State University, Department of Political Science. Kent: Kent State-ETD.

Contributors

Felecia M. Bigard is a graduate of Southern University at New Orleans (SUNO) located in New Orleans, Louisiana with a Bachelor of Science Degree in Criminal Justice and a minor in Sociology. Felecia has over six years experience in a paralegal capacity providing support and assistance to various attorneys on a range of topics. She has graduated from Gwinnett College located in Lilburn, Georgia with a certificate in Legal Secretary and an Associate of Science Degree in Legal Administrative Assisting (Paralegal). Felecia served as a Court Appointed Special Advocate (CASA) volunteer for New Orleans. She was appointed Advocate of the Month and served as a panelist to share her advocate work with current CASA trainee group. In addition to Felecia's exceptional advocacy for abuse and neglect children, she desires to focus on advocating for children and youth rights, respect, safety and education that will be beneficial for every child future.

Vanessa Caguicla Bivens is a Teacher Development Specialist at Houston Independent School District, Houston Texas. She has been an educator for 11 years. Before joining HISD at Hartman Middle School in 2009, she served as a mathematics instructional specialist at Klein Independent School District. Mrs. Bivens hails from the Philippines, where she graduated from the Philippine Normal University with a Bachelor of Mathematics Secondary Education degree and with a postgraduate diploma in Mathematics. She is currently pursuing her PHD in Education at Duplichain University in Baton Rouge, Louisiana. Mrs. Bivens believes that all students can learn and success depends on the effectiveness of the teacher to find ways to meet the individual needs of each student. In addition, she feels that teachers are in their profession to make a difference in their students' lives, to help them become worthy citizens by providing them the best education possible.

Barbara Braun is a Licensed Clinical Social Worker and Primary Therapist for Willowbrooke at Tanner's The Center for Behavioral Health in Carrollton, Georgia which provides outpatient counseling for adults, adolescents and children. Barbara has worked at Tanner for 10 years as a therapist and program manager. Barbara received a Masters of Clinical Social Work degree (MSW) from Loyola University in Chicago and a Bachelors of Arts degree (BA) in Sociology and Psychology from St. Joseph's University in Philadelphia, Pennsylvania. Barbara is an approved therapist recommended by the University of South Carolina/National Crime Victims Research & Treatment Center's Learning Collaborative on Trauma Focused Cognitive Behavioral Therapy sponsored by the Georgia Dept. of Behavioral Health & Developmental Disabilities. Barbara has done in home social services as well as clinical therapy with adults, adolescents, and children in various settings including agency, hospital, and church-based organizations.

Clifton L. Brown, PhD is an adjunct instructor and student advisor at Florida A&M University in Tallahassee, Florida. Dr. Brown teaches introduction to sociology and socio-behavioral courses including Aging in America, Deviant Behavior, Minority Family Systems, Race Relations and Research Methods. As a consultant in the private sector he has coordinated various research projects and job audits, conducted training seminars and focus groups, developed data collection instruments and performed statistical analyses. Dr. Brown is a veteran and located in Tallahassee.

Beverly L. Downing is a native of Washington, North Carolina, where she attended Mother of Mercy Catholic School and Chocowinity High School. At Chocowinity, she was an outstanding student/athlete in the sport of Basketball and Track & Field. Currently she serves as the Chair of the School of Education here at Kentucky State University, she has continued to grow and expand the unit throughout the Commonwealth and the Nation at-large. She serves on the Executive Boards of the Kentucky Association of Colleges of Teacher Education (KACTE), and the Kentucky ACT Council. She also serves on a number of Education Professional Standards Board (EPSB) standing committees and university committees. Dr. Downing was recently named to the EPSB Charter for the Program Accreditation Review Committee.

Alice Duhon-Ross is an Assistant Professor at Walden University in the Richard W. Riley College of Education. Her current research focus is in multi-cultural education and counseling with special interest in conflict resolution.

Rosalind Duplechain is an Associate Professor of Education at the University of West Georgia in Carrolton, Georgia. Rosalind has worked in education for x years: elementary and high school (9 years) and post-secondary (13 years). Rosalind received her degrees in Education from Xavier University of Louisiana (BA) and from the University of Illinois at Chicago with a concentration in Educational Psychology (PhD). Rosalind's research interest is in the impact of traumatic events on the school experiences of children.

Lisa Eargle is a Full Professor of Sociology and Department Head at Francis Marion University. She teaches a wide variety of courses in stratification and inequality, population dynamics, and research methods. Her research interests include community development and adaptation, social justice issues, and educational processes.

Ethel Marie Yeates Fisher, a practicing Speech/Language Pathologist, has worked in the public school system for 36 years. She works for the Calcasieu Parish School System, Lake Charles, Louisiana. Ethel has presented in the area of Bullying in Houston, Texas at a conference sponsored by the National Association for Peace/Antiviolence Education. She lives in DeQuincy, Louisiana with her husband, Donald. They have two daughters, Alinga and Sadari, in addition to their grand-daughter, Jordyn. This is Ethel's first published article.

Kathy Franklin is Vice President of Administration and Dean of School of Liberal Arts and Sciences at Virginia University of Lynchburg. Her current research interests include Higher Education Administration, assessment of student learning outcomes and peace/anti-violence education. She is nationally renowned in her knowledge in accreditation. Dr. Franklin has chaired various accreditation committee team visits.

Kelly Gray was born and raised in McAllen, Texas. She received a Bachelors and Masters degree in Criminal Justice from the University of Texas Pan American in Edinburg, TX. She has been working as an Intelligence Analyst in law enforcement for 11 years; 8 years of that in the FBI. She is presently an Intelligence Analyst at the FBI in El Paso, Texas.

Sherry Harrison is a Program Director in the Master of Science in Education program for Walden University. She is a National Board Certified Teacher with experience as a teacher, special education administrator, and state education consultant. Her research interest focuses on technology and special education.

Marcus Henderson is currently a Master Teacher at L. B. Landry High School, in New Orleans, Louisiana. A lifelong educator, Marcus received his B.S. Degree in Health and Human Performance, with a Minor in English, from Northeast Louisiana University, in 1991. He received his Masters of Education in Administration and Supervision of Education from Northeast Louisiana University in 1993. Marcus is currently a doctoral candidate in Instruction and Administration at the University of Kentucky, where his research is framed in modernity and the use of standardized testing to perpetuate inferiority for marginalized populations and the history of higher education.

Rose Sabina Griffith Hunte holds a PhD in Human Services specializing in Criminal Justice from Capella University and a Master of Human Relations form The University of Oklahoma, Norman. Her research interests cover a range of subjects such as the evolution of criminality in human civilizations, penal policies and prison management, and police management and police-community relations. Although she lived in the United States for 43 years, Dr. Hunte is a native of the Island Nation of Saint Lucia in the Caribbean and currently resides in her home nation. She plans to conduct comparative research of police management policies and strategies reflecting the Caribbean nations in relation to the United States.

Faye Jones received her Ph.D. from Southern University and A & M College in Special Education in 2003. She earned 30+ (Early Childhood)in 1996 from Xavier University and University of New Orleans. She received her Master's degree (Reading Specialist) in 1984 from Xavier University and her Bachelor's degree (Speech Pathology Education) in 1977 from Xavier University.

Maryanne Hunter Longo, Ed.D is a contributing faculty member at Walden University and Grand Canyon University. Dr. Longo is a recent retiree from the School District of Philadelphia after 35 years of instructional and administrative responsibilities with the majority of her practice with Early Childhood Programs in an inner-city school with a diverse population. She now shares her authentic experiences with students pursuing doctoral degrees in Early Childhood Education. She is married and spends her time between Florida where she enjoys reading, golfing, and cruising, and New Jersey where her children and granddaughters reside.

Sylvia A. Mason, Ed.D. is a native of Winston-Salem, North Carolina. She is a Contributing Faculty/Lead Faculty Member at Walden University. She has been with Walden since 2003 in the Reilly School of Education, Department of Teacher Leadership. Dr. Mason also serves as the Director of NCATE/CAEP and Graduate Coordinator for the Master of Arts in Special Education Program at Kentucky State University. Dr. Mason has thirty-one years of experience in public and higher education. She began her career in 1979 as a teacher and coordinator for students with disabilities in the Alternative Education Program with the Durham City Schools and worked at Durham High School, chairing the Department of Special Education until 1988. Dr. Mason went on to the Durham County Schools, where she served as a Speech Language Pathologist, Learning Disabilities and Mentor Teacher until 1990, when she started her administrative career. In 1990, Dr. Mason became an interim assistant principal in the Chapel Hill Carrboro-City Schools. She remained in this role until 1991, when she accepted the role of assistant principal in the Granville County Schools.

Adnan Omar holds a Ph.D. in Computer Science from the University of Louisiana at Lafayette. He joined Southern University at New Orleans in 1995. Dr. Omar is currently Professor and Chair of Management Information Systems in the College of Business and Public Administration at Southern University at New Orleans, Louisiana. His current research areas include Database, Ethics, E-learning, Mobile learning, E-commerce and Information Technology. Dr. Omar also attended and presented many papers at regional, national, and international conferences. He taught for fourteen years oversees at King Saud University, Saudi Arabia and seven years at Northwestern State University at Natchitoches, Louisiana. He has published over seventy articles. He has also written many grant proposals which have generated over $2.6 million as principle and co-principle investigator in grant funding to enhance education at Southern University at New Orleans. Dr. Omar has a great deal of experience as an administrator and researcher in the area of technology. He recognizes the need to develop and enhance the activity of the office operation using technology.

Perla Palileo-Brame is an energetic, enthusiastic educator who is originally from the Philippines, where she received her Bachelor of Arts in Business and Political Science from Holy Angel College and Saint Paul's University. Her Masters of Arts in School Administration and Supervision is from East Carolina University, North Carolina; Perla is currently finishing her Doctor of Philosophy in Education with Duplichain University in Louisiana. Her experiences in the field of education span for more than 40 years where she served as a teacher, department chairperson, student activity director and as administrator for K-12 education. She had served as an educator in the state of North Carolina, Florida, Texas and the Republic of the Philippines. Prior to becoming an educator, she worked as a business manager, beautician, and as a tourist guide in the Philippines. In addition to her interest in finding out the effects of Standardized testing on teachers' instructions, she is also writing her dissertation in the Effects of School and Home collaboration on School Based Programs. She joined the Houston Independent School District Team in August 14, 1984 to the present.

Camacia Smith-Ross, a native of Alexandria, Louisiana, currently serves as the Associate Dean and Director of Alternative Certification and Master of Arts in Teaching at Louisiana College. Dr. Ross has worked on many educational reform projects and initiatives in higher education and K-12; in both the public and private sector. She has self-published two books and been a contributing author in several educational journals and books nationally. Dr. Ross received her specialized training in Louisiana and Florida.

Brucetta McClue-Tate is a New Area Tech High STEM CTTIE Instructor at Xavier University. She is a native of New Orleans, La. She has taught over twenty years in K-12 and higher education. She earned her doctoral degree in 2008 from Walden University in Education. She earned her Graduate Degree in Education in 1990 from Xavier University. She earned her Bachelor's of Arts Degree in 1987 from Loyola University. She has published several articles and books.

Patricia Thurmond has a professional teaching license in Business and Technology with teaching experiences ranging from the primary, secondary, and post secondary levels. She is currently the Interim Program Director and Major Assessment Supervisor in the Master of Science in Education program for Walden University. Her research interest includes topics surrounding technology and charter schools.

Veronica Lynn Doyle Woodard, a native of Eunice, LA, has over 30 years experience in the profession of nursing. She joined the faculty of McNeese State University (MSU) in the fall of 2002 as an Assistant Professor in the College of Nursing. Since coming to MSU she has served on several department and university committees. She has engaged in numerous scholarly activities, some which include: written proposals with approval for two Endowed Professorships, a scholarly poster presentation during the Louisiana State Nurses Association's Annual Convention, moderator during the 39th Biennial Convention for Sigma Theta Tau International Honor Society of Nursing, Power Point presentation at the National Association for Peace/Anti-Violence Education's 13th Annual Conference, in addition to volunteer service to various community and civic organizations. An important aspect of her life is her family—her two sons (proud graduates of Morehouse College and Shaw University), her five sisters and their children, and her two adorable granddaughters (the heart of her being).